The Invisible Man

Awakening the Human Consciousness

by

James Leonard Nobles

CCB Publishing
British Columbia, Canada

The Invisible Man: Awakening the Human Consciousness

ISBN-13 978-1-926585-38-3
Third Edition

Library and Archives Canada Cataloguing in Publication
Nobles, James Leonard, 1960-
The invisible man: awakening the human consciousness /
written by James Leonard Nobles.
Includes bibliographical references.
ISBN 978-1-926585-37-6 (bound).--ISBN 978-1-926585-38-3 (pbk.)
1. United States--Politics and government--2001-2009. 2. United
States--Social conditions--1980-. 3. Popular culture--United States.
I. Title.
E907.N62 2009 973.93 C2009-904782-9

Publisher: CCB Publishing
British Columbia, Canada
www.ccbpublishing.com

New Perspectives on and Resolutions for the Challenges confronting Modern Society in the 21st Century

Time to put keystrokes to Digital

If we don't distinguish the truth from popular myths on our journey of enlightenment we become victims of our own ignorance and followers of false propaganda disseminated by unworthy leaders who serve the unholy status quo

Contents

Introduction

After graduating from college in the summer of 2005, I started working on *The Invisible Man.* I have spent the better part of the last two years reading, writing, editing, researching, and revising my manuscript. At times being the first college graduate in my family feels somewhat awkward because it has made me an outsider. But I believed returning to school to finish my degree provided me with the best opportunity to improve my quality of life by pursuing a career in writing and producing. While at the same time I understand education doesn't guarantee success, it does however enhance the odds. Most of the uneducated poor are hard working, honest, and decent people. And most do not desire the bonds of poverty though the chains of dependency seem almost unbreakable for the majority of the oppressed in America and around the world.

Many of my blind and visually impaired family members, family friends, and my high school friends have accepted poverty as their fate. But I refuse to believe that my circumstances can never change if I face my fears and place the responsibility of my success upon myself. Yes there are always going to be obstacles and I have experienced discrimination in the workplace-along with hostility and harassment for voicing my concerns. Life of the impoverished has always been a struggle for survival. But to surrender to the idea that "it can't get any better" embraces failure and in some ways relinquishes our own accountability.

Rarely is success achieved without hard work and failures along the way. So failures should never be accepted as the end, but as a new beginning-for if we choose to learn from our mistakes, we can open doors to new possibilities. Often barriers provide the underprivileged with an excuse for quitting, but very few paths are unaffected and there will always be challenges for the disadvantaged. Sometimes the fear of success is just as restrictive as the fear of failure. And even though there are conditions beyond our control-the best place to discover who is responsible for our success or lack thereof is staring back at us in the mirror everyday.

During my research, I came across many misused terms by authors with political and social agendas. My agenda is simple. Clarify definitions, establish the facts, review popular myths, and offer some new perspectives. I am not going to say what is popular-I am going to speak candidly for that is who I am. Many authors and reporters avoid controversial subject matter because it doesn't serve their self-interests. But how can we grow as a community or as individuals if we are unwilling to discuss issues that require us to exit our comfort zones and think outside the box?

Before I returned to school, I sat down and listed all of my interests and then I reviewed the accredited college degrees available in Georgia that would best fit my plans. I also evaluated costs and investigated schools academic reputations. It doesn't matter if a student graduates from a small college as long as that particular institution has formidable academic standards. Eventually, at least in the private sector it comes down to job performance not what Ivy League School you attended.

For several years I had been discussing going back to college with family members and friends, but what triggered my response was a meeting with the owner and C.E.O. of the printing company where I was employed. After being passed over for a promotion on several occasions, I scheduled a meeting with the owner to discuss the matter. During the meeting the C.E.O. shouted "You will never be an executive or a manager in my company because you are blind." This wasn't the first time I had experienced this type of discriminatory and unprofessional behavior, but every time it happens I am angered and saddened at the same time. It felt as though my heart was ripped from my chest and I was left with an empty feeling inside. Still like the good solider, I held my composure as I have done on many occasions-for to respond in angry would defeat the purpose and at the same time it would empower the oppressor.

Afterwards, the company scheduled me for an "aptitude test". God only knows why though I assumed it was to discredit me. But if so, their plan backfired because the aptitude test revealed I could perform at any level of management and I had the skills and abilities to excel in any endeavor. Still, they chose to confine me to the lowest level and then began their harassment. Their hostility heightened when I returned to school and it was just a matter of time before they forced me to leave. It is an experience I will never forget and a company I would never allow to print my books.

Maybe forgiveness is a part of human nature, but accountability is also required. Because of the corruption in all western governments, corporate accountability is rare. And morality and ethics have been replaced by selfish desires. Most legislation is manipulated by the ruling class to maintain their status quo. And the two most hated groups in America are politicians and lawyers (a statistical fact) and around eighty percent (80%) of all politicians are lawyers (another statistical fact). Concerned by the disintegration of western cultures, I delve into the abyss-because the time for change is now.

F.A. Hayek in his *The Road to Serfdom* discusses how those in power (totalitarian system) decide what the people opinions are and then through the influence of propaganda convince them these opinions are of their own choosing. And the 2008 Presidential Election where the American voters were persuaded to support Barack Obama by a disingenuous media is a perfect illustration of how the game is fixed. Hayek also asserts, which I agree with, that society's morality is undermined by the blatant disregard for the truth. Usually the end result is the suppression of the truth and subjection to "false truths". By imposing its will, the ruling class can dictate the community's social and moral values while eliminating the majority's and the minority's voices. Thus, social deterioration is the consequence for submitting to an illegitimate regime.

Every community is currently overwhelmed with injustices. The corruption that runs amok has engulfed every nation and enslaved their people. The richest capitalists seek to eliminate all unfavorable criticism while communist governments like Russia and China still rule with an iron fist. Distortions of the truth and dissemination of misinformation has replaced almost all credible journalism. But I refuse to be silenced, I refuse to believe nonsense, and I refuse to drink their *Kool-Aid*. While I try my best to be objective, there is only so much a reasonable person can take. A rise in secularism has spawned an outbreak of immorality and unprincipled behaviors. And deceptive propaganda is continually used to subdue or incite the public. So *The Invisible Man*, takes on the "ludicrous", points out the "absurd", and defies the "illogical". For I am standing up and saying "I HAVE HAD ENOUGH" and my book represents a new voice where "common sense" supplants the "narrative".

1

Indifference

"An awakening occurs when the conscious overcomes its subconscious bias"

Indifference in its simplest form is unbiased. Though, it is much more complex when used to resolve social discourse. As an author I am more concerned with providing credible information. And the journey we are about to undertake is of a peaceful nature that attempts to distinguish the facts from popular myths. Thus, I seek to become indifferent, but my quest is for the "truth".

Unfortunately we all have prejudices that have been developed over time. Our systems of beliefs are strongly influenced through our environmental and social experiences. But a shift in one's belief system can occur if the individual is willing to reevaluates his or her beliefs based upon credible new information. Understanding however, that most of us do not dramatically change our predisposition, we generally move slightly to the left or right of our previous origin. At times my personal thoughts are going to clamor loudly, though I understand the importance of examining varied interpretations.

Many compassionate individuals try to empathize with the individuals or groups that face serious challenges, however this is unrealistic. One can not comprehend the pain, the indignities, the discrimination, the subjection, and the constant challenges I have endured accept for another person who is visually impaired that has traveled a similar path. And I cannot fully understand the plight of other oppressed individuals or groups. However, I can connect at some levels, where similar experiences have occurred. And I often say the hardest obstacle to overcome is some people's resistance to change. For me it is simple because I can't change the fact that I am visually impaired. But I can try to change some people's perceptions of people who are blind and visually impaired.

There are nights when I do not rest for I am engulfed with the unfairness throughout the world. When a child dies of cancer I weep. But when a child molester is sentenced to probation I am angered. While my belly is full, millions are starving. Alcoholism and drug addictions rip at the hearts and souls of families including my own. Many rich and famous criminals go unpunished while some of the innocent poor go to prison. Popular celebrities are idolized and the honest are vilified. Our politicians lie. "God, where are you?" I cry. Only silence fills the room.

During the stillness, I think to myself "God has abandoned us"-for I can find no peace because so few have plenty and so many haven't any. Yes I desire like most to improve my quality of life, but how much is enough? Once I was told "Don't worry about things you cannot control." Still, I worry. If we detach ourselves from all emotions aren't we less human? As I wrestle with my thoughts I feel an agonizing pain in my stomach. And my ulcer says "Forget about others and think only of yourself." "No" I say. Then I grimace as another spasm intervenes.

Each night my body signals "Turn off the set and go to bed." And I obey blindly, but sleep evades me. Is it wrong that I care about those less fortunate than I? To be human is to care. As minutes become hours the clock continues to move forward. Tick tock, tick tock. I am alone in thought. My consciousness is overflowing with data and my analytical processes are in an algorithmic mode. Like a computer, I am weighing all the options and searching for the most rational solution. To be objective without succumbing to subjective bias is a very difficult task for anyone.

As I lie awake, millions of nerve impulses pass from one neuron to the next. The synapses are in a rapid fire mode and there is no off switch. Each issue weighs heavily on my on mind as I try to separate the facts from the written and spoken propaganda. Twenty-seven years ago my political science professor said "Believe half or what you hear and ten percent of what you read." That would mean ninety percent of all that is written is a fictional recreation of the truth. But I continue to toss and turn as though I were on a sinking vessel during a severe storm. My only peace comes when I finally dose off three to four hours after I have lain down.

After one issue has reached a conclusion another issue starts the process all over again. Eventually I feel my body slipping as a dull numbness is occurring in my arms and legs. Still, I fight to stay awake for the issue I am debating is important. I say "Not yet, I am not finished." But the voices are softer and softer and the sounds are becoming muddled. Silence comes as the Sandman sprinkles his sleeping dust. Eventually I drift into a deep sleep and my dreams occupy my time until I awake.

The next night, I try to recall my thoughts from the previous night. I review my conclusions and start with the next item on my list. In the interests of fairness I strive for neutrality. Though compromising our beliefs is not an affective format. It denotes a winner and a loser. And the tumultuous task is to find commonality in belief systems that articulate opposing points of view. For in commonality there is a center where common sense and logic replace idealistic bias.

Meanwhile leaders of faith shout from the pulpit "Put your worries in God's hands." Has that worked yet? Are there no more homeless? Does poverty no longer exist? Can people travel freely around the world without fear? It appears God is not listening to his apostles anymore. As I change the channels the "idiot box" provides no rational answers. Channel after channel is filled with programmed robots spouting mindless rubbish. Wait, I thought I heard English, but I do not understand. Their language is foreign to me. Eventually, I press the off button and return to my reading.

What can one person do to change the course of history? "Plenty" say I. One voice can become two and two voices can become ten. Ten becomes hundreds and hundreds become thousands and so forth. Before you know it, a single voice becomes a social movement. There is no law that says we have to accept the disintegration of society as our "manifest destiny"-for life is a journey of an undiscovered future. And any movement that benefits the whole is revolutionary. For it is progress, it is just, and it is an awakening.

Resolutions

Listening is as important as speaking. Reading is as important as writing. In our tabloid oriented society, separating facts from fiction can be a difficult task. Do not surrender to propagandas hate rhetoric. Research the material using credible sources. When listening to opposing points of view, be respectful and open minded. Do not respond to an emotional issue in a moment of passion without rational thought. Do not allow others to think for you, think for yourself. Taking back America and reclaiming our world from the greedy capitalist oppressors requires self discipline and self sacrifice.

Because I believe in God and I also believe the *Bible* is a reputable declaration of how humanity should strive to live, I am conservatively biased. But at the same time, I believe Karl

Marx, Charles Darwin, and Carl Sagan offer many interesting observations. I also enjoy the writings of Sun Tzu. So I am much more complex than just a simpleminded Southern Baptist. Blind faith without question, the general behavior of most conservatives, is illogical. While selective faith, the common practice of most liberals, is irresponsible.

Carl Sagan suggests our gods and demons assist us in our efforts to make sense of our troublesome world. And there is both truth and logic in his arguments. But if you are looking for heaven above and hell below or to the left or right then you're looking in the wrong places. *Heaven*, *Hell*, and perhaps *Purgatory* are parallel universes where our energy (spirit or soul) transfers when we die. And I agree with Sagan that aliens have replaced demons and witches in our cultural folklore, but I still believe it is scientifically impractical to dismiss the possibility of other intelligent life forms in the universe. Furthermore, there is no doubt that many religious surrogates have used fear to commit unforgivable acts against the innocent throughout history.

However most moderates recognize that there are two sides to every story, but truth and justice can not be debased. And the most effective method of assuring equality is to always consider how decisions affect humanity as a whole. Fairness can eventually be achieved through this process of putting the community ahead of the individual-for the majority of us, at some particular time in our lives, have been subjected to unjust treatment, but the challenge is to move forward. And there may never be a "utopian world", but there is always hope for a "better world".

2

The Truth about Liberals and Conservatives

"Trying to serve two masters is like trying to walk forward and backward at the same time"

Before I began dissecting the issues that are dividing our nation, I must first breakdown the fictional depictions of *Conservatives* and *Liberals.* Liberalism is a secular doctrine while Conservatism is a religious doctrine. Both belief systems are the antagonists of one another and each requires devout obedience. Just like good's alter ego is evil, one cannot exist without the other. Thus we have a complex duality competing for our will and both seek to indoctrinate.

Ann Coulter argues that liberals are godless. But over ninety percent of all Americans believe in a divine creator (God). I am but one amongst the masses. Since this is a statistic fact, it means ninety percent of us are actually conservative from a religious standpoint. The degree of conservativeness is the discerning variable. Based on the issue, a person might fall under a kaleidoscope of categories or labels.

More than 90 % of Americans believe in a ***Supernatural Force***

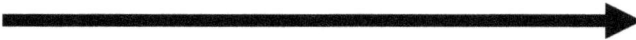

Extreme Left Liberal Moderate Conservative Extreme Right

Extreme Conservatives generally believe everything in the *Bible*, the *Koran*, or the *Torah* is true and scientific discovery is a tool of pagans. Anyone or anything that disagrees is evil (a symbol of Satan) and some consider the enemy. They don't care that all religious texts were reinterpreted by men, who's intentions may have been honorable, but their biased agendas on many occasions dictated what was written as

"God's or Allah's words." Most extremists believe the world is only six thousand years old. An unrealistic idea since science has proven the world is billions of years old and the human species has been around for close to two hundred thousand years. If a train is roaring at a high speed, does one step off the track or stand there believing it will magically stop? Faith also requires usage of common sense.

When it comes to the *Ten Commandments*, I would probably be labeled as extremely conservative. I believe that God laid the foundation for all men and women to live by in these simple words:

> Romans 13:9 For this, Thou shalt not commit adultery, Thou shalt not kill, Thou shalt not steal, Thou shalt not bear false witness, Thou shalt not covet; and if there be any other commandment, it is briefly comprehended in this saying, namely, Thou shalt love thy neighbour as thyself. Exodus 20:12-17.

I admit I fall short on numerous occasions of how God desires us to conduct ourselves. We are all flawed and imperfect. No one, but Jesus, walked without sin. But if society rejects the Ten Commandments, I believe there is little hope left for humanity to reestablish its moral character.

Conservative's belief system is God. Still, many have trouble letting go of some religious notions because they are tied to traditions and one thing I am sure of is Americans love traditions. We celebrate anything and everything. Birthdays, weddings, patriotic holidays, births, and deaths our festive and religious traditions fill our yearly calendars. Regrettably Americans spend more time celebrating than they do praying which is a sad commentary on our priorities. And one tradition I do not believe in is the mummifying and burying of our bodies. This practice of ancient pharaohs and kings was adopted by the religious sects. Our bodies are shells and our souls ascend to heaven or descend to hell in alternate universes where our life forces continue throughout eternity. Accordingly, the body is meant to return to the dust from which it came.

Therefore cremation would be a more logical choice after an autopsy has been performed. And we live on in the memories of those who knew and loved us and our good deeds are not in vain. Americans use enormous amounts of land for burial sites which could be used more effectively. Some possibilities might include homes for the poor, parks for children, campgrounds, recreation facilities, and animal reserves. Still, the most wasteful use of land is the ridiculous number of golf courses throughout the western hemisphere. It is a foolish consumption, but I guess rich people will not be satisfied until they own and control every inch of the world.

On the issue of heaven and hell, I am a conservative. I believe there will be a "*Judgment Day*" when each one of us stands before God to answer (atonement) for our sins. Though I also believe the harsher the crimes, the worse the punishment will be in hell. Just because we are forgiven for our sins doesn't mean we are excused from our evil deeds. Our salvation rests in God's hands and the seriousness of our disobedience will dictate our fate. The cliché "Think before you act" is wise advice we should all adhere too-for Dante was right the seriousness of our sins will determine our eternal punishment in Hell.

When it comes to the issue of prayer in schools, I would also be labeled a conservative. Ann Coulter is absolutely correct in her assertions that liberals have taken over our educational systems. When I was in school we prayed and pledged our allegiance to the flag everyday. We also gave thanks before every meal and we had discipline and dress codes. And the vast majority of students respected our teachers. Most of the blind and visually impaired students of the resident school for the blind came from poor and uneducated families. While we didn't have much, we had one another and we had our faith. I am very thankful for the positive impact of a conservative faculty that understood compassion, motivation, self reliance, respect, and discipline are all critical components of the maturation process of young minds-although there were a few extremists that probably should have been terminated along with our high school career guidance counselors who were more concerned with their thirty-five year careers with the state than they were in assisting the blind and visually impaired students. For whoever serveth self does not serveth the LORD.

With *Moderate Conservatives* there is an ability to separate fact from fiction. Here, religion and science co-exists. The middle, often referred to as the center, is where most Americans identify themselves on the majority of the issues. However, many often misrepresent themselves as moderates too. Pro-abortion is not a moderate view. It is a liberal view that excludes God's revelations and the unborn child's rights from the argument.

Both conservatives and liberals appear to be confused about "*pro-life*" and "*pro-death*". Conservatives are pro-life when it comes to abortion and pro-death when the issue is the death penalty. Yet, liberals are pro-death on abortion, but pro-life on the death penalty and war. Common sense says one should either be pro-life or pro-death. And based on their doctrines, conservatives should be pro-life and liberals should be pro-death.

I am pro-life. What I believe distinguishes me as a moderate conservative, on the pro-life pro-death issue, is that I believe there has to be "exceptions to the rules". And though I strongly oppose abortion, you will not find me at any clinic harassing women. God will judge them. Nevertheless, I do feel in my heart, my soul, and my bones that abortion is one of humanity's most hideous crimes.

On the other hand, *Liberal Conservatives* put more faith in man. They are not godless as Ann Coulter suggests. But I believe they are misguided and often confused by anti-religious propaganda. And I have many liberal friends who consider themselves to be Christians. Most of them are honest and decent people, but they have been persuaded by mounds of propaganda and "hate slogans" that seek to invoke doubt or create emotional outrage. Nevertheless, liberals try to incorporate God into a secular belief system. But this is a serious mistake for trying to serve God, while embracing a secular lifestyle, is an impossible feat.

Sometimes I am amazed that intelligent people can be coerced by a doctrine that seeks to remove God from all aspects of life. How can people be so gullible? "*The Separation of Church and State*" slogan is a fictional myth. Just like a crooked defense attorney, who knows his client is guilty, the liberal agenda is not concerned with the truth. It preys upon people's good will and desires to be fair (inclusive). And the liberal doctrine solicits angry, hate, guilt, and fear disguised as empathy. Thus, emotional responses are generally irrational because a reaction without thought lacks substance. Though the extreme conservatives are also guilty of using mindless dribble or hate rhetoric to propagandize their flocks as well. At times it is very difficult to detach our emotions from decisions but fairness depends on our objectivity.

In *The Purpose Driven Life,* author Rick Warren said:

> Many people are driven by guilt. They spend their entire lives running from regrets and hiding their shame. Guilt driven people are manipulated by memories. They allow their past to control their future.

Injustices of the past overwhelm many liberals thereby allowing their guilt to influence their decisions. At the same time, they have forgotten that conservatives have always been at the forefront of social equality. *Abolition, Voting, Civil Rights, Education*, and *Employment Opportunities* would not have changed without the support of the majority of American conservatives. Every reasonable human being whether he or she be liberal, moderate, conservative, and even progressive or godless desires fairness for all, but we cannot fix the past.

Today gay marriage is one of America's most controversial issues. Even though I believe the gay lifestyle is an immoral choice, consenting adults have the right of choosing their partners. Again, I will let God judge them-for we do not have the right to hate or mistreat anyone because their belief system differs from ours. Besides most of us, especially me, have lapses of morality everyday. Thus, I am for *Gay Civil Unions* sponsored by the state. But I still believe marriage should remain a religious ceremony between men and women. On this position, I might be characterized as a liberal conservative. Personally I view myself as trying to be open-minded. We have the right to disagree with the gay lifestyle, but homosexuality is not a crime.

Most *Extreme Liberals* that believe in God don't believe his rules apply to them. Many of these extremists are on the edge of insanity. They are the polar opposite of the Extreme Conservatives. And criminals that commit heinous acts such as torture and murder, poison people with drugs, launder blood money and diamonds, steal and exploit the poor, promote legalized prostitution, gambling, and pornography are going "straight to hell." And I will not lie for I too have watched my share of adult porn in my day. I have also gambled and I still like to play small stakes poker every once and a while. When I was younger, I drank heavily and I still swear too much. But I also understand I will have to answer for my shortcomings, there are no free rides. Those who lack any remorse for their crimes against humanity and rebellion against God will face his wrath. No, you will not pass Go, you will not collect Salvation, and you will not enter *the Kingdom of Heaven*. Truthfully, the allure of these temptations are extremely powerful aphrodisiacs and our resistance requires enormous self control.

But it is an illogical myth for extremists to do whatever they desire and then believe all will be forgiven. Just as good deeds do not go unnoticed; evil deeds will not go unpunished. And just as extremists turned away from God, he will strike them from the roll. I actually believe there may be a place called Purgatory where God allows repentant souls to gain redemption. If not, the majority of us including myself are skating on thin ice.

Still I can't find much in the extreme liberal conservative's ideology that I agree with other than the fact they recognize the existence of God. Though, vigilante justice does seem to be the only real justice left for the majority of law abiding citizens. I grew up fighting and I have been pushed to the brink many times by despicable people masquerading as human beings. But as I grew older, I realized that violence empowers those in control and imprisons the oppressed. I still get upset, especially with hypocrites, but I am now more able to control my emotions much better than when I was younger. It is ok to be passionate about our beliefs however, we must also be civil. Again, I will continually reiterate "We have the right to voice our opinions publicly, but we have no right to force our opinions upon others."

Resolutions

We must be willing to reevaluate our belief systems on a continual basis. Liberals and conservatives must work together for the good of the whole. I get extremely aggravated with politicians double talk. Barack Obama said in his book *The Audacity of Hope*:

> But the essential idea behind the Declaration-that we are born into this world free, all of us, that each of us arrives with a bundle of rights that can't be taken away by any person or any state without just cause.

But his stand on abortion contradicts this proclamation. Abortion obstructs the unborn child's unalienable rights. Barack is a gifted storyteller, though he seems to be the same old typical politician "Be everything to everyone". Saying he fears women might use unsafe methods if abortion is overturned is a copout. The phrase "I'm a Christian" means nothing. How we conduct our lives says everything. And I am far from perfect, but as I told a former college professor and good friend once I am who am I-honesty and integrity mean more to me than worrying about offending someone.

Sometimes conservatives irritate me just as much as liberals. *Universal Healthcare*, *Education*, our *Environment* (especially *Global Warming*), and *Equal Access* based on merit are a handful of moral issues that affect the majority of Americans. But these are not liberal, moderate, or conservative values; they are American values and noble causes that call for reasonable personal sacrifices for the good of the whole-*for a united village is built by contributions from all.* Moreover, our conversations should be focused on the most efficient and effective ways of addressing these and many other important challenges we are facing in the midst of an unstable future instead of using them as political sound-bites to stimulate a desired response from a targeted audience. Our economy is in flux with record setting housing bankruptcies, the cost of postwar reconstruction, the retirement of baby boomers approaching, billions in personal debt (credit cards and high interest loans), trillions in trade deficits (especially China), outsourcing tens of millions of livable wage jobs to foreign markets, future healthcare costs of medical conditions associated with obesity and the poisoning of our environment, the costs of a steadily growing oversized inefficient government, tens of billions in wasteful spending by Washington politicians, rising costs of health insurance, the costs of national emergencies due to the increasing numbers of natural disasters directly linked to global warming, record numbers of corporate bankruptcies, the mismanaging of retirement funds-for the list of economic volatility seems endless. All the warning signs are here, but we continue to listen to these market analysts on television who are paid to forecast sunshine even though a storm has been verified. And if we do not start preparing for this unprecedented storm, we are going to witness its wrath first hand.

In June of 2006 I had an amazing dream. I was riding along with a friend on the interstate when all of a sudden there was a loud clap of thunder. I had never heard such a great roar of thunder. All traffic stopped. Suddenly a large figure appeared in the sky. Flying like *Superman*, the figure could be seen from afar and I knew immediately who it was. A bearded man wearing a royal blue robe trimmed in gold with brown sandals filled the sky like a balloon from a Macy's holiday parade, it was *Jesus.* As I jettisoned from the car leaving the door open I proceeded toward the emergency lane pavement near the grass, I dropped to my knees. Then I awakened.

I was reminded of this dream around a year later (August of 2007) because of a different dream. *Satan* appeared to me, but the representation was not the horned menace that is frequently portrayed in religious art or Halloween customs. And the ingrained depiction of the *Devil* that I had often imagined as a child resembled the face of media correspondent and ABC analyst Sam Donaldson. Instead the most beautiful woman I had every seen stood before me. She had flowing thick bright apple red hair and light pinkish skin that was as soft as butter. Her naked body was perfectly sculpted and her voice was sweeter than any I had ever heard. She looked more like an angel or goddess rather than the fictional demon I had believed Satan to be. Again I awakened.

Truthfully, I have never put much stock in dreams. For me, they have always been like a movie I am watching and sometimes staring in. In the tens of thousands of dreams I have dreamt a few have actually come true. Still, that has more to do with statistical probability so I never dwell on it. But these two dreams got me to thinking if we cannot get beyond our stereotypical beliefs, liberals and conservatives will never be able to work together unless a mediator intervenes.

3

Fiscally Conservative

"Debt imprisons the irresponsible to a lifetime of Servitude"

Fiscal conservativeness must not be confused with religious conservatism. It is an idea centered in financial responsibility. It involves planning and budgeting. The majority of Americans have accumulated more debt, especially credit card debt, than they can afford. And the facts clearly indicate that most Americans lack the discipline or the knowledge of being fiscally conservative. I have tried, with little success, to simplify this notion to my own family. If one's net income is fifteen hundred dollars per month, one's cost of living can not exceed this amount.

On one hand I feel sorrow for people in financial disarray and on the hand I acknowledge there seems to be a lack of self-responsibility. I am constantly reminded of an old cliché "Give a man a fish and he eats for one day. Teach a man to fish and he eats for a lifetime." About ten year ago, I fell into the credit card pit of debt. I worked a lot of overtime to pay off half the debt and I refinanced my home at a lower interest rate and paid off the other half. At the time I was very angry at myself because I am good with numbers and managing finances. But the "debt trap" can lure even the shrewdest financial minds if we are unaware of the dangers. Many conservatives, moderates, and liberals in western cultures are drowning in an endless sea of debt.

Numerous credit cards with large limits, paying the minimal payment, and barrowing high interests loans will lead to a lifetime of servitude. God calls upon all of his children to be fiscally conservative. Planning, budgeting, and managing our finances is an absolute necessity in our current economy.

Now I have one major credit card with a set limit that I use sparingly and I pay off quickly. The consumer can set a lower credit limit on any card. Don't allow these companies to increase your limit. When I was finishing my degree, I worked as a paraprofessional at the residential school for the blind where I graduated. My net take home was around a thousand dollars per month. My rent was half my net pay. I was able to live on the rest because I lived within my budget. So, if the working poor can survive on so little, why does our government continue to waste our tax dollars? That is very simple, our government and politicians are not fiscally conservative. Most politicians and government bureaucrats spend tax dollars as though it were "Monopoly money".

One should remember that if the majority of us who own a home lost our current job, a strong possibility with the erosion of the American job market (livable wage jobs), and had trouble finding another with a comparable salary, we could potentially lose most of our possessions. That is why being fiscally conservative is a necessity because it prepares us for the unforeseen future. Requiring our government to be fiscally responsible is the right of every taxpayer. Each elected official and government agency should be scrutinized and held accountable for every tax dollar collected and spent. Senator Byrd's (D) West Virginia earmarks are a prime example of the wasteful spending in Washington. He will find only torture with no idol sanctuaries built unto himself in *Hell*. Why in God's name do the West Virginians, a community of hard working decent folk, keep reelecting this irresponsible senile old fart? The only irrational behavior more astonishing is the reelecting of Ted Kennedy (D) by the Massachusetts voters. Robert Byrd should have been caged decades ago. And Senator Kennedy is one of the best examples of what the influence of a family's wealth and the media can achieve in a corrupt two party system. Both senators illustrate why there should be term limits for all elected officials.

Most of the liberals, along with their coconspirators the democrats and the majority in the media, believe in throwing money at every social problem. An unwise and ineffective use of our taxes with minimal ROI (return on investment) and that is why the people need fiscally conservative representatives. Elected officials should be guardians of the American taxpayer's dollars. Instead both parties spend our taxes with no fiscal restraint. And the wasteful insanity of Washington angers the majority of us. So voting for new Democrats or Republicans will not change the corruption because they are a part of the corruption. Every time I see someone on television saying "We can vote them out of office if we are unhappy with a politician's performance and that is a democracy at work", I lose it. If we had four more choices such as a conservative, a moderate, a liberal, and an independent to replace the irresponsible Democrat or Republican, this statement might make more sense. Thus, limiting the number of candidates, who are subservient to their wealthy financial contributors, is contrary to the meaning of a "democracy".

Another common misuse of the taxpayer dollars is oversized governmental bureaucracies. These government bureaucracies provide a buffer between the wealthy and the poor. Ann Coulter was right on the money when she said our educational systems are trying to *baptize* our youths into the doctrine of liberalism. I know this is so because I went back to college a few years ago and finished my Bachelors Degree in Communications (New Media) while I worked as a paraprofessional. But the doctrine of liberalism is being used in all government agencies. And the majority of employment opportunities and advancement are predicated on one's indoctrination.

Also the liberal doctrine opposes both religious and fiscal conservatism. When writers like Anthony Signoreli attempt to link liberty and liberalism, I mock their ridiculous notions. *Liberty* represents freedom in a revolutionary context; it calls for rebellion against the oppressors. Our oppressors are the western corporate capitalists. Our politicians (Democrats and Republicans) are their puppets. And they use their corporate controlled media industry to create illusions of truth through spin, misinformation, and hate propaganda. Still, I believe the majority of liberals are good, but they and many conservatives are being manipulated by the propaganda machines of the richest pagans in the world. It is imperative that we do not allow others to think for us because the world will not change unless we change.

Resolutions

Because most Americans are spinning out of control when it comes to being fiscally conservative, we need consumer protection-laws that will limit interest rates that can be charged, laws that limit the number of credit cards, laws that limit the individual's credit based on income, laws that imprison predator lenders, laws that exclude late fees that are underhanded, laws that prohibit foreign investors from purchasing our debt, issuing credit, or charging Americans interests, and laws that imprison corporate executives who mislead investors.

Another helpful solution would be to create a free national education program, taught by volunteer financial advisor retirees, that teaches the public how to invest, save, and live within a budget through free workshops and educational seminars for all citizens as well as a required national program for all high school, technical school, and college students. This plan would include mandatory meetings for all politicians with top economists, retirement fund managers, and a panel of financial advisors from the educational program that would educate Congress, state, and local politicians on how to be more fiscally conservative. It would be cheaper to incarcerate every Democrat and Republican for life than to continue to allow the irresponsible and increased spending habits of these jackals to go unchecked.

Taking baby steps in the beginning is very important. Each one of us can change our spending habits. Americans compulsive buying goes far beyond our needs. There has been so many times when I have purchase an item I don't really need and later wonder why I bought it. Don't depend on Social Security. Invest in your own retirement plan. All Congress does when it supposedly fixes Social Security is overtax the middle class. With the decline of the middle classes standard of living there won't be an available resource in the future for Congress to exploit unless they turn on their masters. At the same time we should demand fiscal conservativeness from all politicians. The pork and earmarks are a crime against the American people. Changing our behaviors can positively influence others throughout the world faced with similar circumstances.

And we must also be willing to learn from others such as the *American Jewish Community.* There are two life-lessons they seem to comprehend better than most other cultures and communities in the US. One is the importance of a quality education and the other is sound financial planning. Jews, Muslins, and Christians must put aside our differences and work together to build a united community of responsible and compassionate believers. And yes the less traveled path is not always the simplest or easiest route. Though, if we are going improve on our fiscal conservativeness, we must not be afraid. You are not alone because I and many others will be sailing on the same voyage.

A 9 trillion dollar national debt and over 1 trillion in trade deficits is more than irresponsible; it is criminal and both the Democrats and Republicans are guilty as charged. So with the economic crisis confronting America over the next several years, how can a Presidential candidate make promises of *change* by aiding trillions in debt to our ten trillion dollar overdraft already sucking the life out of the American middle class while enslaving many future generations? The truth is he can't, but Barack Obama has a large portion of the democrat's liberal media posse riding shotgun; deflecting any questions concerning fiscal responsibility involving common sense except when it comes to Iraq. When Democrats had no answers they blamed George Walker Bush or Iraq, but I want to hear details of how elected officials are going to approach our economic crisis not hate rhetoric. And now that Barack has become our 44th President, how long will the "blame Bush scheme" work before angry Americans revolt? Moreover, God calls on us to be fiscally conservative. Sometimes we forget this, but we must reverse the current debt dependency or it will eventually collapse upon us and America will suffer a great depression a thousand fold worse than the *Stock Market Crash of 1929.*

A World Gone Mad

What happened to our world?
Has it always been this way?
Maybe God gave up on us.
Or language has nothing let to say.
Hatred flows like a river.
And anger dominates the day.
Our streets are filled with violence.
And children have no safe place left to play.
Suits poison our waters.
While mindless speech circles the globe.
But fear dictates our silence.
And the atrocities of thieves go untold.
Many seek refuge in addictions.
But no solace can be found.
Immorality has become commonplace.
While the impoverished are abound.
Our destiny looks quite gloomy
For mankind has embraced the dark side of humanity.
And the truth is lost in deception.
So it must be the end of our sanity.

4

The Godless Minority

"He who walks without faith believes in nothing and travels a lonely path"

Less than ten percent of the American population falls under the *Godless Line.* Here the rules change because there is a lack of moral guidelines governing most belief systems. Radical ideologies replace reasonable convention. Survival of the fittest, might makes right (an idea of the Roman Empire), lawlessness, and dictatorships are some of the extreme ideas of the godless. Without God there is no accountability. Thus, rules seldom apply to the non-believers.

Less than 10 % of Americans are ***Godless***

←

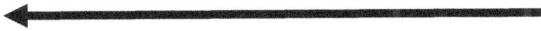

Communist Fascist Socialist Progressive Liberal

Godless liberals tolerate everything except a conservative point of view. Since there is no God, they don't have to answer for there sins. Drugs, pornography, gambling, adultery, homosexuality, violence, lying, theft, murder, rape, child molestation, vulgarity, for some of the godless liberals there are few boundaries. Whatever feels goods is right. Many liberals use trifle victimology as a reason for unruly anti-social behaviors. And most aristocrats ignore the lawlessness until it penetrates their exclusive inner sanctuaries. Greed is their master and I will continually refer to the wealthy elite as godless or pagans. And the basis for my belief is what Jesus said in Mathew:

> Mathew 19:24 And again I say unto you, It is easier for a camel to go through the eye of a needle, than for a rich to enter into the kingdom of God.

This profound statement by Jesus is as close to zero as one can induce. If Ann Coulter had characterized the greedy capitalists or liberal non-believers as godless, I would have been more inclined to agree. Though I feel sorrow for the godless because they journey through life alone and the "*Angel of Death*" will bring forth unimaginable suffering in the *Underworld* as the toll for their sins against God and mankind.

Godless Progressives are politically motivated. Their agenda pushes for a secular world view through legislative or judicial decrees. Lawlessness, with no self discipline, and no consequences for misconduct is a huge part of their doctrine. Many western cultures have legalized everything except for murder and that depends on who is being murdered and where it occurs. It is not hard to understand why many Islamic followers view most western societies as deplorable. I too, am disgusted and appalled. The disintegration of morals and values in every western nation is unbelievable. But the seduction of sin is an alluring trap that I have fallen into many times. Temptation knocks on everyone's door. However, there are still lines even I would never cross and most are extremely liberal or progressive.

Often Progressives misrepresent their views as progress. Progress is the advancements that contribute positively to humanity. Its contributions are based on improving our quality of life. Just because a friend jumps off a cliff doesn't mean I am going to follow. I'll find a new friend. When countries like Holland and Sweden legalize drugs and prostitution, it doesn't signify progress. It demonstrates an erosion of their moral constitution.

Socialism is a government controlled society. All production and wealth would be overseen and redistributed by the government. This idea centers on all men being equal (elimination of class). Karl Marx and Friedrich Engels developed their theories in the mid 1800's. *Fascism* is slightly to the left of socialism and the right of communism. It is a centralized government that suppresses opposition. Hitler and Mussolini were fascists. Sadly, the current most popular hate rhetoric used by liberals, labels conservatives as fascists. Though quite ridiculous since socialism and fascism are forms of communism which is a godless ideology. *Communism* is a political doctrine based on Marxian socialism.

It is the most extreme form of a socialistic government. Here the government is a dictatorship of one party or one person and there is no opposition. Any attempt to oppose said government is met with serious consequences (imprisonment or death). Russia, China, and Cuba are communist governments. Russia is not a democracy as some in our western bureaucratic governments and the media industry are now spinning. This is a fictional creation born from capitalists that desire to exploit foreign markets with less restrictive environments. These untapped markets before 1990 offered low wages, fewer safety and environmental restrictions, and labor exploitation which fit the corporate goal for excessive profits.

Yes, I am a fan of Karl Marx's writings. Do I agree with everything he says? Of course not, but his ideology grew from the class warfare he observed and suffered through his entire life. Many great writers such as Charles Dickens and Mark Twain have written fictional works that imitated real life conditions of their eras. The bourgeoisie (owners of production and employers of wage labor) or robber barons of the industrial revolution are described as the oppressors in Marx's *The Communist Manifesto.* Marx and Engels were looking for a better system of fairness. However, they made two critical mistakes in their search for equality. (1) No society will ever be successful without moral guidelines (God). And (2) a government without outside (independent) oversight will never represent the best interests of its people-for its self preservation (survival) will dictate its policies.

Any government can serve a purpose if it is structured correctly. But all governments are accountable to the people they represent. We need a government to reasonably regulate and monitor corporations and businesses. There is also a need for consumer protection, environmental protection, and employee protection. And there must be protection for all citizens against the unlawful. But the oversized inefficient governments of the western societies have run amok. If the American citizens reclaimed our government and political system from the wealthy influential corruptors, other western nations would eventually follow our lead-because we have the moral and legal authority to do so.

I have struggled with the existence of God my entire life, but I don't believe this is uncommon for many of us are searching for the truth.

And I understand what Joseph Smith (founder of the Mormon Church) was going through when he observed the corruption in many of the *American Christian Churches* in the 1820's. Today the corruption of most *Western Christian Churches* is worse than any time in world history or that is the way it appears to me. But just because many believers are dissatisfied with the direction of current churches doesn't mean we can rewrite the Bible. And I do not believe God or any Angels appeared to Joseph Smith and there were no *Golden Plates.* Just like many false prophets before him, I believe he lied and then began to rewrite the Bible to fit into his world view similar to the way liberals try and fit God into their lifestyles. And besides a Church of God would not be worth over thirty billion dollars for *Jesus's Churches* are built on service and compassion for our brothers and sisters not wealth, power, and influence dictated by repetitious propaganda.

That doesn't mean I am right, it means this is my interpretation. But if anyone tells me they are hearing voices I would recommend them for counseling because they maybe unstable. And it is true the *Roman Catholic Church* started the canonization of the *Holy Bible* which was finished by King James, however, that doesn't empower us to redefine scripture. Although the meaning of verses may be interpreted somewhat differently by those with different religious experiences and backgrounds in religious history, we (including clergy) do not have the authority to rewrite God's words. But it is also true the Catholic Church, with its centralized dictatorship in Rome (Italy-the Vatican), is another corrupt religious *Empire,* though I believe they started out with good intentions and were corrupted by the Roman Emperor Constantine in 324 A.D. And thus began the Roman Catholic Church's movement toward the dark side through unholy alliances that still exists today. Therefore I must believe in God or all the suffering in the world would be meaningless while greed, lust, and power would be the dreams of most and the only social discourse left for the oppressed would be violence.

Resolutions

The godless are a part of humanity too and we must not turn away from them. There are some rich people doing good deeds. So it is up to us to appeal to the goodness in the ruling upper class. The majority of us have kindness and love lurking somewhere deep within. Many capitalists lost touch with their inner self as did the Catholic Church when they became focused on power and wealth. By ignoring their hearts, greed became their god, and the lust of what wealth could purchase consumed them. Wealth is not necessarily an evil achievement. How financial success is attained and what the financial gains are used for determines one's atonement.

Most wealthy people start out with good intentions similar to politicians. However, the problem is not where you start but where you end up and how you got there. Often judgment becomes clouded by determination. Right and wrong are redefined. The media continuously over uses the term "*gray area*" to spin unlawful acts. All of a sudden wrong becomes right through propagandas advertisement blitzes. And so I say to you "The ends will never justify the means but God's punishment will fit the crime."

Without moral guidelines, progressives are lost in a maze of deception. Every time I hear one of the Hollywood liberals comment on the legalization of all drugs, I can't help but get upset. Are people oblivious to the damage that alcohol has caused in our society? Alcohol and drug usage has seriously damage my family and our personal relationships. There have been many holidays spent at my mother's home, where I have endured immeasurable suffering for the sake of peace. If America gives into the pressure of a few radical idealists, the social, psychological, and criminal damages may be irreversible.

Hasn't the crime rates and violence increased in these so-called progressive countries? What were they thinking? Sinful addictions cost enormous amounts of money. The wealthy establishment can afford these deviant habits, but the rest of us can not. Thus criminals who are usually poor must con, steal, push, assault, or murder to participate. The day I take advice from an uninformed *Hollywood crackpot* who has been smoking weed for the last forty years is the day I submit to counseling. Truthfully I smoked marijuana up until the age of twenty-three and I did inhale. But we put away childish things as Paul said when we become men and began to understand our responsibilities. And there are some knowledgeable people in the entertainment industry, but unfortunately the majority of these extremist constantly demonstrate their ignorance every time they open their mouths and speak. Nevertheless I enjoy Bill Maher's HBO show *Real Time* though some of his guests are beyond counseling.

Almost everyone desires a fair social and economical system. Regrettably everyone is not willing to do their part. But extreme liberals and progressives are anti-social. They desire chaos, a society with no rules. In their minds, God's and man's laws do not apply to them. At the same time, Dictatorships are restrictively dangerous, but they can also be more effective because they don't have to deal with bureaucratic nonsense. Though for me any successful community must establish solid moral ground and an ethical code of honor as its primary foundation for an inclusive society.

5

The Quagmire of Iraq

"He who rushes in encounters tragedy
while he who approaches cautiously understands the meaning of valor"

The Iraq War is a quagmire for there are no good solutions to the complexity of its challenges. It is true we were misled by falsified intelligence. But it was not the first time and it probably won't be the last. FDR allowed the attack on Pearl Harbor to sway public opinion on the war. And he was also sending war supplies to Great Britain on passenger liners two years before the Japanese attacked. Lincoln goateed the Confederates into attacking Fort Sumter. Johnson and McNamara constantly lied about Vietnam. Truman dropped two atomic bombs on a defeated Japan when it wasn't necessary although some argue it saved lives, sadly we will never know. Reagan declared the "*Cold War*" was over, but doesn't Russia still have enough nuclear weapons to wipe out the entire world hundreds of times over and hasn't Russia sold weapons and nuclear technologies to terrorists and its comrade China. JFK and RFK abandoned freedom fighters of Cuba during the "*Bay of Pigs*" and signed off on the assassination of Fidel Castro because they were misled by top officials in the CIA. Grant and his administration committed hideous atrocities against Native Americans and White Southerners. I suspect Clinton may have divulged technological secrets to China. Unfortunately lying is what politicians do especially Democrats and Republicans.

But I have a question. What did Iraq do other than agitate the U.S. and UN? China has disposed of its toxics waste materials in American foods, healthcare products, animal foods, and toys, but that's just what we know about. I guarantee China has unloaded poisons in more than just the products identified to the public-for if more information leaked out our government would have some serious explaining to do. Poisoning the American people is an act of "*War*" and campaign contributions from communist sympathizers to Democrats is an act of "*Treason*". At times it appears Americans are as stupid as the rest of the world thinks we are. And Russia's selling of weapons and nuclear technology to terrorists is an act of "War" against all western nations. But members of the UN lack the courage to stand up to Russia or China- for both have always committed unspeakable atrocities to their own people and others throughout the world. And while it was true that Saddam Hussein was ruthless, he posed no significant international threat. So if Iraq really wasn't a danger then what else could the conflict be over other than oil?

The UN and America didn't intervene in Rwanda (1994) and now we are allowing the same genocide in Darfur. After World War II, the *World Community* said "Never again." I guess they meant "No genocide where it interferes with our economic interests". Today Putin is indoctrinating the youth in Russia the same way Hitler and the *Nazi Party* brainwashed the German people. And China has built the largest military in the World which it uses to oppress any freedom movements. But western corporations are more concerned with their business interests in Russia and China. So they use their media conglomerates to suppress the truth.

Meanwhile, journalists who speak out in Russia and China are murdered or imprisoned by their governments. Moreover, any good news in Iraq is rarely reported. But the *Western Media Empires* continue their assault on the American men and women who are putting their lives on the line and that is the sad truth about today's irresponsible journalism. Many of these liberal loonies are products of the drug crazed generation of the 1960's and they have been indoctrinating the western youth over the last forty years with anti-military propaganda. But the U.S. Military is not the problem, the politicians and their policies dictated by their capitalist masters is the reason why America and other western governments have interposed themselves in the Middle East against the will of their people. Thus, our dependency on oil has brought us to *The Iraqi Quagmire.* But the question isn't whether the Iraq War was necessary because that is hindsight. Therefore I believe the question should be "How can we most effectively resolve the crisis in the timeliest manner?"

Everyone can speculate on what is going to happen when the U.S. military eventually leaves, but that doesn't matter. It is the Iraqi people's "right to settle their own disputes and solve their own problems" with limited oversight by the *International Community.* Imposing our belief systems on other sovereign nations is imperialism not democracy. America should always lead by example instead of might-for no nation, no corporation, no military, and no man have been given the authority to subject others to their will.

Resolutions

As I said there are no perfect solutions to Iraq. But there are some options that seem to make the most sense. First, Iraq should be divided into three (3) provinces. Each would have representation in a single Parliament and share in the oil revenues based on the population percentage of their District. Then we must reach out to the International Community for assistance in developing a plan to stabilize Iraq's Government (of its own choosing by its people), law enforcement, and military until they are able to operate sufficiently without international support. While we are offering the olive branch to the International Community, we need to start bringing our troops and civilian workers home in the most responsible and humane way-for there are no winners or losers the situation is just one big "stinking mess". And I don't believe it is necessary for the United States to have a permanent base in Iraq. Of course I am against having embassies or military bases in any foreign nation for it is time to put the CIA, KGB, and other rogue government agencies out of business.

However, the world is focused too narrowly on terrorism by a few radical fundamentalists we can monitor while trying to workout peaceful solutions. For we have the technology, capable law enforcement, and proficient military personnel to handle any crisis. And it is not our given right to impose our beliefs systems on nations in the Middle East or anywhere else. But we do have a right to discourage oppression, injustice, and terrorism through international sanctions and it is America's duty to support and protect free allied nations such as Israel, though this can be achieved from a distance. Furthermore, we should always reserve the right to use military intervention when any sovereign nation harbors terrorists, drug traffickers, arms dealers, murderers, or any criminal trying to escape American justice.

Unfortunately the world is ignoring Russia and China and I believe that is a crucial mistake-for their alliance reminds me of Germany's and Japan's alliance in WWII. And Iraq is a quagmire created by poor political policy just like Vietnam, but verbally attacking those who serve our nation is unpatriotic and if one crosses that line in my home, his next stop would probably be the dentist (exception to the rule). It is also sickening to watch the anti-military protests in Berkley for if there were no *America Military* there would be no "freedom of speech" or educational institutions in America. And as *Chinese Soldiers* patrolled our streets and suppressed our rights while the *Russian Secret Police* (new name for the KGB) invaded our homes, these fools might regret their ignorance.

6

Religion

"The test of one's faith is a measurement of one's character"

Religion has played a major role in society for thousands of years. Many have died in the name of religion or because of their differences of opinion in religious ideology. For the majority of us religion is a spiritual journey or connection. A pilgrimage, a peaceful transition, or an awakening can dramatically change one's life. And thus I say to you "Anyone who commits an act of violence in the name of religion sins against God for God is love."

There are three major factions of religion today. Judaism, Christianity, and Islam dominate conservative groups. Each faith has splintered into multiple denominations. When conflict arises, members leave the group and form new congregations. Adults should never behave this way because it turns off nonbelievers. So when reading the Torah, Bible, or Koran one must use rational logic to interpret the meanings of scripture. Muhammad said:

> When you meet the unbelievers, smith their necks, then, when you have made wide slaughter among them, tie fast the bonds; then set them free, either by grace or ransom, till the war lays down its loads,

When examining this one small verse, it opens the door for numerous interpretations. One of the Ten Commandments is "Thou shalt not kill" and it is also a crime, under manmade laws, to take another life without just cause. Thus murder is an act against God and humanity.

For the last year or so, I have been leaning toward the Islamic faith. I have started reading the Bible, the Koran, and the Torah in an effort to broaden my understanding of religion. An outside observer objectively viewing western cultures might question the validity of our proclamation of faith considering our lack of morality. Anyway, my patience is being tested as is countless others whom are witnessing the "wickedness of the west". I am not without fault because I have been a participant in sin on many occasions. Most decent people are searching for the right spiritual fit. And even though I was raised as a Southern Baptist, my tolerance for the current representation of Christianity has withered.

Nevertheless, religion in its purest form is the moral backbone of mankind and the Bible aluminates the wisdom of God. Many have turned away from God for idol worship, but at the first hint of turmoil they seek the "Almighty". That is why I often refer to liberals as hypocrites because they think God serves at their convenience while at the same time liberals pick and choose which of the Ten Commandments apply to them. Accordingly, it is almost impossible to get extremely religious people to review any credible information that argues against their beliefs. They know their beliefs are true "For their religious texts tells them so." Any modern science or any opposing point of view is discarded as anti-faith propaganda. I understand their conviction. Some extremists are so frustrated with the real world that their faith becomes their delusional world. I too feel their pain. What religion often provides is an escape from a world gone mad. Though, believing in exaggerated myths will not relieve extremist's agony.

Regardless, when it comes to religion being identified with holy war, I do not like the idea of being a religious pawn in the battle between *good* and *evil*. How can we say that if three million souls go to heaven and six billion souls go to hell, God wins? This just doesn't make sense. Besides God is the symbol of love and Jesus symbolizes hope. While war is symbolic of killing which is the opposite of what God commands, and peace is the opposite of war and makes more sense. Therefore believers should never be involved in violent conflicts. To believe is to seek peaceful resolutions that do not support any acts of violence.

Shamefully humanity can't seem to learn from history so we continue to repeat the failures in history. Religion is a dynamic part of history. It doesn't have to be the end of history. Thus, religion provides a baseline for moral and ethical laws-for unwise decisions usually lead to serious consequences. And our faith guides our sensibility. So all religions should advocate love, hope, and peace for they are commanded to do so.

There have been several instances when my mind is overwhelmed and my heart is heavy. During these times I usually put forth my questions to God. Sometimes an answer comes to me and my mind is put at ease. No I do not have a phone line to God, there is no burning bush, no angel cometh, and God doesn't speak in my ear or appear in a dream. It is a peaceful awareness, a synaptic impulse (thought), and the answer is always perfect.

I remember the last three years of my stepfather's life the only father I ever knew. He was in and out of the hospital frequently before he passed. During one of these visits he slipped into a coma. The doctors told my mother to start making funeral arrangements. They said his brain wasn't functioning and even if he came out of the coma he would be unresponsive. A quiet calm came over me. I turned to my mother and said "Mama it aint his time". As I touched my stepfather's hand his eyes opened gazing around the room and he spoke gruffly "Give me a swallow of water." He looked at us as if he knew we had been there waiting for him the whole time. Suddenly a room full of somber had become a place of unspoken joy. A few days later he went home. So I do not profess to be a righteous man, though I am an honest man and I know there is a God for who else could be responsible for the answers I often receive.

Resolutions

At the end of the day, religion boils down to faith. God lives in one's heart. Yes, I am very disgusted with the injustice throughout the world, but that doesn't mean I don't believe in God. Right or wrong, I just find myself questioning the unfairness and I don't understand why he calls upon me to be thankful for all the unpleasantness. There is no equality in consequences. The idea that those of us who pay the highest price will be rewarded in heaven just doesn't cut it. Jesus came two thousand years ago and gave the oppressed hope. But today there seems to be little hope. For the wealthy that reign are of a godless nature, and until they answer for their crimes against humanity or they have a change of heart, the world and the majority of its people will remain hostages of their oppression.

What religion provides is a road map for self discipline and awareness. I use strong language throughout *The Invisible Man*. It is my way of venting my frustration and angry with the corruption that seems to have engulfed our world. The ends are now justifying the means. Morality, decency, character, integrity, kindness, caring, fairness, and equality are forgotten words. And the people are being herded to slaughter as though we were a flock of animals by the *Sons and Daughters of Satan* leading the secular progressive movement.

Religious leaders throughout the world are wearing thousand dollar suits and ten-thousand dollar watches. They are driving luxury vehicles while lodging at elegant hotels and dining at extravagant restaurants. There are only a few religious leaders today that I have confidence in for most have traded their souls for fool's gold. So I say to you "Do not cast your lines into empty streams. Do not invest your salvation in false prophets. Seek God and you will find him."

Eventually I believe *Religion* has to become *One* and cultures have to be willing to work together for the good of the whole. Religion doesn't commit violent atrocities people do. And religion is not perfect, but it represents the goodness in society. Those who love and serve others, serve God. Webster defines religion as beliefs and practices of faith to a supernatural form. I believe religion is *a moral boundary that requires selfless commitment.* Unfortunately, incidents such as Roswell, the JFK assassination, Hoover's FBI follies, and countless investigative government cover-ups breed doubt amidst good people.

Again, I do question the fairness in good and bad consequences for individuals that make the choices. Sometimes people that make good choices have blessed consequences while the majority struggle their whole lives. While a few that make bad choices pay the piper, many never get what they deserve. So the accountability issue is a difficult question for Religion to provide a satisfactory answer for me. Maybe at my *Day of Atonement*, God will reveal all the answers to my questions. I do know this much, "When Religion becomes ONE; I will return and do my best to serve." But the current hypocrisy in the majority of the religious sects leaves little for me to believe in or subscribe too.

7

Creation

"The power of God is incomprehensible in the simple minds of humans"

Genesis 1:1 In the beginning
God created the heaven and the earth

I believe there is a high probably that all things were designed by a higher form of intelligence we refer to as God. There is no scientific theory plausible, probable, or possible with the knowledge of current science today. God is in all things. Maybe I am not one hundred percent sure there is a divine creator, but I am ninety-nine point nine-nine-nine percent (99.999 %) sure God exists.

The fact is that no species on this (Earth) planet, including humans, could have developed from nothingness. Simply put, every species came from somewhere.

> John 1:3 All things were made by him; and without him was not anything made that was made.

Where did the human species come from? Well I can only speculate and pronounce my own beliefs. While the "*Creation Theory*" may seem far fetched for a few in the scientific community, it is much closer to the truth than any theory in science. Although the evolution of all species does have validity and it is also a part of the equation so we cannot disregard theories of evolution. Charles Darwin said:

> All the individuals of the same species, and all the species of the same genus, or even higher group, are descended from common parents; and therefore, in however distant and isolated parts of the world they may now be found, they must in the course of successive generations have traveled from some one point to all the others.

This statement solidifies the religious proclamation that we are all descendents of Adam and Eve. And common sense tells me that Cain and Abel either married their siblings or there were others in the Garden with Adam and Eve. The Torah says that Adam and Eve had another son named Seth and many more sons and daughters were born afterwards. The original humans probably looked much different than humans in the 21st century. And the nomadic wandering of humans was God's punishment for Cain murdering his brother Abel. These movements throughout the world, in varying climates, over close to two hundred thousand years is why there are differences in hair, skin color, and body shapes and sizes. Furthermore, diets based on food sources of these regions were also a contributing factor. What I surmise is that a superior being(s) transplanted or created, whichever one prefers, every species that has evolved on earth from the beginning. And this superior being(s) is studying (observing) our evolution the same way our scientists study rats in a laboratory.

Charles Darwin's idea that man evolved from apes is interesting though impractical. What separates mankind from all other species is our consciousness. The *Torah* states:

> Genesis 2:7 the Lord God formed man from the dust of the earth. He blew into his nostrils the breath of life, and man became a living being.

But animals act instinctively for survival without rational thought. And even though humans may act instinctively and irrationally at times, they are aware of the consequences that accompany their actions. So the moral consciousness of the human being is the difference. Truthfully there are some human beings today that have minor physical resemblances to apes and chimpanzees, but many prehistoric humans also had some of the same physical characteristics. Thousands of generations of genetic mutations and adaptations to a particular region or environment determined body structures. Thus, the physical appearance of humans has nothing to do with the evolution of animals. Each species, including man, has evolved over hundreds of thousands of years or they became extinct.

And the universe, not just earth, did not come from nothingness. It had to be developed by a higher form of being(s) that far exceeds the intellectual capacities of the human mind. Our measurements of time would not be remotely compatible with the creator(s) of such an intricate design. One millisecond, for this supreme designer(s), might be a billion years for modern science in the 21st century, or at least one day equivalent to seven thousand years or so. The latter would mean the world is around 15 billion years old. There is no way to actually quantify time measurements of God with man's standard measurements. Therefore, I would suggest that a superior being(s) is the only answer possible and so I ask this; "If not *God*, then who?"

> Hebrews 1:10 And, Thou, Lord, in the beginning hast laid the foundation of the earth; and the heavens are the works of thine hands.

But Man's arrogance is his weakness. We think if we can't see it or feel it, then it doesn't exist. Yet, God exists in our hearts and minds and he represents all that is good. The difference between us and other species is that we have a soul. And that means we are responsible for all our actions.

So think of *Judgment Day* as going to court, but there is no dishonest lawyer there to get you off. If one lawyer makes it into heaven, it would be a miracle. Every sin you have committed from the day you understood the difference between right and wrong will be brought forth. And God is the Judge of the highest court and only his mercy can save us. Moreover, the only witness in our defense, that can be called, is Jesus. I have never been to a funeral where people were honest and said "That son of a bitch is going to Hell." It always phrases like "He is in a better place," "she was such an angel," or "he will not suffer anymore." If he or she went to *Hell* for his or her sins, then he or she is surely suffering for eternity. The Koran phrases it this way:

> But God shall not turn towards those who do evil deeds until, when one of them is visited by death, he says, Indeed now I repent, neither to those who die disbelieving; for them We have prepared a painful chastisement.

For all of us will be visited by death that is an unchangeable fact and how we live our life will determine our fate in the afterlife.

It doesn't make me right because I am reasonably sure of a higher power. And God knows I screw up every day. But where I struggle most with faith is the injustice throughout the world. How can thousand of drunks drive home every night and one has a wreck and is criminally charged? I think God should put them all on the same expressway and let these irresponsible jerks kill each other. Why does God allow children to be born into poverty? The impoverished should never bring more children into a world of hopelessness for it is not a right, but it is a selfish act. Truthfully, I know corrupt capitalists aren't getting into heaven, but why should we suffer for their atrocities? Most of the people that generally die from disasters caused by these arrogant pagans (global warming) are the poor that have no means of fleeing to safety. If God is as angry as most of us then God should strike down some of these wicked retches with a few thunderbolts of justice. And a good place to start is Washington D.C. for Washington has more crooks than a New York crime family. Maybe God could bring ethics back into law. I know that's a lot to ask for, but people need hope. Unfortunately the world that God has created, in the midst of a much larger universe, is under siege by a few dishonest wealthy power seeking men and women who neither recognize nor respect God's Laws.

> Psalms 8:6 Thou madest him to have dominion over the works of thy hands; thou hast put all things under his feet.

God's trust has been violated by these robber barons of yesterday and the capitalist thieves of today while the people seem powerless to respond. These wealthy few control the lawmakers, law enforcement, the courts, the militaries, and the governments throughout the world. It seems as though God has given up on man. Maybe Mars was the first human experiment that failed. It could have easily have been destroyed by nuclear technology or global warming similar to the path of earth today. And maybe God created other beings besides humans. Who really knows, but all the injustices throughout the world could easily make any believer question his or her faith.

Personally, I do not fully understand why we are commanded to worship God. Even though I believe in God bending to his will feels like I am being forced into mandatory servitude. Why can't we just love one another, serve those who are less fortunate, treat everyone the same as we wish to be treated, and work for the betterment of humanity? Without God we would not exist, but faithful devotion where reasonable questions are prohibited is oppressive bondage.

When we do things we know are in opposition of goodness, isn't that the same as worshiping Satan? Satan said "It is better to reign in *Hell* then serve in *Heaven.*" To me, this statement does make sense. It seems as though we are in a constant struggle between representations of good and evil. What if humanity rebelled against both? Then we would no longer be pawns in the battle between good verses evil. Wealth and power would no longer be considered important. While all weapons would become obsolete. And hatred, angry, vanity, jealousy, lust, and fear would become distance memories. WOW! Utopia!

Resolutions

Believing in the creation theory makes me a conservative. But I am reasonably sure that the world is more than six thousand years old because men and women have existed for close to two hundred thousand years. And I also assert with a fair amount of certainty that either more than two people (Adam and Eve) lived in the *Garden of Eden.* Or it would be reasonable to surmise that the children of Adam and Eve married one another. Thus my beliefs signify I am moderately conservative.

There are many times when I question my religious beliefs. In a world of apparent hopelessness anyone might submit to the dark side. Still there are many radical religious cults that journey far beyond mainstream conservatism. The handling of poisonous snakes is not a sign of faith it is a testament to fundamental ignorance. For God doesn't call on us to be stupid, he prefers we use common sense.

Maybe *Satan* is a female because there is no way a *God* who created man in his own image and a *Goddess* of whom woman were born could have lived together for eternity. And surely there were female angels in heaven. It would be hard to believe that heaven was just full of male angels. All men, maybe homosexuality and the oppression of women started in heaven or when God created woman from man as a companion, he said "Dang, what the heck was I thinking? I should have saved these beautiful creatures (women) for my posse (Angels) and me."

Seriously though, there is a high probability that a superior being(s) created the universe and all its dwellings. But, I am not sure that means we have to bow down and be grateful for our suffering and misery. Accepting our place in the world sounds more like an idea of the rich and powerful, but faith can move mountains. Therefore our belief in God, our unity, our self-sacrifice and self-discipline are the keys to overcoming the capitalist's hostile takeover.

No I can't prove or disprove the existence of God. Though I can say I believe there is a *Creator* we have named God. Unfortunately, the religious texts have been rewritten so many times, by the powers that be

(PTB); some truths have been omitted or replaced by socially constructed ideology. Usually the dominant ruling class of the world records history in a favorable way that rarely reflects negatively upon itself. And religion is just a piece of the newly constructed reality.

But all doctrines require devout faith. The *Creation Theory* is born from religion. However, one of science's biggest problems of trying to disprove the existence of a divine creator is his son. For it is a fact that *Jesus* walked this earth over two thousand years ago. And he was more than a humanitarian and a healer. Jesus Christ gave mankind hope. Sometimes the pieces of a puzzle are in front of us and we continue to look elsewhere. Thus I say to you my brother "Look no further than the miracle of thyself".

What makes me reasonable sure an invisible being is watching over us? Of course, one of my arguments revolves around miracles. And I say Helen Keller was a miracle of God for few could have overcome her disabilities and achieved so much. Her faith was her driving force for she knew while the body might be imperfect a soul pure of heart is perfect in Heaven. If someone with so many reasons to be angry at God could love and believeth in God because she understood he had a purpose for her life then who amongst us can argument against such profound logic.

Therefore every time I find myself wallowing in self pity, I look around and see so many others less fortunate than I. My sight for a visually impaired person is good and my mobility and health are great. Also my mind is always soaking up knowledge like a sponge for the lessons in life never end. I have family and friends that I love and care deeply about and I know they feel the same. And I have a roof over me head, clothes on my back, and food in my pantry. So I understand no matter how bleak life appears there are always others in need that would trade places with me any day.

8

The Church

"The House of God is not a physical entity it is a place of serenity"

When the wealthy moved into and took over the Church, God moved out. A structure subservient to gold is a temple of Satan. Even though many decent believers attend these structures-they must stand up against the influence of wealth for their silence supports the immoral act. And worship predicated on idolatry is false worship. Therefore I say to the believers "Any minister who seeks wealth to build his sanctuary to God or his son Jesus (the head of the Church) builds an empty house unto himself for he is a false prophet and he will lead his flock astray".

What bothers me about religion today is that it has become a business. Somewhere along the way, churches lost sight of their mission and became extensions of social and political ideologies. The original mission of churches was to preach the teachings of God and provide salvation for lost souls. Yet, somehow the mission became focused on growth of wealth, promoting agendas of reinterpreted philosophies, and preservation of self.

First, most churches have become so obsessed with wealth, that they are willing to compromise the nature of spiritual scripture for lust of greed. Basically large churches, of all denominations, have become big businesses (corporations) that are run by the wealthy elite who are intent on controlling all aspects in our lives (the masses). In essence, what these churches have done is sold out the poor and oppressed for a slice of the financial pie, which has a tendency to corrupt both hearts and minds of some decent people.

When churches operate under a business model, their financial portfolio becomes more important than their mission. Therefore large donations that come with strings attached should be declined. Once exceptions are made, the process becomes easier with each bribe. After a while, denial and excuses are the end products. Thus, the church has been commercialized and commodified by a controlling entity (wealth) that relies on submission without question. Therefore, if something appears to be too good to be true, it usually is-so walk away my friend.

This leads to the second problem of religion. It has reinterpreted the word to meet its own social agendas. If we, as a religious society, hold the Bible as truth, then that truth can not be changed because individuals want it both ways. There can be no amending God's Laws! Though many religious leaders seem to claim this as their right; they are not authorized to do so. As I will continually say, I am no angel and I probably won't ever be. However, if what is offered as religion today is the choice, then I have no desire to be a part of this masquerade. I choose not to participant. When religious leaders and followers are more concerned with social tolerance of ideologies, that exclude or circumvent religious principles, they have become hypocrites.

And they are substituting their own beliefs for the word of God to make it fit into their social circles of convenience (many modern liberal philosophies).

While it is true that it is not our right to judge others solely on religious ideology, that doesn't mean that people have the right to reinterpret religious scriptures to exist in modern society. The only two choices in religion, that we have the right to claim, are whether to believe or not to believe. Then we can choose either to obey or disobey God's commandments. But, do not misinterpret this idea as the right to mistreat or judge others. One doesn't have the right to force their beliefs on someone else. Expression of one's spiritual beliefs is fine. But, don't expect everyone else to feel the same way.

Fanatics, whether conservative or liberal, are nuts that escaped their cracked shells and lost touch with reality. These extremists actually believe the verbal nonsense seeping from their leaking appendage (tongue) as truth and moral convection. They are the lunatics that have somehow avoided the asylums of insanity. Yes, a lot of these idiots seem to be lawyers and religious leaders, who are supposed to be intelligent. But somewhere along the voyage of common sense, they got lost in a world of ideology. Here they believe their path is righteous. By becoming entrenched in some self-proclaimed noble cause, they become the idol of their false illusion. The problem here is they probably will never admit their misguided beliefs are wrong. Thus, they are trapped in a maze of denial and their only escape is death.

Many churches throughout history have dictated their own agendas to maintain power and control in the community. The *Roman Catholic Church* is an abomination to *God.* It is the *Church of Satan.* Because of the financial repercussions they might endure, along with social embarrassment, the Catholic Church chose to cover up molestation of children by their own priests. Forgiveness is one thing, allowing these pedophiles to continue their psychotic behavior, in the ministry, is unforgivable. There is no cure for these sick individuals who molest children. The Roman Catholic Church will continually be criticized for this atrocity throughout history along with its many other evil deeds, and rightly so.

Another aspect is violence and murder, such as the *Religious Crusades* and *Jihad* or any *Holy War* in the name of God is absolute blasphemous in nature and does not follow the teachings of any religious theory of God for GOD IS LOVE. And suicide is an unforgivable sin. There are no virgins waiting for you and the perpetrator is damned for eternity. Chastisement in Hell is the reward that awaits suicide bombers that target the innocent to insight fear and terror. Even though the Roman Catholic Church chose the "path of shame," I still believe Islam is a religion of peace that a few misguided radicals are reinterpreting out of frustration. Many western churches have endorsed false acts that do not represent sacred principles for the sole purpose of self preservation. Thus, when self preservation becomes more important than God's mission for the church, its credibility is lost, and society as a whole suffers the consequences.

If there is a God and his son is Jesus, then no one can buy their way into heaven. Any Church that has its members paying financial restitution for salvation should be ashamed. This is a crime against humanity. The ten percent that God requires is for spreading the gospel and reaching out to the oppressed. What some Churches are doing today resembles the same model of organized crime. It doesn't matter whether it is called protection, insurance, or restitution. These solicitations of funds have become a racquet that even western governments are now using. And accepting contributions of money marked by blood or evil deeds does not please God-it serveth the wicked and stains the Church.

Take the lottery for example. Linking the lottery to education is a devious marketing scheme, while the truth is the lottery is an underhanded taxation scheme, of the poor, by our government. And the chances of winning are so astronomical, but the addiction of playing, by those who can least afford it, is a predictable outcome. Just like must addictions the addict spends all their hard earned wages or supplemental incomes on the illusion of one big score. And just like an addicted gambler, they are digging a deeper hole of debt with no escape. While at the same time, only a small portion of the lottery revenues (around 20%) goes to education. But the clever marketing would have us believe, that a large majority of the funds collected are allocated for education of the disadvantaged.

Another important fact that has eluded the questionable tactics of the lottery is that most of the students that qualify, with families who can't afford tuition costs for their children are eligible for financial aid. Thus, the lottery is nothing more than a legalized numbers running racquet which organized crime ran for many decades after stealing it from criminals in the black community. So, when I witness church members asking what number fell today, I am somewhat confused why ministers would not preach on the entrapments of gambling and the consequences (reaping what they sewed) of this inappropriate behavior. Could it be because these same ministers are also playing the lottery? What does that say about supposed servants of God and leaders in the community? I even buy one ticket, a couple times a year, when the jackpot is over one-hundred-million. But I know my chances of winning are slim, and if there wasn't a lottery I would be just fine. Every church should be at the forefront of banning lotteries in every state.

But the ruling upper class formed an unholy alliance with corrupt governments and the Roman Catholic Church thousands of years ago. Since the fourth century, ***Satan's Place*** has endorsed wars, murder, torture, and rape of its faithful members while protecting unworthy priests that molested young children of God in exchange for profit and power. During the process they have aligned themselves with organized crime families, wealthy pagans, and many dishonest politicians proclaiming their faith. Although their educational institutions are larger than most due to their enormous financial clout-many are as corrupt as the Mother Church (Vatican in Rome). And while there are many faithful servants in the Catholic sect, most unknowingly serve the Devil. And yes I understand some Catholics will be angered by my words, but I would ask them why because my words are true.

The Vatican in Rome, Italy is the left hand of the Devil. So I say to those believers who seek the truth "Find another place of worship for your salvation will be lost in a "pool of deception" if you remain in the "*House that Satan Built*".

And a physical building does not symbolize Jesus Christ. For *God* symbolizes love, *Jesus* symbolizes hope, and the *Holy Spirit* symbolizes peace. Thus, a church built on false principles is an unstable structure. And any place of worship where the pure of heart gather is God's house. Imitating big businesses, appeasing a secular world and serving thyself has nothing to do with God, it places man's desires first. Hence I say to thee "God must come before all else".

In the seventh century the Roman Catholic Church focused on expanding its Christian Empire into Western Europe. At the same time the Catholic leaders, who were very proficient in politics, demonized Islam. By portraying Islam as a dark force that threatened the west, the Catholic Church divided Christians and Muslins followers and their actions lead to centuries of bloody battles that to this day have negatively affected a trustable relationship betweens Christians and Muslins.

During the eighth century, Charles the Great forced Catholicism on the illiterate poor that he conquered through a choice of baptism or death. Muhammad also practiced indoctrination or death which I disagree with but I also understand why. Furthermore the aristocratic rulers of the west and the Church were constantly fighting for the power of persuasion over the people. Eventually in the thirteenth century the Church seized power and initiated the Fourth Crusade while committing horrific atrocities during the *Inquisition*.

There is no such thing as a "just war" for war should always be the last choice. But when genocidal maniacs like Hitler rise up from the depths of Hell the world must rise up and face the challenge. However, when any religion endorses or sanctions war it has defied God's will.

Peaceful resolution is the only path of enlightenment for any religious community that truly represents "The Almighty" for Allah is saddened by man's violent nature that the curse of Cain has descended upon us.

Resolutions

The future looks bleak and most feel powerless as they watch the digression of America. Many Western Churches integrity are questionable. Their moral backbone has been broken by false prophets and secular beliefs. While technology has quantum leaped our expectations, the manufacturing jobs for the middle-middle and lower-middle along with the upper-lower classes, mostly blue and white collar labor, are being outsourced to underdeveloped countries for wages no America could live on. At the same time, the wealthy elite are pushing their globalization agendas down our throats while mocking our inabilities to fend off their atrocities. It is like being raped mentally and knowing no justice will befall the accused. These corporate bastards are screwing the American people and destroying our environment without any fear of repercussions. They are very well rehearsed in spinning negative publicity and harmful information into misunderstandings, unfair representations, and isolated incidents that are under review. Thousands of corporations like *Wal-Mart*, *Nike*, *Ford*, *AT&T*, *Microsoft*, and many others are directly responsible for the "*Reign of Oppression*" against the American people in the 21st century. With cost of living increasing and wages decreasing along with jobs, or at least jobs with livable wages and affordable health insurance, we are in serious trouble. If one thinks things are just grand, either he or she is wealthy, ignorant, or in a state of denial. Maybe some feel that God's wrath is our only hope.

Regardless, I am a believer in peace and peaceful solutions. But if the extreme radical fundamentalists of Islam were truly serious about their convictions, they would destroy all the oil production and refinery facilities. This would impact the wicked west more than any other action. Adversely, they wouldn't target the innocent-they would exterminate the capitalist pagans that rule a secular world. Some of these wealthy nonbelievers are members of the Royal Families living in the Middle East-for they have not only adopted western ways, they have turned away from Allah for the lust of wealth from oil profits and most do not share their fortunes with their oppressed brothers. I would never condone such violent actions, but from a logistics standpoint these strategies would be more practical and representative of their fundamental ideology. Again, many believers are outraged by a world spinning out of control, but we must strive for peace until there is no alternative left.

Sometimes the radical Islamic principles can be confusing. While I do believe, they are correct, in their view that Western Cultures have gone too far under any religious ideology. Killing one's self and other innocent people (men, women, and children), who have no control over governmental policies, goes against any religious philosophy ever written. Sometimes principles, and the conditions of the principles, are confused as representations of social discourse. And a human life would be more valuable in pursuing peaceful solutions for a lifetime instead of dying in vain for a fifteen second reference on the news. As I was reading in the Koran, I came across this passage;

> And those who have taken a Mosque in opposition and unbelief, and to divide the believers, and as a place for ambush for those who fought God and His Messenger aforetime-they will swear 'We desire nothing but good'; and God testifies they are truly liars.

Those churches and religious leaders that deceive their congregations do not deceive the All-knowing and All-wise. The believers must challenge the *Ungodly Houses* for their fate lies in the hands of evildoers. Those who enter the LION'S DEN naked will surely perish without God's protection.

There is only one way to reverse this power of illusion. We have to rebuild the church starting at the bottom (foundation). There can be only one denomination. A Church of God, with individuals who believe in God, and who live a life of servitude for God is the key to salvation. I believe in God and I am moderately conservative, though I am not a Christian-for I am also a sinner, but I have lost all faith in modern Christian churches. There are many decent people that attend these structures who are faithful servants. I know this because I have met and became close friends with some of them. Although I still contend that many of these church goers are hypocrites living in denial.

My mom is a strong believer in God and all it has gotten her is a life of pain, misery, and suffering. She raised all of her children my siblings and I up the right way and she is not responsible for our mistakes. If anything, she deserves a place in heaven because she has spent a lifetime in servitude of others while living in poverty. So many times, she was beaten down through verbal abuse and repetitious rhetoric that told her she was not valued as a human being because she was blind. Throughout my life, I have felt her suffering and she has endured mine. It has been a long hard road though I have always looked forward because hope lies ahead. This is why I am so focused on becoming successful, though I refuse to forget those who have traveled similar paths. Hopefully, one day I will be able to ease her financial burdens and allow her to enjoy a better life here. If that's wrong; then I am prepared to answer for it. No one should have to live in poverty or depend on a corrupt government for crumbs of enslavement.

For I believe God lives in the hearts of the believers and Jesus guides these believers through treacherous waters-for he is the lighthouse. And the Holy Spirit serves as the consciousness of the awakened believers. Thus, the resolution lies in the rebirth of the Church and the unity of all believers. Truthfully, even I must admit, the Holy Bible serves as blueprint of how one should live and conduct his or her life on a daily basis. Even if some texts have been manipulated, the foundation is there-we have to be willing to work together for the Good of the Whole and by doing so we serve God. So I say to the believers "If you can find a nondenominational church where wealth and race do not matter, where the leadership is willing to take a stand on immorality in the community and abroad, where all believers and nonbelievers are welcome, and where the members serve God and the less fortunate instead of themselves-then go there for you have found a gem amongst a mountain of worthless stones."

Hear me well my brothers and sisters "A Church of great wealth is not a true Church of Christ. Any believer that denies Jesus as the son of God will not enter the Kingdom of God. Jesus is our arbiter and only he has the authority to hear our confessions and grant us absolution. Believers who are misled by false prophets will face God's wrath-for we have a moral obligation to seek out the truth and our desire to belong must not overwhelm our sensibility. Do not put your faith in the doctrines of the deceivers or you will reap severe consequences for your foolishness. Those who listen and do their best in following the righteous path will regain their salvation, but those who reject these warnings and continue down the same path will suffer the chastisement."

9

Scripture

"A challenged life is an enlightened journey"

Many teachings of God's laws become misused interpretations as a form of power and control. It is true that the husband is suppose to be the head of the household the same way *Jesus Christ* is the head of the Church.

> Ephesians 5:23 For the husband is the head of the wife, even as Christ is the head of the church: and he is the savior of the body.

However, that doesn't mean he is to rule with an iron fist. The passage later reveals that the two are to become one flesh. What I find in the meaning is there is a partnership between both spouses. The husband may make the final decision, but his decision should take into account his wife's point of view as a part of the process. Then if there is a disagreement, the husband should pray for guidance and then make the best decision possible based on logic and common sense. Often, women think with their hearts which is predicated on wishful thinking and doesn't include a rational approach.

Many act as though this is a degradation of women, but it is not (most *Rap* videos debase women). Men and women are genetically structured (wired) differently. Most men tend to be more analytical. And maybe the reason men on average excel more in math and science has more to do with genetics. While at the same time, most women are loving and caring vessels. In theory, putting the two together equals a loving heart and a reasoning mind working as one body. When women use sex to get their way; this is a form of control and will lead to problems in the marriage because sex was never meant to be used as a device to gain the upper hand in important family decisions. This behavior is a childish way of trying to manipulate a desired outcome without any consideration of the possible ramifications. And selfishness is not the right way of achieving a harmonious relationship-for it is the opposite of what God desires.

Equality does not mean men and women are the same. While we may have similar interests and belief systems, we are still different in many ways. In his book *Men are from Mars Women are from Venus* Dr. (Ph.D.) John Gray says:

> Without the awareness that we are supposed to be different, men and women are at odds with each other. We usually become angry or frustrated with the opposite sex because we have forgotten this important truth. We expect the opposite sex to be more like ourselves. We desire them to "want what we want" and "feel the way we feel."

Meanwhile, women are trying to domesticate men, but men fight to maintain control. Listening to television talk show garbage like the *View* or *Oprah* only increases the conflict. For God made us different and that will never change.

Another critical teaching involves the discipline of children. The Bible says "To spare the rod is to spoil the child," but this does not literally mean to beat a child with a rod.

> Proverbs 13:24 He that spareth his rod hateth his son: but he that loveth him chasteneth him betimes.

My understanding of this text is that children must be disciplined lovingly. And yes, using a switch, belt, or paddle should be lawful, though we should not act in a moment of angry. But common sense has to be used and the punishment should fit the inappropriate act. Regrettably, we have allowed the State Apparatus to intervene and impose its will unlawfully upon us when it comes to disciplining of our children. I will discuss this *Bureaucratic Monster* later. Nevertheless, the most important thing to remember about disciplining children is to again use common sense.

Over the last twenty-five years, we have seriously damaged the last two-and-a-half generations of children because of unprincipled psychologists and corrupt liberal bureaucrats with self-serving agendas of control that infringe upon our unalienable rights as individuals. I sometimes debate "Who has damaged society more, psychologists or lawyers?" For psychology is nothing more than s "BS" degree in common sense. Many of the students of psychology are as loony as their chosen field. Somehow psychologists have convinced people that we can no longer think for ourselves. If there is a God, the liberal psychologists, along with corrupt lawyers, politicians, and religious leaders are damned for eternity and they will suffer immensely for their sins against society. And their atonement is coming and I feel sorry for these pagan fools.

When I was a student at the residential school for the blind (Georgia Academy for the Blind), we were forced to go to church every Sunday. If we skipped or missed church, we were put on restriction. Not having a choice left me angry and confused about religion being forced upon me. I was ok with prayer in the classroom and grace before meals, but my church experience in Macon was not a joyous one. During Sunday school for children, we met in a big classroom and then we were separated into smaller groups. The blind and visually impaired children were segregated from the other children. It felt like they feared us and we were isolated as though we were a contagious disease. At my grandmother's church in Bainbridge, my brothers and I were not isolated from other children. So this religious experience was confusing and didn't assist my spiritual growth.

From the beginning Vineville Baptist Church left a bad imprint on my subconscious. As we grew older we attended adult church services. Here we could sit where we wanted. I usually sat in the back near the doors where I could exit quickly when services were over. It seemed as though the preacher's first priority every week was money. "We need funds for this and funds for that" God it never ended and I was left with an untrustworthy feeling for this pastor's God was "*The Almighty Dollar.*" Another confusing experience was the white and black blind and visually impaired children attended different churches. I always questioned this segregated practice because our two schools had fully integrated when I was twelve. "Why were we shuttled to different churches on Sunday" I often wondered?

Later in college, I was baptized in a small Baptist Church in Americus. However, I did not feel that God or Jesus was going to save me from oppression or make my life perfect by excluding all painful experiences. Although I must admit, I became friends with some good people in the church. This was important because it showed me that some people do care about those who are different. I realized at this point that it is the leadership of a church that determines how a church operates and is perceived. There are many righteous men and women in churches, but if their leadership is corrupt the house is empty, the trees are bear, and the ground is unfertile-for God has exited the building.

What I have found and observed during my life is that people settle or become satisfied with their status because they accept it will never get any better. Accepting that my vision will not change is one thing, but accepting a life of poverty by living from paycheck to paycheck or having to depend on a supplemental income such as SSDI (Social Security Disability Income) with no chance for improving my quality of life is not a glorious option. This mythical notion of being poor and happy or rich and miserable is a lie with no valid foundation. For I know no one who is poor and happy, yet I know many that have accepted being poor as their fate. Being wealthy is not a bad thing as long as it was achieved honestly. It is the individual's willingness to give something back to society in appreciation for his or her blessed outcome that shapes the person's humanistic growth. Thus, religion makes it easier for people to deal with their suffering in life-it also prepares them for death and the afterlife. If we had to face the probably that we suffer for nothing, well that would be a reality that many would not be able to handle. And so what religion basically provides is a "Cushion of comfort." Nevertheless, I still believe in an afterlife.

And yes that means I believe there is a supernatural force. Though I feel it allows us to make choices and then we reap the consequences, good or bad, based on our decisions. But, I have a question; one man commits murder and gets the death penalty, another man commits murder and never gets caught, how is this fair? Sometimes there seems to be no logical answers for outcomes because the consequences for bad choices are not always the same. So, I understand with all the unfairness throughout the world why people question the existence of God.

But I also believe that someone named Jesus did exist over two thousand years ago. However, myths of miracles always get exaggerated over long periods of time. Thus, I cannot prove or disprove any of the alleged events of that era, but I know three things; Jesus was a healer, he was a holy man without sin, and he was the son of God. And I, as do most, believe in the message of hope, peace, and love for all mankind and a respect for nature and its resources. Many fictional theories of Jesus, like *The Davinci Code*, are interesting entertainment and some feminists would like to believe the tale because it gives them some delusional form of empowerment. However, the importance here is that Jesus appears to have really connected with the poor and oppressed and that seems to be lacking in our religious communities today.

Unfortunately the *Religious Apparatus* (especially the Catholic Church), the *State Apparatus* (especially the Western Governments), and the *Aristocratic Apparatus* (especially the Capitalists) have joined forces (a partnership) to maintain control and influence over the masses. This control has a lot to do with structuring of religious and manmade laws. Those in power ordain what is lawful and what is unlawful. So they (these 3 apparatuses) determine what is written as history, religious texts, laws, canonized literature, educational texts, scientific discovery, and any written material that constitutes social order.

Personally I wonder about the one wife law; "Did this come from Jesus or was it a political agenda of the religious order?" I suspect the latter. So, I surmise the ruling male aristocrats, influenced by their jealous wives, used its power over the church to initiate the polygamy ban. Every great Biblical leader of the *Old Testament* had more than one wife. Honestly, the fact is that when men see beautiful women, they fantasize about having sexual encounters. All men fantasize about other women, some just lie about it. Do women also fantasize about other men besides their partner? The fact is that one person can not meet or satisfy all the needs of another. After two to three years, everything becomes old hat, and there is a shift in opposite directions.

Truthfully, the probability of connecting spiritually, intellectually, and physically is almost impossible. Yet society's answer to this is an old phrase; "Marriage is hard work." Socially constructed idealism does not solve a problem. It tries to impose its will upon us. Thus, the results are predictable because the problem was never resolved. It is merely a form of control when people are forced to live in constructed "norms". I believe the majority of the world would agree that murder, rape, molestation, stealing, and physical abuse are wrong and should be prohibited. However, people have different views on the ideas of marriage, religion, family, government, and so forth. And remember, I said we have the right to express our opinions, not impose our belief systems on others.

For the vast majority of women marriage is viewed as a commitment. For most men marriage is comparative to a prison sentence because we feel our freedom has been taken away. John Gray says:

> Falling in love is always magical. It feels eternal, as if love will last forever. We naively believe that somehow we are exempt from the problems our parents had, free from the odds that love will die, assured that it is meant to be and that we are destined to live happily ever after.

The truth is marriage is not a fairytale or fable. There is no Prince Charming or Snow White. We are all flawed individuals and sometimes our expectations do not correspond with reality. Understanding our differences is the key to overcoming conflict.

Therefore I am all for gays getting hitched. Let them be miserable like the rest of us. From the first day after the honeymoon, women start trying to change their spouse into what they think he should be. If you marry a jackass that is what he will be. There is a reason for women out living men. They nag us to death. If a man marries a witch that is what she will be. Both women and men are often delusional about changing one another. Men relate to men and women relate to women because they think similarly. Sometimes I just want to watch the game in peace without interruptions from someone who doesn't know anything about sports. Marriage is more than hard work-it is a stressful relationship between two people who do not think alike and have very little in common. Thus, religion provides a common bond.

And many people stay married because they fear being alone. Others stay for the children or the financial security. Some stay married because of religious beliefs. So the point I am getting too is, originally men were allowed to have as many wives as they were able to financially support.

What happened? The clergy with the aid of their unholy alliance (Aristocrats and Big Brother) may have changed this law themselves without God or Jesus consent. For some reason, religious leaders and government bureaucrats think they can determine what is best for society. The truth is, many religious leaders can't even figure out what is best for their own local ministries. And bureaucrats are a lost cause. Maybe Joseph Smith was not as crazy as some religious historians might suggest. Although I believe the Mormon Church is not a Church of God, it is a ministry that rebelled against an immoral society in the nineteenth century. The majority of us have a strong desire to belong and on many occasions we naively fall for misrepresentations. That is why con artist target good people. Some college and professional athletes are very skilled in hustling coaches, teachers, administrators and owners. Their success depends on our desire to be fair or our inability to see through their deceptions or our willingness to ignore the warning signs.

Still, statistically there is no denying that many children with two parent families, on the whole, seem to be more successful in life-especially the families with a quality male role model leading the way. But that might work with a three or four parent family; "Who has the right to say?" Prisons are full of people that either had no father, or an abusive father figure. Children being raised by single parents or abusive parents, have a higher risk of abnormal behaviors that eventually may lead to criminal acts. Many boys, especially in the white community, raised by single parent mothers, tend to be soft (pussified). They lack survival skills and common sense that a quality male role model generally provides. Others rebel and join gangs, more so in the black community, as a father supplement. However, children need to understand at an early age that enduring harsh social condition doesn't give them the right to disregard society's rules. Most poor people suffer, but the majority of us do not use it as an excuse to violate the law. Usually we fight to overcome our oppression and improve our quality of life through mechanisms such as education.

But this idea of marriage is a socially constructed concept defined by religion. We do not have to be married to have a meaningful and intimate relationship though it would go against scripture. If we maintain our own space during a relationship-generally it is more beneficial and provides more harmony because we are different (men and women). This is why dating is much more satisfying than marriage. If we can resist the social pressures of "being married", then we might experience more happiness in our lives. And if we choose marriage, then we should understand two people do not become one. There are still two people with two unique personalities. The idea of "two becoming one" may mean two people becoming one team that work together for the common good of the relationship and family (goals). However, it is a necessity for children to have quality adult role models in their lives. It doesn't guarantee success, but it drastically improves their chances.

18th December 2003 I awakened abruptly around 5:30 A.M. Something had awakened me as I sprung out of my bed from a deep sleep. My heart sank because I knew my stepfather was dead and a minute or two later the phone rings. Somehow I knew before I answered it, it was my brother calling to confirm my intuition. First, I called my mother-she was alone in the room crying with my dad. Since I knew my mother didn't have the strength-I called my sister. Often the bearer of bad news is not received well, but I wanted my sister to go to the hospital because my mother was alone. Next, I called my wife-sadly I said "Come get me (I was working and going to school in Macon, Georgia). Bill just died and mama is in the room by herself."

Normally my prayers are argumentative for I am distressed by the lunacy of the world. This time however, I said a short prayer. "God have mercy on Bill for he did the best he could with what he was given. He kept a roof over our heads, clothes on our back, food on our table, and was there whenever we needed him; for this is what a good man is called to do. While he had little education, he had more common sense than most men. Even though he did not express love well, I always knew he loved us. And only your grace can pardon his mistakes. Amen." There are only a few family members I can vouch for that I know have a first class ticket into heaven. The majority of us including myself will need God's grace. Every time a close family member or friend passes away my mind drifts to *Psalms* 23:1-6; and the song *Amazing Grace.* Psalms 23 is one of the few Bible verses that never leaves me and I fell in love with the helm Amazing Grace the first time I heard it as a small child.

Resolutions

When reading any scriptural text, we must apply rational thought to the meaning. Yes, I do believe God's design calls for men to humbly lead with the support of our women-for there are many women that possess leadership skills and abilities. But the majority of the liberal doctrine is in direct opposition of Christianity. If women of faith don't believe men of integrity are supposed to guide households and nations with their assistance, their faith rests in foolish arrogance and selfish pride, not in God-for a woman without virtue is like a well without water, but a woman with virtue is more precious than any treasure. In Proverbs God says the wicked women that are today's gold diggers, prostitutes, porn stars, stripers, unscrupulous celebrities, liberals, progressives, and feminists who destroy the character of righteous men will be judged severely. For there was a time when women were the backbone of Christianity and the glue of the western family, but today many women are succumbing to the liberal progressive secular propaganda spawn from an anti-religious media and a handful of influential female leaders who are determined to rule a godless world in defiance of God through the emasculation of all decent men who dare question their agendas. And the moral majority of women that resist their treachery are ostracized or labeled as religious fanatics. Truthfully the aggressive nature of men often leads to irrational violence, but evil women are the instigators of conflict.

And the rising divorce rates in Western Cultures can be directly linked to an antagonistic liberal media. If the Media isn't dividing people racially, then it focuses on dividing men and women along gender lines. Relationships are difficult enough without the liberal agenda intrusions of an antagonistic media. I don't understand how women can be manipulated by shows like "*Oprah*" and "*The View*" because most of these programs are nothing more than male bashing nonsense. And relationships are not about "taking charge;" relationships are a partnership of two people with similar belief systems and common interests working as a team of one. Maybe if we didn't rush into marriage and took our time finding our soul mate-we might discover happiness and even though I believe we can experience intimacy without being married, I confess it goes against the will of God.

Often, the word "fight" is used in the Koran. For me "fight" doesn't always literally mean physical confrontations. I see resistance to evil, speaking out publicly against immorality and godless temples, challenging hypocrites, or working together for peaceful solutions as representations of "fighting". And a call to violence should always be the last choice when all other options have failed-and only then will Allah call "HIS WARRIORS to ARMS".

Many believers have been deceived. For Joseph Smith and Brigham Young were false prophets and thus the foundation of the Mormon Ministry is built on false prophecies. But, I have never met a Mormon that wasn't a kind and caring person-still that is not enough. Our "need to belong" can not take the place of our "ability to seek the truth". And faith in a false ministry is not faith-it is a foolish waste of time.

Exodus 32.33 "But the LORD said to Moses, "He who has sinned against Me, him only will I erase from My record." Living a lie is the same as sinning against God-for God is the "Truth" and his "Word" is our Shepard. All people, not just conservatives, must be able to see beyond today's propaganda. The media seeks to indoctrinate through repetitious artificial narratives. For us to find the truth, we must be able to distinguish the facts from fictional rhetoric. And by seeking the truth we seek God.

Most of humanity's toughest problems can be resolved by working together. While at the same time, I am not sure we can ever gain consensus on every religious principle because many were added or omitted by the political and religious hierarchies of the last several thousand years. An example is the *Gospels* of *Thomas, Mary*, and *Philip.* They were left out of the *New Testament* because some of their scriptures might have contradicted passages in the revised edition of the Holy Bible. But that doesn't mean we disregard the rest. It is imperative for all people of faith to find common ground for God has put his trust in us. And when humanity lets God down-he also suffers unto himself.

Blueprint for World Dominance

1. Divide the people racially, economically, religiously, biologically, politically, socially, and by generations.
2. Control all world markets.
3. Ownership of all mediums throughout the world.
4. Control all governments, militaries, law enforcement, and courts.
5. Use governments as a buffer for the people's animosity.
6. Control all political entities.
7. Exclude individualism, criticism, and dissention.
8. Exploit, destroy, and imprison.
9. Destruction of all religions.
10. Disenfranchise, marginalize, frustrate, and confuse.
11. Lie, steal, and kill.
12. Cheat, use, and abuse.
13. Seduce, lure, entrap, and enslave.
14. Limit choices.
15. Change historical facts into creations of popular fictions.
16. Restrict independence and encourage dependence.
17. Polarization; divide the whole into two opposing halves.
18. Indoctrination.

The ruling upper class is well aware of the power of unity. Divided we offer insignificant opposition. By controlling world markets the capitalists can minimize restrictions while maximizing profits. Karl Marx said:

> The history of all hitherto existing society is the history of class struggles.

Throughout history there has always been the oppressor and the oppressed. Today, the irony of globalization is that capitalists and communists are now business partners. Propagandas rhetoric has the capacity of influencing outcomes. Sun Tzu said:

All warfare is based on deception.

The takeover of all mediums guarantees the truth can be suppressed and replaced with prepackaged fiction. Our society is currently involved in two major struggles. (1) Rich verses poor. The gap between the rich and poor grows with every passing second of every minute of each day. (2) Morality verses immorality. Unfortunately, the erosion of morality and disregard for ethics has weakened our inner resolve.

Many corrupt governments, described as *Big Brother* in George Orwell's *1984*, and politicians shield the aristocrats from the people's hostility. These governments enslave their people through generations of dependency. Mary Shelley may have written *Frankenstein* but FDR created the Monster. Our politicians are purchased through individual and corporate bribes redefined as campaign contributions. The word "*Team*" is often referenced by government branches, but its true meaning lies in devout obedience. Thus, individualism is ostracized and opposition is forbidden taboo.

The majority of us watch in horror while our planet is raped and pillaged by these greedy capitalists. Many impoverished people are entrapped by addictions to porn, drugs, alcohol, and gambling which has been legalized in many progressive societies that lack moral integrity. And as a result, we have become prisoners of debt, servants of creditors, and slaves of sin.

Every legitimate religion has been deemphasized through vilification by a liberal oriented campaign supported by the western media. At the same time, some religious institutions are using corporate business models to increase their wealth and influence in local communities. And most religious leaders lack the intestinal fortitude to speak out against the seduction of sin. Thus, many religious organizations have become pawns of their aristocratic benefactors.

By using polarization the masses can be easily divided. For or against, red or blue, liberal or conservative, right or left, protagonist or antagonist, and good or evil have created an illusion of only two opposing point of views. Such gimmicks as limiting our choices are control mechanisms used to manipulate a desired result. Whether it is used to divide nations or influence the outcome of an agenda oriented poll, polarization is one of the most effective divisive tools used by the ruling upper class.

Under the Blue Print for World Dominance, the final phase is our indoctrination. *Indoctrination* is the most critical aspect. Before we drink the Kool-Aid, we must be convinced it will not harm us. Frequently mind control through repetitious rhetoric of a deceitful nature or "brainwashing" is the preferred methodology. If the same message is repeated over and over again on the television and radio or is written in newspapers and magazines "The fictional myth becomes a believable truth". And our minds are being reprogrammed like computer chips that respond to commands. Thus, authority is unchallenged and rational thought has been deleted.

Therefore *the Blueprint for World Dominance* is no laughing matter. Currently the globalization of the world threatens our *individualism* and *independence.* But, drowning in our own sorrow will not change the course of history. I say rise and be heard because your life, your heart, and your voice are meaningful-*for divided we are a weakened many, but united we are a strong one.*

10

Democracy

"Freedom is not a guaranteed right, freedom is an abstract idea"

A "*Democracy*" is a *Government* of the people, by the people, and for the people where the majority determines the mission. The word "*Freedom*" is the desired result of a democracy. And "*Liberty*" is a symbol of freedom. Thus, I say America is not a Democracy; it is a two party "Aristocracy." The ruling upper class controls the legislative, executive, and judicial branches at every local, state, and federal level. And tragically voters must constantly choose between a Democrat and a Republican as their elected representative. By limiting the voter's choices the ruling class can maintain social order.

Both the *Democratic* and *Republican Parties* sold out the American people a long time ago. Now, less than half of all eligible voters vote today. I do not vote anymore unless there is someone I consider a moderate because I feel no matter whom I choose, the outcome will be the same-constant watered down legislation with billions of dollars in pork and earmarks is the common practice of our current politicians. Shamefully the current mission of "western capitalists" is "*World Dominance.*" These aristocrats do not covet an environment of unrestricted independence except when it benefits their agenda.

Around forty percent of the actual voting participants identify themselves as independents. However, the problem is there are rarely any independent candidates on the ballots. This is by design. The Democrats and Republicans have made it almost impossible, through exclusionary legislation, for anyone who is not one of their own party affiliates to run against them. And the media, which is owned by the same capitalists who control both parties, rarely offers an opposing political voice other than the Democrats and Republicans. It is insane to believe that voting for one of two jackasses will make a difference.

Each election year comes and goes and many voters are left with the feeling of hopelessness for the numbers of Democrats and Republicans may change but the way they do business never changes. Washington is a cesspool of liars, crooks, and hypocrites who only care about themselves and the wealthy cliental they serve-we do not matter to them. But contrary to the myth we do have the power. When we begin demanding more choices on the ballots and quit voting for Democrats and Republicans-we might actually experience some genuine progress-for common sense is lacking in today's political arena and politicians rarely act unless they are afraid. Specifically the most common fear of both the political whores in the US is the "fear of our unity". If Americans stood together, we could even the playing field in Washington and redefine our political history.

In 1998, I graduated in "The Partners in Policymaking" advocacy training. It taught us to work within the current system. While networking with others who had similar concerns was a wonderful experience, I am not one to follow any group's agenda unless it is beneficial to society as a whole. Many citizens are so frustrated with the corruption of the American Political System and our oversized government they have begun organizing local and regional movements. Unfortunately, when their personal beliefs dismiss any opposing views, they minimize their objectivity. The end result is usually an exclusive group oriented agenda focused on a narrow goal. Thus, selfishness often replaces selflessness.

At meetings clichés like "Win one battle at a time", "Roman wasn't built in a day", "Catch more flies with honey", and "Patience is a virtue" were some of the ineffective catch phrases often repeated. Theoretically it is impossible to change a corrupt system unless the influence of the corruption is removed. For America and other western nations, that means eliminating the influence of wealth and denouncing any political movement or social discourse which doesn't represent the best interests of society as a whole. Continually groups portray their oppression as the most tragic atrocity in history. The fact remains no one has a patent on oppression. And what about people with disabilities aren't we human beings too?

Often I ask "If an individual has creative ideas, but never gains access to demonstrate his skills and abilities, what purpose does he serve if he cannot achieve a voice in the determination of his own fate?" I do not wish for someone else to speak for me because I am more than capable of speaking for myself. And my message is clearly different than a person who has not walked the same path of oppression. How can an individual reach his goals if the door of opportunity is locked by a controlling entity that doesn't recognize the individual's existence?

Still a few members of society can not admit that there are some people with disabilities more talented, more creative, more knowledgeable, or more athletic than they are. Many of these same persons, view people with disabilities as broken or damaged goods. So it becomes almost impossible for them to view us as equal or more capable. Admitting their beliefs are mere fabrications is a difficult pill to swallow for a prejudice few. The superiority complex has deep roots in all western cultures. In the kingdoms of the endowed ignorance is used to perpetuate the fallacy of the myth as the truth.

Unfortunately the real tragedy of these socially restrictive environments is that society is losing creative genre or art that might achieve canonization if it acquires equal access. I have often struggled with my faith because I don't understand the injustices and unfairness throughout the world we live in. It is not enough to say people's sufferings will be rewarded in heaven. This cliché does not sooth my soul or perpetuate my spirit to a supposed form of enlightenment. And though I still believe in God, religion doesn't always provide satisfactory answers to unnecessary hardships. All most people with disabilities want is equal opportunity (access) based on merit.

While reading Anthony Signorelli's *Call to Liberty: Bridging the Divide between Liberals and Conservatives,* my first thought was "This guy has drunken from the liberal fountain of secularism." Though I agree with his characterization of the word "polarization", his attempt to define "liberty" and "liberalism" as one and the same was an enormous reach. And criticizing Ann Coulter's conservative views, while at the same time pushing a liberally biased agenda, is hypocritical. Mr. Signorelli claimed that the media validates conservative writers and attacks liberal dissention. This is a blatant misrepresentation of the facts. His assertion that the liberal voices on the left are reasonable illustrates his personal bias and his attempt to redefine who liberals are was outrageous. In fact, five major corporate conglomerates own close to ninety percent (90%) of all mediums in the US. And the FCC just voted (December 18th of 2007) to allow the buyouts to continue even though over seventy percent (70%) of the American people are outraged by these hostile takeovers.

These "*media corporate empires*" are Disney (ABC and HB0), NBC (General Electric), Time Warner (CNN), Viacom (CBS and MTV), and FOX. They control almost every television program, newspaper and newsroom, radio program, magazine, and most of the entertainment industry. There are few independent media sources left and without marketing dollars which is the collusive plan of media consolidation, they either sell or go under. And it is true, many talk radio station's hosts are conservative and some are extremely conservative. Though the main reason is there is a large audience on the right that many capitalists recognized was being underserved. Sometimes lustful greed trumps the lust for power-for they are the "walking damned."

Only FOX News can be characterized as a conservative voice of the right. But that is just the news for their programming is as liberal as NBC and ABC. And Disney, NBC, Time Warner, and Viacom are all liberal voices on the left. Also, the two most influentially recognized newspapers in America are *The New York Times* and *The Washington Post*, both are extremely liberal. Similarly one might think NPR (National Public Radio) and PBS (Public Broadcasting Systems) would be neutral, but they too are slanted to the left. And I can testify from personal experience of trying to publish my work for going on two years, the vast majority of the publishing industry is extremely liberal. Accusing the opposition of what the accuser is guilty of is a deceitful practice. But, it has become a popular method of disseminating misinformation as "the truth" for the sole purpose of inflaming their core bases by extremists on both sides.

Though in my view, the unfortunate outcome of the corporate buyouts is the loss of independent voices. When the corporate conglomerate takeovers of all the mediums are completed, including the internet, our voices will be replaced by their prepackaged rhetoric and slogans (subliminal advertising). And our "*Freedom of Speech*" (*1st Amendment*) will be abolished by the shrewd planning (control of all mediums) of these deceitful rich devils. By eliminating "*free speech*" the ruling class has also expelled any hope of a "democracy" while guarantying their stooges will not be challenged (similar to a dictatorship).

Right now the "political correctness" being forced upon us by our corporate controlled government and media is one of the most serious attacks on our 1st Amendment Right. George Orwell's *1984* described the horror as the "*Thought Police*". A hostile takeover of our minds, thoughts, and speech is one of the many important issues Americans face today. Like a thief in the darkness they lay in wait-for to silence all opposition ensures the truth will be buried and no individual voice can ever be heard over the noisy hate propaganda.

Therefore, I have lost much of my tolerance for the constant hate rhetoric spun on a daily basis by our current irresponsible media outlets. I may disagree with some people philosophically, but I don't allow my differences in opinions to affect my humanity. Western civilizations have more to worry about than just the "*War on Terror.*" This is another propagandas hate slogan (by right extremists). Some of our biggest threats are "globalization", the effects of "global warming", abolishing our "Freedom of Speech", "imperialism" disguised as "democracy", and the most corrupt politicians and governments in world history. That doesn't mean that the threat of violence by tens of thousands of misguided radicals isn't real-it means that labeling it as "A War on Terror" is a scare tactic that solicits fear.

Resolutions

Personally, I have a lot of respect for the former Senator, professional basketball player, and Rhodes Scholar Bill Bradley, but he is a member of the "establishment". So naturally his views of democracy and a two party system (Democrats and Republicans) are going to be different. As a member of the "ruling class" he has access to unrestricted freedoms. Therefore, his belief in bipartisanship is a logical answer for today's gridlock. But the view from above is always more serene while the forecast below is always more severe.

The illusion of democracy is the "carrot on the string in front of us" and we are the mules that keep going in circles hoping to retrieve it, but never quite get there. Our "*Founding Fathers*" laid the foundation for a democracy, but the upper class seized the moment after Thomas Jefferson's presidency-for wealth is power and the misuse of power is a sin. And the corruption in Congress today is rooted in the early 1820's. Andrew Jackson tried to halt the corruption, but the aristocrats challenged his character by criticizing his wife which probably contributed to her death. And he knew the corporations were going to take over America and limit the poor man's ability to prosper, but the Bankers and an Aristocratic Congress were too much for an honest man. And no "*Old Hickory*" was not a perfect man for some of his wrongful deeds against Native Americans and slaves can not be justified. But no man in this era achieved success without blood on his hands and without Andrew Jackson's leadership and bravery; today we would be known as *British America.* Until we are able to eliminate the influence of money, democracy in its pure form cannot be achieved. Clearly, the attack on our freedom of speech while forcing political correctness upon us violates the *Constitution.* But remember, the aristocrat's control the courts, so the decision will not be based on constitutional law-it will be determined by the financial influence of the powerbrokers.

Sometimes it is easier to believe a lie than it is to face the truth. Don Imus was fired for incentive remarks he made about the women on Rutgers University basketball team. No one is defending his comments, but I am angered by the current double standard. Many black radio hosts such as Al Sharpton and Jessie Jackson make racially divisive remarks all the time and they are not fired. Except for the former Hurricane in Miami Lamar Thomas, black radio and television personalities are rarely held accountable for their racist comments or unprofessional antics. And gay activist Rosie O'Donnell constantly spouts off with unacceptable racial and gender rhetoric. Most rappers and comedians use offensive language that crosses every unacceptable line of race, gender, religion, ethnicity, and sexual orientation. It appears that white males and white conservatives are the only ones being held accountable by the thought police. I am personally torn on the censorship issue because it infringes on every American's right of free speech. By creating racial, class, gender, and religious divides, the earthy kings (upper class) can reign without fear.

In Newton's *law of inertia* for every action there is an equally opposite reaction. Thus, if there is a "War on Oppression" there is also a "War against the Oppressors". And a duality can easily be created by a disingenuous media whose true motive is profit. Since the current media is so irresponsible, it almost merits some restrictions on "free speech". But, a simpler way of handling the media's untruthful propaganda is to remove their shield of free speech which they hide behind and make them criminally and civilly liable. Many wars and social unrest can be attributed to a sensationalistic media that lacks any moral integrity. And their unholy alliance with the Democratic Party has become a serious national problem.

The disintegration of western cultures by excluding morality and ethics is partially responsible for inflaming religious extremist's hostile actions. It does not validate their violence, but it provides insight to their anger. Western nations do not have the right to dictate policy to any sovereign nation. Since our so-called "democracy" is a sham, how can we establish democratic governments in other regions of the world? The people of each nation have the right to establish their own belief systems regardless of outside opposition. The only time other nations should intervene is to prevent mass genocide, provide medical assistance, distribute food and clothing, eradicate drug production, arrest international terrorists, oversee any nuclear programs, or at the request of that government. Any such undertaking should be done collaboratively with international oversight.

Instead of looking for peaceful solutions, western governments incite the terrorists and thereby place their military personnel, law enforcement, and citizens in "*Harm's Way*". And the *United Nations* is nothing more than a bureaucratic nightmare that has outlived its usefulness. We need an IFP (*International Federation of Peace*) with three incorruptible representatives from each continent. These twenty-one leaders would work in the best interest of humanity. If China and Russia refuse to reform their human rights policies, then the IFP would use international sanctions until they comply. But the main reason the western governments act irresponsible is to solicit fear. By creating chaotic hysteria, these governments reestablish their self-worth. These horrific acts superimpose their master's objective of world dominance while at the same time-it allows them to restrict our freedoms. If we don't start holding our governments and their bureaucrats accountable we will continue to suffer for their sins and our lack of courage. And even though there is a Government Office of Accountability (GOA), it is in name only for there is little accountability in most U.S. government bureaucracies.

11

Politics

"Absolute power only corrupts those who are corruptible"

"The world doesn't need another great athlete, the world doesn't need another charismatic politician, and the world damn sure doesn't need another greedy capitalist; the world needs more humanitarians of faith-keepers of God's realm."

Politics has become a dirty word in society today because it is a controlled mechanism of the wealthy. Our two party political system does not represent the views of the people; it limits the choices as a way of maintaining social order. Republicans are supposedly Conservative while Democrats are supposedly Liberal. It is a serious mistake when we attempt to identify ourselves as conservatives or liberals in a political context. These politicians only care about getting elected or reelected and they will say whatever is popular with the group or individuals they are addressing.

Who represents the majority, or the *Moderates*? Neither, but that is where the election outcomes are determined. Both the democratic and republican parties are bought and paid for by the largest corporations (American and Foreign), the world's wealthiest individuals and families, along with powerful special interests groups with self-serving agendas. And we, the eligible voters only matter when an election is near.

What about the over fifty percent (50%) of eligible voters who often don't vote? Including people like me who are fed up with the current corrupt system, so we rarely vote. It feels like I am trying to choose between the least of two evils. Of course, there is only worse and "the worse." Both parties sold their souls to the Devil many moons ago. And most of our politicians think we are all stupid and there must be some truth in that assumption because we keep reelecting the same old lying ass hypocrites.

Our freedoms are slowly being eroded and any opposition is being vilified. Slogans such as "A woman's right to choose" or "War on terror, crime, or drugs" are designed to confuse and frustrate the masses. This soliciting of fear is used by both parties. The Democrats have used "welfare" and "Social Security" to their advantage for the last seventy plus years. At the same time, Republicans are using "terrorism" and "morality" to solidify their base. Neither gives a damn about the poor or the working class. And the majority of American politicians worship power and wealth.

Still the middle is where common sense flourishes and people still use their mental capacities for reasoning. As the reader might surmise, this is where I choose to dwell. Unfortunately, there are no moderate politicians, but there are Democrats and Republicans that pose as moderates. Often I have wondered why so many college professors get hung up in liberal philosophies instead of the rational approach of the middle which would seem a more logical choice. I understand advocating for social change when necessary, but most liberal professors become so biased that they are blinded by conviction, and thus they lose sight of reality and "the good of society as a whole." And college should be the one place where all sides are explored. When I returned to college, a large majority of my professors were liberal. For me, educational institutions should be unbiased and a leader in reshaping our current corrupted political and bureaucratic systems.

What these two parties are doing is dividing the people by preying on their emotions and using modern mediums that spin language which incites angry and irrational responses. By limiting choices and creating divisive language, it is easier for the controlling elite to maintain their status quo. They desire no change and legislatively they restrict any opposition for change. And their lies, deceptions, manipulations, and ungodly acts do not support their claims of faith-for God knoweth their hearts and the people bear witness to their evil deeds. Barack Obama assertion that Republicans hijacked religion is a lie because neither party works for God. Both sides use the media to deceive the people about their faith.

Approximately ninety percent of the media is controlled by five corporate conglomerates which use their influence to sway voters. Four of the five mediums are controlled by rich liberals who represent a very small percentage of our population. When the Democrats lose in the elections, they try to manipulate constitutional law through the judicial system. This is the .behavior of a spoiled child that did not get his or her way, so they throw a tantrum. Here a good whopping as a child might have produced a decent citizen instead of a jackass. And the Democrats also use their media influence to constantly criticize their opponents, but more and more of us have slowly begun to recognize their deception.

Now the Republicans on the other hand want to preach religious ideology on Sunday and live the good life by embracing the corrupt political system from Monday through Saturday. Sound familiar, it should, I have witnessed these ridiculous behaviors throughout my lifetime. When an individual compromises his or her beliefs for a piece of the corrupt corporate or governmental pie, this person has sold his or her soul for a stake in this glutinous capitalistic system. The Republicans unethical and immoral behaviors are the main reason for losing control in the Senate and House in the November election of 2006. The voters weren't embracing Democrats as their liberal media puppets suggested; they were angry and sought retribution through the ballot box. There is no room for God in either party for their Lord and Master is the ruling upper class.

Honestly, Democrats and Republicans have lied so much to the American people that we have come to expect it. Every time one of these liars opens their mouths-I am repulsed. These soulless servants of Satan don't give a damn about the average citizen and they only use the poor for their own personal agendas and then discard us like a piece of toilet paper they just used to wipe their filthy butt with. Unless you are wealthy, you do not exist in their world-for politicians are the lowest form of creatures that God hath made.

And the majority of western politicians are corrupt, not just American politicians. They give in to the temptations because they are corruptible. Everyone sins, but most decent people draw lines for immoral behaviors that we dare not cross. Unfortunately billionaires including royal families of false faith in the Middle East run and rule an ungodly world and most are deceivers. Their crimes against God and humanity exceed repentance-for men with no good in their hearts only serveth themselves and thereby serveth Satan.

Nevertheless, America was founded on moral *Christian* principles. Yes, slavery and the oppression of women were wrong. But all men and women are born of sin and each will disobey God's laws countless times during their lives. Those that drafted the *Declaration of Independence*, *Bill of Rights*, and the *Constitution* of the United States were products of their era. They were men of character and men of faith. If we continue to live in the past instead of learning from the past, there is little hope for mankind-for yesterday is gone and it can't be fixed.

Moreover it is a myth that white people will not vote for a black presidential candidate. I would vote for General Colin Powell for in him I see honesty, integrity, leadership, and a man of faith. Though I would not vote for Senator Barack Obama for in him I see allusive, unprincipled, ambitious, and a religious hypocrite. But the irony of Barack's campaign is that he is using the same hustle (making promises he can't keep for votes) that Bill Clinton used in 1992. And I admit I have my reservations about voting for a woman. We live in a very complex and volatile time in history. Any hesitation or poor negotiations could mean ruin for the United States. NAFTA, the UN, corporate influence, a dysfunctional educational system, Democrats and Republicans, an oversized bureaucratic government, China and Russia, a weakened military, and an endless list of intricate failures have America on life support. So for me to consider voting for a female candidate she would have to be a woman of faith, character, sincerity, insightfulness, and humility. And no, this does not include Hillary Clinton. Hillary is intelligent but not insightful, she is outspoken but lacks humility, and while she is cunning she lacks character. The former First Lady changes with the wind so she lacks sincerity and her liberally progressive ideology weakens her declaration of faith. The only difference between Hillary Clinton and Howard Dean is she has balls. And I would personally like to see a new amendment to the Constitution. (*New Amendment*) From this day forward, no Clinton or Bush can run for the office of President of these United States for at least one thousand years or until Hell freezes over.

When I was a young boy the older boys usually bullied the youths that were strong, intelligent, and athletically gifted. In turn, we mistreated others who were weaker. As I grew into a teenager, I became a protector of the weak from bullies but it never made up for my shortcomings. I have always regretted my transgressions and these memories serve as a reminder of my shame. Many times when I have reflected on my life, I have wished that I could have changed many of the mistakes that I had made. It is not enough to say "I am sorry" for our sins impact others lives not just our own. With each passing day I strive to be a better human being because I know I can't fix yesterday. But I also understand that if I don't learn from my mistakes the chances are highly probable that I will repeat them.

Resolutions

There are many resolutions for our dishonest politicians, judges, and bureaucrats. First, we can start by sending the corrupt ones on a long ten to twenty year sabbatical at the local state penitentiary, instead of the federal vacation spas generally used. And we should also prosecute top executives of corporations for price fixing, fraud, hiring illegal immigrants, and bribing political and government officials. Next, we can change patent laws if companies do not comply with more competitively (much lower) set rates. If quality health care, including all prescriptions and treatments, were free and guaranteed for all American citizens, it would allow us to sleep better at night. At least American taxpayers might actually benefit from paying their taxes. Instead we are witnesses to all the wasteful spending and it frustrates the masses who feel powerless to do anything about the abuses.

Repealing or dramatically revising NAFTA (*North American Free Trade Agreement*) is another change Americans must demand. If we are going to have trade agreements with China, Japan, Korea, India, or any nation, they must be reciprocal. The American job market continues to suffer because of these foreign deficits. While corporate profits are on the rise, livable wage jobs are declining. And politician's debate minimum wage increases while American workers have become the sacrificial lambs of corporate irresponsibility. By placing tariffs or fees on all products not manufactured in the US equivalent to the cost of producing the products in the United States, or taxing corporations that move American jobs overseas, we could reenergize the American job market. And there is no doubt we should also have a *National Minimum Wage* as well as an *International Minimum Wage* that represents the cost of living. Every Democrat and Republican who is responsible for passing NAFTA (that includes the former President Bill Clinton) should be removed from office and exiled to "*The Fairyland of the Foolish*" for they betrayed the American people's trust in the interests of corporate greed.

Meanwhile lobbyists of corporations and special interest groups have become a fixture in modern politics. So the best way to handle this is to outlaw lobbying and solicitation of all elected officials because this is just another form of bribery which is already supposed to be illegal. The absurdness of things going on in the American Political Arena, are mind boggling. And term limits should be *National Law* because politics should have never become a career; politics is supposed to be and should have always remained a service of the people, by the people, and for the people. Instead politicians have become the bitches of the ruling class and thereby prostituted their integrity for a few pieces of silver-just like Judas

Every county, state, and national office should have term limits and a two term limit at any level is more than reasonable. This includes judges; all judges should be elected, not appointed by other elected officials with political agendas and that includes the Supreme Court. There should also be an age cutoff for service around the age of eighty, especially for judges. It sounds simple, is a reasonable solution, but it would put a lot of lazy and incompetent jerks out of work. And it is easy for these power grubbing whores to waste trillions of dollars that they literally steal from the working poor and middle class in this country because they don't see or know us personally.

Similarly I am not sure which country is gayer, Great Britain or Canada. But Great Britain's gun control policy is far more effective than the United States. And France surrenders at the first sign of conflict, but France and Canada have superior health care systems. Fifty-four countries throughout the world have better educational systems. These facts are shameful considering the United States has superior financial resources. There is no disgrace in evaluating more efficient systems in other countries and then implementing new policies and procedures that replace our current failing systems.

Politics isn't necessarily a dirty word; it is the people in politics who are dirty rotten scoundrels. There are only a few Democrats and Republications I consider decent people. However, those few are chained by loyalty to their affiliations and they are whipped by their masters when they forget their place. Their speech is restricted and they follow the script-those who do not comply are abandoned. Ask Joe Lieberman for he is one of those I admire. Observe John McCain (another I respect) being forced to reconstruct his beliefs to become a more viable "Republican" candidate. Both parties require devout obedience and therefore nothing of significant importance is every achieved.

And our current stagnation in the American political arena is by design. The ruling aristocrats do not desire men and women of integrity-they seek the weakest links. Next, they use their mediums to create fictional political characters for the sole purpose of deceiving the voters. By polarizing a nation into two opposing factions, the godless capitalists can rule without fear. A vote for most Democrat or Republican is a vote for "no changed". Frequently we look for a doctrine of ideology in the two parties, but there is none. Thus we are left confused and disenfranchised-for western politician's houses are made of sand and their loose particles scatter in all directions when the wind blows.

Now that the votes have been counted some more than once, Barack Obama has a unique opportunity to change Washington. But so far, it looks like the same old partisan politics that led to the downfall of the Republicans in 2006 and 2008. And I would argue that George W. Bush has damaged the Republican Party so greatly, it may never recover. Unless a new Moderate Party of reformers is established to stop the liberal agenda of a few Democrats on the far left, our nation is headed for *Economic Armageddon.* That is why I didn't vote for President Obama for I believe his radical ideas are going to accelerate the 2nd Great Depression and possibly lead us into a global conflict of horrific tragedies never before witnessed by mankind. When the honeymoon of adulation is over, hopefully the American public will began to smell what Washington is cooking before our *Golden Goose* is deep fried in hog fat.

12

A New System

"A wise man seeks advice while a fool listens to no one"

It is impractical to think we can change a two party system of Democrats and Republicans, but we can start three new parties that represent the masses. Conservative, moderate, and liberal parties, including independent candidates having access to the ballot; is the logical solution for changing our failed political system. There are also several cornerstone ideas that each new party should include: (1) No individual contribution to any party candidate can exceed five-hundred dollars per year. (2) No corporate or small business contributions to an individual candidate can exceed one-thousand dollars per year. (3) No campaign contributions from any union or group for any candidate can exceed seven-hundred-and-fifty dollars per year. These include unions and groups such as the NEA (National Education Association), NRA (National Rifleman's Association), UAW (United Auto Workers), CC (Christian Coalition), NAACP (National Association for the Advancement of Colored People), etc. (4) Term limits. (5) No discriminatory exclusion. (6) And possibly the most important recommendation is to use every safeguard imaginable to prohibit the wealthy elite from ever being able to purchase any party or candidate. Through group discussions and intellectually inclusive think tanks we can positively impact our political system that has betrayed the people it was supposed to represent.

Truthfully we can not overthrow the current corrupt social order with violence because the powers that be (PTB), or ruling class, control the militaries, the courts, all law enforcement, the government bureaucracies, the media, most churches, almost every western corporation, the politicians, or basically every political, social, influential, economical, and enforcement entity of modern society. Our power is in a non-violent unity which Dr. King recognized in the late 1950's. That is why Dr. Martin Luther King Jr. was assassinated because the aristocrats fear anyone who can unite all races, classes, cultures, ages, religions, and genders for a common cause that benefits all of humanity. When we use violence, we lose and the powers that be gain more power. They continue to impose new restrictions on our already limited freedoms through unconstitutional legislation that their courts uphold. Frequently statistical data provides insight into how we were bamboozled if we stay alert and pay attention to the trends we can regain our moral authority.

Approximately eighty percent (80%) of the state and national politicians are lawyers. The large majority of the rest are doctors and there is a correlation. It is not coincidental, these individuals are products of what greed and power can produce through an exclusionary modeled political system. With a three party system of *Conservatives, Moderates,* and *Liberals;* at least ninety-five percent or more of the population would actual be legitimately represented and those not represented could run as *Independents.* While this might seem to be an enormous undertaking; political reform should be expected and demanded by the voters. Maybe we should consider not allowing lawyers and doctors to run for public office because the majority of these corruptible parasites have mucked up everything they attempted to fix.

On the other hand, the criminal element ranges somewhere between one and two percent of the populous. Criminals don't believe in hard work or care about their fellow countrymen. They are always looking for "easy street" through cons, rip-offs, selling legal and illegal narcotics, prostitution, gambling, pornography, bribery, stealing, and they will use any means necessary while pursuing their obsessions. For years I have tried to convey this message to family, friends, and students; "*The road to success for most of us who are poor requires hard work, sacrifice, and persistence-for there are no free rides.*" But criminals never "get it" because their moral decency has been extinguished by their immoral desires. Thus their road usually ends in tragedy-for that is the path they have chosen and the consequence for unlawful behaviors are severe for the uneducated and unprincipled poor.

That's why a political revolution is our best chance to restore law and order. Our current laws, protects the criminals and suppresses the victims. Most poor people can't afford an adequate defense and most public defenders are unequipped to handle dirty cops, politically ambitious prosecutors, or dishonest judges. Once those sworn to uphold the law violate their oath, they lose all credibility and thereby become the loyal subjects of their corruptors.

Shamefully organized crime has purchased policemen, politicians, and judges for over a century in the US. This is especially true in large cities such as New York and Chicago. *Organized Crime* bosses and families have purchased many mayors, law enforcement agents, and district attorneys in Chicago and New York since the early 1900's. The *Entertainment Industry* corrupted the politicians and police in the Los Angeles area when Hollywood became the Film Capital of the world. Don't believe that "Tough on crime slogan nonsense." While it is a statistical fact that murders and the crime rate were lower under Mayor Rudy Giuliani-he is given far too much credit. Tougher laws with harsher punishment passed by Congress under President William Jefferson Clinton, which stopped liberal judges from slapping violent criminals on the wrist with unbelievably light sentences, is the main reason for the decline in the crime rates. Locking up a few homeless people of color and then declaring the city safe is a disgraceful recreation of the truth. Don't get me wrong, I love big cities like Atlanta, New York, Chicago, L.A., and Miami, but I don't like the corruption in these cities. In 2008, our Presidential Election would have come down to Rudy Giuliani (R) against Hillary Clinton (D) if the early projections of 2007 had held up. And that would have been freaking great; a choice between the *Mafia* and the *Antichrist.* "Lord please have mercy on us for we have truly lost our minds and our destiny lies in the hands of the fools."

What in God's name did Giuliani do that somehow made him a hero? Did he stop the planes from crashing into the Twin Towers? How many people did Rudy save by going into the structure as it was collapsing? Who are the terrorists that Rudy Giuliani caught? The policeman and fireman that lost their lives while trying to save the people during 9/11 are the heroes. Rudy Giuliani is an illusionary hero created by a liberally biased media in the Northeast. The amount of bickering and corruption involved in the rebuilding of the Twin Towers is appalling. What about the fighting over payoffs for surviving family members of 9/11? The greed and the enormous amounts paid out for the silencing of family survivors tainted one of the greatest tragedies in American history since Pearl Harbor. All Rudy did was his job and from my vantage point, his job performance is nothing to boost about.

Besides Rudy Giuliani is a liberal posing as a Republican. He lacks the values of a conservative and he dang sure isn't a moderate. I can't help my feelings that Rudy maybe a pawn of organized crime and didn't he have an affiliation with the ACLU or was it a legal conflict of interests? How in the hell has this liberal politician disguised himself as a Republican? David

Copperfield move over for Rudy is the greatest illusionist in the world. That's all we needed in the White House was another pussy hound, Dick chasing Jane, fumbling the football while trying to score. I may not see as well as others, but I see through people's phoniness better than most.

America needs new leadership not the same old deceptive hypocrites. But when it comes to the most important job in the world, *the Presidency of these United States of America*, I examine every candidate's qualifications, experience, and record. John McCain and Joe Lieberman have taken principled stands for America against their own party as well as the other party on more occasions than any representative in Congress. They are without question the most honorable representatives of the people. Moreover, the *American Presidency* is not the *American Idol*; the merit of a candidate is more important than a candidate's popularity.

And just because Bill Clinton benefited from a strong economy doesn't mean he was responsible for it. Because any honest financial planner would say "Economies are influenced by market cycles. It has nothing to do with any one individual." And weren't taxes raised to offset the deficit first by Bush (which along with Ross Perot cost him his reelection bid) and then again by Clinton? Some people's obsession with former President Clinton amazes me-for I am personally troubled by his many unethical and immoral acts. Besides, weren't most of those 22 million new jobs created low skilled minimum wage positions and wasn't that so-called economic prosperity tied to the dotcom explosion (of the 1990's) which collapsed into bankruptcy and cost millions of investors the majority of their retirement portfolios?

Why did President Clinton pardon some of his wealthy criminal financial contributors? Those contributions to his library were disguised payoffs. This is a misuse of power and an embarrassment to the Presidential Office. How is it that every illegal scandal Bill and Hillary were linked too miraculously disappeared? Without a biased liberal media that is joined at the hip with the Democratic Party, such atrocities would not vanish so easily. But our disingenuous media representatives had a *love-fest* with Hillary that turned into an *orgy* for Obama. Thus, in the majority of election contests throughout the United States the Republican candidates are running against the Democratic nominees and the liberally biased support of the media. However, the Presidency of the United States is a *Symbol of Freedom* and the *Guardian of Humanity.* It is not a Democrat or Republican. He who worships false idols builds a prison unto himself-here he will remain because he is confined by the delusions of his own construction. William Jefferson Clinton is no hero and his friends in the western liberal media cannot make him so. And if celebrity becomes more important than merit (experience) then the *Obama Express* is steamrolling America toward the *Dark Days of the Apocalypse.*

Bill Clinton becoming President is a direct result of the disintegration of America's morality. We have placed our personal needs above all else. Dick Morris wrote a book called *Because He Could.* He comments:

> But the Bill Clinton story has taught us a new and different lesson: that we must learn to attend carefully to the scandals and controversies that arise during a person's pursuit of the presidency, for they are likely to provide clues we need to understand what kind of a president he or she will be.

All the evidence was in front of the American people and we chose to ignore it. Listening to a Clinton friendly media, many voters drank the *Devil's Coolaide.* Dick Morris said later if we had paid more attention we might have elected another person. I challenge anyone who says they are a Christian who voted for Bill Clinton or is considering Hillary-for you are only fooling yourself, not God. Both have escaped the criminal justice system, but they will not escape *Judgment Day* and those who follow will join them in *Hell.*

Similarly popularity has nothing to do with credibility. Barack Obama is not qualified to be the President of the United States of America in 2008. Truthfully I know I lack the necessary experience required for the Oval Office, but it appears Obama and his media whores believes the Presidency is based on *Affirmative Action.* And I am always suspicious of over hype and it is just a matter of time before his closet door is opened and the skeletons start tumbling down. But because of his momentum the media will bury any information that might affect Barack's chances. For our media desperately desires the Democratic nominee to be an *African American* or a *Woman* and they will do anything to ensure this outcome including withholding the truth. God must truly be pleased with America. The only Presidential Candidates I would even consider voting for in 2008 is John McCain, Colin Powell, or Al Gore for they are the three most qualified candidates. And the media takes pleasure in crucifying conservatives, so *Christians* need not apply.

Moreover I am concerned about China's censorship aided by *Microsoft* and *Google* that suppresses human rights. As soon as America elects a liberal feminist or unqualified minority with a left-wing extremist's agenda, we will pay a heavy price for our insanity. First of all, China with the aid of Russia will begin to manipulate American policy the same way they did when Bill Clinton was President. Putting aside Bill's lying under oath, the campaign contributions from China was a criminal and treasonous act. In the last ten years China has taken over the American economy because of NAFTA (North American Free Trade Agreement) which Bill swore he would veto if he were elected.

Once America has been neutered through liberal negotiations, our significance will be lessened even more by the idiots in Congress who have no spine. Anyone who thinks Russia is no longer a threat and holds no animosity toward the US is either a liberal extremist or has fallen for the fictional propaganda. Who is supplying the majority of the weapons used in international terrorism? Who sold nuclear technology for oil and cash? Yes, I too dream of a utopian world, but that is not the reality of our world in the *21st century.* Senator John McCain, General Colin Powell, former Vice-president Al Gore, Secretary of State Dr. Condoleezza Rice, and Senator Joe Lieberman possess the required experience and they personify the meaning of a person with character, but most importantly they are qualified to lead America. It is true I do not trust Hillary Clinton though I do respect her qualifications, but it is an unarguable fact that Barack Obama is not qualified, and John Edwards made his fortune as an ambulance chaser. So how could I in good conscious vote for any of the current democratic choices? Besides I would not trust Barack Obama or John Edwards leading a local municipal, much less a country. And just because the New York media portrays Giuliani as a savior doesn't mean I believe it either because *donkey dung doesn't float down south.* Yet, you can bet the leftist media is going to push for a joint Presidential ticket of Obama and Hillary even though the best Democratic choice because he is the most qualified would have been Al Gore a champion for the environment and a leader with both experience and character (another I admire and respect).

Regrettably integrity is no longer a required characteristic of today's media. Their operating procedures are the same as the Entertainment Industry. By using their deceptive influence, the media can create fictional characters out of despicable human being to further their own economic, political, and social agendas. Barack Obama is mimicking Bill Clinton. He is making promises he can never keep while saying what the audience wants to hear. At the same time the liberally biased media is using short soft interviews with Barack and Hillary to politically define them as more admirable characters. Neither is one of us and their political ambition is repulsive. And Oprah and Jessie endorsing

Obama seems racially motivated which is sad, but voters in the *African-American Community* often block vote for self interests. Many black voters have been asked "Why are you supporting Barack Obama?" And the general response is "he is inspirational". But this isn't a church social; the *American Presidency* is the most important political office in the world. It is a poor refection on any uninformed American voter who believes inspiration somehow trumps merit and substance Thus we have a responsibility as American citizens to use every peaceful solution possible to interrupt the lies, slogans, and deceptions of an out-of-control spin-monster that has created a movement based on popularity while excluding the facts.

However don't misunderstand my displeasure with the Democrats for I am just as disgusted with the Republican hypocrites. In 2008, Republicans tried to nominate Mitt Romney a stiff white guy claiming to be a Christian wrapped in the American Flag. It doesn't take a genius to figure out the scams of both because they use the same one over and over. Stopping the madness means putting new players into the game while exiling the corrupted. Washington is like a barrel of rotting apples- the only way to get rid of the bad ones is to discard the whole barrel.

Therefore I believe the three main groups of voters in the US would be better served by a new political system. They are the moderates or the major majority, the conservatives or the minor majority, and the liberals or the minority. The majority of the rest could be represented by independents. It is time to put aside our differences and take America back from the ruling class.

Even though God will punish the unholy capitalists in the end-our focus must be on rebuking them now before it is too late.

In early 2000, I was more politically active. I scheduled an appointment with my local state representative, a republican, because he didn't like being bothered outside his office by his constituents. A funny thing though, despite his complaints about being pestered and the low pay of a state rep, he continually runs for the position. I called his office the day of my appointment to confirm our scheduled meeting. From my house to his office it is a fairly long walk. During my walk I was besieged by a torrential down-poor, but I continued. Upon arriving at his office his secretary informed me he had conveniently left for the day. The truth be told, I knew he was trying deliberately to avoid me because I had some tough questions about what he and others in the State House and Senate were doing to improve employment opportunities for people with disabilities?

It wasn't the first time so I contacted the state run Republican office which was headed by Ralph Reed. Well we now know that Ralph isn't all that he claimed to be but in 2000 I was going through the supposed proper channels. I explained what had occurred and asked "Is this how the Republican Party treats its constituents?" Nothing is how they responded except for a phony apology in a letter that was sent only after I had repeatedly called their office because Reed hadn't responded to my letter voicing my concerns.

Outwardly my local rep claimed to be a Christian but I guess expecting lawyers to be honest is too much to ask for-though the experience opened by eyes to the truth about the Republican Party-for many are not conservatives they are lying hypocrites just like the Democrats. Afterwards I investigated running as an independent. It was depressing to find that the Democrats and Republicans had legislated barriers to make it almost impossible to run as an independent. But to run as a Democrat or Republican all one had to do is pay a fee on a set day at the state capital.

Resolutions

America's best chance for a revolution is through the political process. No, not the current political system, it is broke and it can never be fixed. A new three party system that represents Conservatives, Moderates, and Liberals (yes the liberals have a right to representation) is our best chance for political reform. We have been hoodwinked far too long by the Democrats, Republicans, and a sensationalistic media. Our government agencies have abused their powers that were entrusted by the people they swore to protect. Almost everything we were taught to believe in was a lie. Our salvation has been traded for an illusion of "silver". Now is the time for us to stand up and let the world witness our faith is stronger than any party, corporation, or bureaucracy.

In other words a political revolution can restore our country and redeem our souls. However, a new three party system only works if safeguards are put into place to ensure the

Aristocrats only have one vote just like the rest of us. We need to outlaw all lobbying and that includes special interests groups. No government matching funds, limited campaign contributions that prevent the influence of legislation, and independent oversight for every government agency. No more war unless America has no other options, make social discourse from the bench an act of treason, and bribery of any government official should be considered a crime against the people and punishable by a minimum of twenty years to life in a state prison. Repealing *Double Jeopardy* with independent oversight of all felony cases and competitive tariffs or fees on all corporations that do not produce their products in the United States where they are sold. There are thousands of resolutions that can change the current *Corrupt Capitalist Climate* if we are going to take back America from the few that intend on sacrificing our well being for their corporate greed, but we must stand together.

Sadly, most Democrats and Republicans are more concerned with their reelections than actually doing what is right for America. If we don't create a new honest political system that represents the people, America is going to fall just as the Roman Empire and all those before and after it. The ruling class and their puppet politicians will be hiding in secure underground sanctuaries with a few scientists, military leaders, and security personnel, while the rest of us will be doomed above ground in a chaotic bloodbath with Russia, China, and radical terrorists. It is time for a new government formed of decent ordinary men and women who understand the difference between right and wrong-there are exceptions but there is no gray area. America needs honest people who care about our country and the world and they must be willing to take the necessary steps to reclaim our sovereignty.

In November of 2008, voters bought into the "change" message that President Obama articulated. Many disregarded his inexperience and troublesome associations because of his eloquent demeanor. But there were other contributing factors that included President Bush's unpopularity, the media's hype for Obama and lack of journalistic integrity, the stock market crash, the bank bailout, the unpopular Iraq War, John McCain's poorly run campaign, corporate greed, the outsourcing of middle-class jobs, Obama's $600 million dollar advertising blitz, and the mainstream media's branding of the Republican Party as the villain. Voters were angry and they voted with their emotions.

Some might say it was the perfect storm that allowed a media backed celebrity to steal an election. But one must give David Axelrod credit for running a brilliant Presidential campaign. And we cannot dismiss the historical relevance of electing the first Black President. However, I would also argue that the Presidential Election of 2008 was wrongly influenced by the PTB (Powers That Be). Though if you break down the voting data, it was White women who decided the election and they will share in the success or suffer for the failure of President Obama because choices have consequences.

After the election, I had great hope for President Barack Obama even though I didn't vote for him. But what I had envisioned of "hope and change' at the early stages is very troubling. For President Obama's Administration reminds me of Grant's Administration which was the most corrupt Presidential Administration in American History. And the Democratic controlled Congress of 2009 resembles the Congress of the Reconstruction Period during the same era that was the most corrupt Congress ever. We are on the brink of collapse and President Obama is still campaigning. If President Obama doesn't find the courage to reevaluate his cabinet and can't summon the integrity to stop Nancy Pelosi and Harry Reid, America will soon be in an economic crisis that reaches far beyond corrupt politics and harebrain policies.

13

The Constitution

"Those who push the boundaries of decency work against the good of humanity"

The Declaration of Independence

When in the Course of human Events, it becomes necessary for one People to dissolve the Political Bands which have connected them with another, and to assume among the Powers of the Earth, the separate and equal Station to which the Laws of Nature and of Nature's God entitle them, a decent Respect to the Opinions of Mankind requires that they should declare the causes which impel them to the Separation.

The *Western Democracies* of today are the *European Imperialists* of yesterday. Currently they are forcing their values of greed, power, self-gratification, and selfishness upon us like a plague that will eventually infect all. And they don't care whom they hurt, how they make their money, or what their toxic poisons do to the environment. For them, tomorrow is not important-they live in the "now" and are consumed with "self". These pagans own the justice system, so they rarely answer for their crimes. And though they may have the world at their mercy, God will show them no mercy-for they have gone too far and their suffering will be immense.

As citizens of the United States, we must separate ourselves from this corrupted two party system of injustice. Our bondage by the Democrats and Republicans has to end-for hope depends on our rejection of both. In the eyes of God, we are all equal, but in the immoral world of Satan's disciples, we are not considered equals. However, *The Declaration of Independence* clearly acknowledges our Founding Fathers depended on their faith in God for the pursuit of independence.

> We hold these truths to be self-evident, that all Men are created equal, that they are endowed by their Creator, with certain unalienable Rights, that among these are Life, Liberty, and the Pursuit of Happiness.

The popular slogan "*Separation of Church and State*" is a creation of the *Secular Doctrine.* For their goal is to remove God from all aspects of life-thus they serve Satan. The irony for men and women that serve Satan is "They believe by serving Satan, they in return will gain favor. But they are sadly mistaken for *Satan's Army* is the *Fallen Angels.* Those mortals who serve Satan will be punished severely in Hell as their cries are mocked-for no sin goes unpunished. And the severity of the crime against God and man will dictate the "terms of torture" in the "pit below"-for that is the unbreakable agreement between the LORD and LUCIFER. Our forefathers knew that faith is the key to developing a moral and ethical system of government for and accountable to the people.

And our *Bill of Rights* or the first ten amendments laid the foundation for the *Constitution of the United States of America.* In the first amendment Congress was forbid to prohibit free speech of religion, the press, and the people. Thus, Lyndon Johnson's restrictions on religions political activism by denying their tax exempt status is unconstitutional and the judicial system failed the people. Today's judicial branch is filled with social activists that make decisions on personal ideology rather than the constitutionality of the law. And the judges that are appointed by Governors and the President have no accountability to the public they have sworn to serve. If you listen closely to what the Federal Judge in Michael Vick's case said; he provided Vick with many opportunities for contrition. After Vick's defiance the Judge rightfully sentenced him to twenty-three months. But when the Mayor of Atlanta, Shirley Franklin (D), wrote to the Federal Judge and pleaded for reconsideration, I wasn't surprised. If we consider Marion Berry, O.J. Simpson, Barry Bonds, or Michael Vick the majority in both the black and white communities view the outcomes quite differently. Unfortunately this is what our judicial due process has become; a manipulative process where the wealthiest capitalists and celebrity criminals can fix the outcome while spinning the truth.

I have two family friends, one is visually impaired and the other is blind and they both are lawyers. They are the only two lawyers that I know that are men of faith with unquestionable character. Now there maybe a few more decent lawyers that I don't know, but I am reasonably sure ninety-nine percent are *the disciples of the Devil*-for their oath of allegiance is not to justice it is to power, wealth, and winning. It doesn't matter if their client is guilty or not-for the process has turned into a game where the final decision is influenced by money, fame, or the power of the institution (Entertainment Industry, Sports Leagues, Corporations, and Governments). Afterwards, with the cooperation of the corporate owned media, their public relations machines began their assault on our intelligence.

Therefore we must not forget the phrases, "Innocent until proven guilty" and "beyond a reasonable doubt", were our forefathers attempt to create "justice for all", but there is no justice for the common man in today's judicial system. Most poor people are "guilty even when the evidence overwhelmingly supports their innocence" while the rich and famous "are innocent even though the evidence against them undeniably supports their guilt." There are many dishonest attorneys that manipulate the judicial process to get their guilty celebrity clients off. Of course this would not be possible without the assistance of the media. And they generally start with "allegedly", "entitled to due process", support from their inner circles (fraternities like the NFL, NBA, and MLB) "this is not the person I know", and the public relations spin goes on and on for months redefining the unlawful criminals as the victims. But every once and a while a rich or famous person gets shafted by our corrupted judicial system-Martha Stewart and the Duke Lacrosse players. And an irresponsible media runs with it because it is easy to stir up racial emotions by blaming rich white people for all of society's problems-totally ignoring the facts while disregarding their responsibility as representatives of journalism as they disseminate misinformation. Still, the irony of this indefensible act is the majority of the medium owners are white aristocrats-though most are liberals who allow "*the guilt syndrome*" to influence their social activism.

Normally I would support the "freedom of speech" in regards to the press, but today's western media lacks substance, credibility, and a moral code of ethics. So maybe its time to remove the media's shield of protection behind free speech until they learn the meanings of honesty, integrity, and character-for the media today serves its pagan owners and itself. And because of the media's irresponsible journalism, the people can no longer trust their prepackaged rhetoric. Thus, there can be no doubt the media of today is the most powerful weapon in Satan's arsenal.

And who, over two hundred years ago, could have foreseen the cultural disintegration of morality in America? Seriously, I doubt our founding-fathers could have ever imagined that pornography would be shielded by today's interpretation of the 1st Amendment by a corrupt judicial system. How did freedom of speech turn into freedom of sexual exploitation? As I said before, I have watched my share of porn and maybe someone else's share as well, but I am at a loss with how it is protected under our freedom of speech. Unfortunately, while Congress sat on their thumbs, the judicial branch rendered elasticity in the laws-thus increasing their power unconstitutionally. By doing so, the judicial branch has upset the balance of power that was created to prohibit such a treasonous act-for "freedom of expression" is a play on words similar to "a woman's right to choose". Where are the Thomas Jeffersons of today because America needs new leadership with his foresight and courage?

In the *Preamble*, God is referred to as "our Lord". In *The Declaration of Independence*, God is referenced as Nature's God and as all men's Creator. And in the opening statement before Article I of the *Constitution* the words blessing and ordain are used. In Article VI, it prohibits religious tests as a qualification of holding any public office or trust, but that simply means a person is judged on merit and his faith has nothing to do with his qualifications. Its sole intent was to prevent discrimination based on one's religious beliefs. Thus, the "separation of church and state" is a false representation of what our forefathers believed, but our judicial branch is out of control and we must reign them in or suffer for their unconstitutional power grabs.

Another part of the Declaration of Independence clearly invokes: "when a Government infringes on our unalienable rights, we the people have the right to alter or abolish it". The politicians, judges, and bureaucrats have violated their oaths, sold out the people they govern, and it is time for us to hold them accountable-for there are some who are honest, but the majority has betrayed our trust. And our system of checks and balances is out of balance and leaning disproportionately to the judicial branch where many have abandoned God for a secular belief system.

During the process of trying to find a publisher, I came across a small publisher who gave the impression he was interested in publishing my work. First he wanted me to read some texts in an attempt to convert me into his liberal doctrine. So I read the books because I enjoy looking at others ideas, but I warned him my beliefs would not change-for I am not an impressionable teenager. And what I discovered was he wanted me to substitute his beliefs for my own. This made no sense to me because it would change the authenticity of my work and if he wished to express his beliefs and opinions he should write his own book. After I told him I was seeking other publishing alternatives he seemed to be very angry. It is mystifying when extremists think their point of view is all that matters and they get upset with anyone that disagrees. That is why most decent folk don't like to discuss religion or politics-for extremists lack the civil skills of debate.

Resolutions

Our Founding-Fathers never intended for there to be a separation between the church and the state. For the foundation of the Constitution was cemented in faith and forged in the moral consciousness of all decent men. This is a secular notion created by those in high places who seek to destroy religion and the ACLU is *The Little Engine That Could.* Under the Constitution, we are guaranteed the right to alter or abolish our *Government System* when it no longer serves the *People.* Our two party system does not serve the people and the bureaucratic corruption of our government has violated the trust of all Americans. Now is the time for the powers that be to reap what they have sewed-we must rise to the challenge and erase their unconstitutional acts from the records.

If we desire change then we must become socially active to positively affect change-for we can no longer stand on the sidelines of injustice. In The Declaration of Independence it says "all men are created equal" and that says to me that everyone is entitled to "equal access based on merit". And Dr. King said "We are all God's children". Thus, whatever good or evil deeds you do unto a man or boy you do unto your father, your brother, and your son or whatever good or evil deeds you do unto a woman or girl you do unto your mother, your sister, and your daughter-and thereby your deeds are also done unto God and his son Jesus.

When judges, especially in high courts, make decisions outside their realm of responsibility defined by the constitution, I believe it is an act of treason in which they should be immediately removed from the bench and they should face the death penalty for violating the constitution and their oath of office (exception to the rule). That is the reason why no Judge should be appointed because it allows them to bypass accountability for their unconstitutional and immoral decisions. But what we are experiencing today is Judges making decisions based on personal beliefs and this can no longer be tolerated for it is a violation of their oath and doesn't reflect the majority of the people's expressed wishes. If all Judges are elected and we created an independent oversight committee that has the power to remove social activists from the bench and charge them with treason, we could restore the checks and balances of power-for Congress is supposed to be the lawmakers and the courts are suppose to judge on the constitutionality of the law. This can be easily achieved by allowing the President and Governor to present their choices to the public. Then the voters vote Yes or No for each appointee on state, regional, and national ballots. By allowing citizens to the opportunity to voice their opinion through the ballot box-we can create a legitimate form of accountability and an independent oversight committee can weed out the vermin that slips through the cracks.

Thus I say to my Muslin brothers and sisters do not hate your brothers and sisters in the west or east for must of us are paralyzed by the evildoers. Our people are constantly under attack by a corporate owned media that continually bombards us with repetitious fiction presented as the truth. Originally, I thought George Walker Bush was a man of faith, but I now see him for who he really is-President Bush's faith is in "oil" and his doctrine is "imperialism" counterfeited as democracy. How could someone that is borderline retarded graduate from two Ivy League Schools? I hope Laura's Masters is in Special Education because teaching George must be challenging. Maybe George's graduation from Yale and Harvard begin the decline of education in America because it defies all logic-for the Lord works in mysterious ways, but this miracle is truly amazing.

And when President Bush gave his "*Axis of Evil*" speech, I believe he made a mistake-for the true culprits (evildoers) are the three C's. *Capitalism*, *Communism*, and *Catholicism* are the real villains in the 'global world". For Capitalism represents "greed" while Communism is "power" without opposition and Catholicism exchanged God's mission for "influence" achieved through wealth and position. Dr. Charles Stanley says "Don't sacrifice your future for the pleasure of the moment." So the Democrat's Stimulus Package passed in February of 2009 maybe the biggest legislative mistake in our brief history. But this is *never ending war* in America between corrupt Bureaucrats and greedy Capitalists. And any time someone mentions the word Communism, the media and its liberal posse begin their character assassinations by referencing McCarthyism-totally ignoring its suppressive nature and the ruthless violations of basic human rights by its dictators. At the same time, they attack our Muslins brothers because evildoers do not relish

Theocratic Governments even if it is the will of its people. So I say to my Muslin brothers "I understand your concerns with the disintegration of morality in the progressive west, but do not use this as an excuse to oppress your women-for the wicked media and social bureaucrats in the west will use this to label and characterize you as evil." And I also say unto you "Don't hate other believers or nonbelievers-despise our sins for we are all imperfect people."-forgiveness and peaceful resolution is Allah's will. Thus, you must convince the radical Islamic followers to let go of their hatred and join us in a peaceful movement that respects all men and women for we are all brothers and sisters in the eyes of the Almighty.

And regardless of our animosity, all people of faith are called to love thy neighbors; enemies or friends. It is not an easy achievement for most of us have been treated unjustly by a dishonest hypocrite posing as a righteous person. Often I have personally struggled with this Commandment, though over time I am usually able to find peace-even though the experiences are locked away in my memory. But our unity in reclaiming America and the world will require sacrificing our emotional weaknesses of the now for hope of a better tomorrow. Our *Founding Fathers* authorized the people to replace our government when it no longer reflects the values of the majority. Through a peaceful political revolution-we can oust the corrupted judges, politicians, and bureaucrats. And we can reestablish ethics and the moral consciousness of decent folk that our Constitution was built on-for we are America and justice can be served.

Nevertheless, the majority of blacks, feminists, gays, and the godless block vote for the Democratic Party. Maybe the majority of decent whites should start block voting for our own self interests. Because if other groups are unwilling to unite for a more diverse America, then white Americans should say "We will no longer allow this insanity to go unchallenged." And if young voters can't distinguish between media hype or understand the meaning of integrity, character, and merit maybe we should raise the voting age to thirty. Because when you are 18 you think you know everything, but when you are 40 you realize how foolish you were. And every man and woman of every race who died for our right to vote are saddened by our declining values and lack of reasonable judgment.

Western Totalitarian Social Order

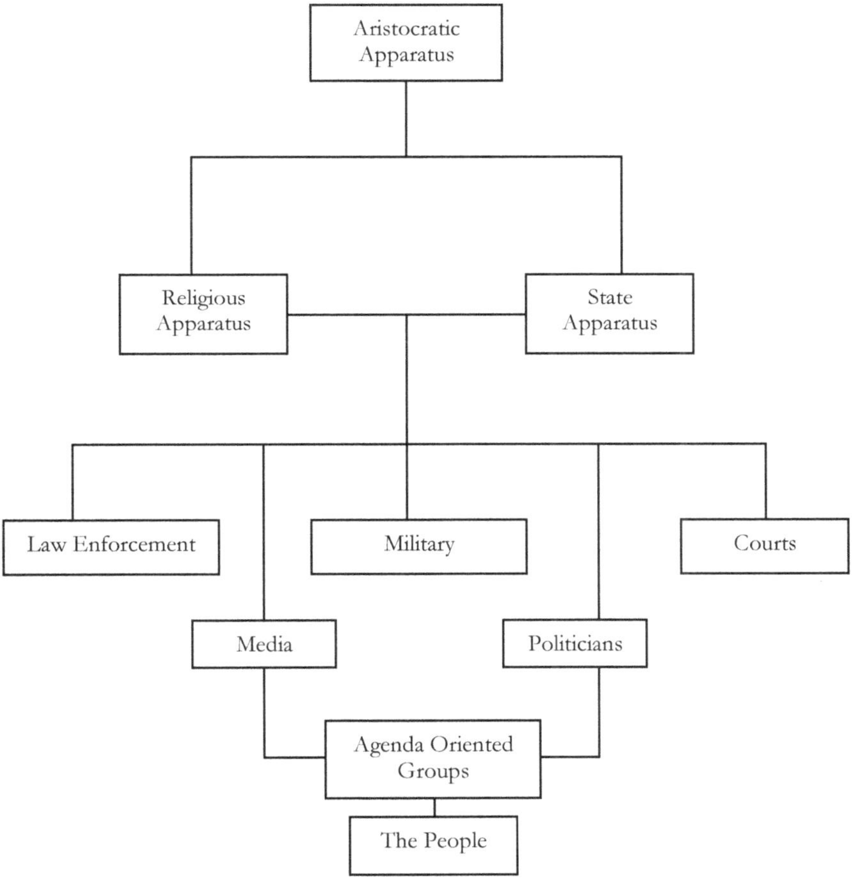

The *Western Totalitarian Social Order* is controlled by the wealthiest individuals and families throughout the world. Under the totalitarian model there are three controlling apparatuses in our modern world. The *Aristocratic Apparatus* is the most influential apparatus of the three. It controls all aspects of life and death and everything in between. These aristocrats are driven by a thirst for greed, power, and sex. They are the masters and the rest of us are their slaves and we are required to serve at their beckoning calls or suffer unduly for our dissention. While creating their earthly *Kingdoms*, they have placed themselves above God. And now they seek to remove God from all aspects of life through secular or progressive movements lead by their loyal subjects.

Many of these hypocrites like Arthur Blank create public perception of decency. But these capitalist icons are far from decent and most have sold their souls. Arthur Blank and Rich McKay cleaned up behind Michael Vick for years. Their lack of concern for character is as evident as their lust for greed. Still, Mr. Blank is not alone for many of the owners in the NFL, NBA, MLB, and every professional sports league throughout the west are focused more on image because that is what affects their corporate bottom lines. So the owners, commissioners, and player unions constantly enable athletically gifted athletes with questionable character and unlawful behaviors to participate for ridiculous salaries with minimal accountability. I don't know Mr. Blank personally, but until I see some contrition and humility on his part I will continue to boycott the Atlanta Falcons and *Home Depot.* Most of us don't have the usage (access) of the local or national media to reestablish our image. So I am not impressed and until the owner of the Falcons addresses the lack of character of the players they draft, sign as free agents, or trade for, his claims lack sincerity. But this enabling would not be possible in the U.S. without the aid of most College University's athletic departments. Unfortunately sports have become one of the most economically powerful regimes in the unprincipled cultural shift of the west. With corporate sponsors and unlimited media access, integrity and sportsmanship have been replaced by lying, cheating, cover-ups, and a "me attitude". And the current Congress of Democrats and Republicans will never intervene unless the public rises up and demands change because many have been purchased by these aristocrats.

Despite the fact that Congress approval rating is around eighteen percent and the President's approval is around twenty-nine percent, depending on the day of the poll, nothing changes because voters only have two choices on the ballot (Democrats and Republicans) and the Aristocratic Apparatus will use every means available to fight any change in our current two-party system. Their (Aristocratic Apparatus) control is achieved through financial influence and manipulation of the media. How do you think that fat drunken unscrupulous prick, Ted Kennedy (an

Obama supporter), is constantly reelected? Ah I forgot his alleged improprieties are often misunderstandings and besides he has never been charged or convicted. Imagine that, an innocent rich man whose family has a large stake in the corporate media conglomerates throughout the United States. John and Robert rebelled against the aristocracy of their birth and they were murdered because they actually believed in government reform and justice for all. Their brother Ted, who will not be joining them in *Heaven,* believes in *Big Brother* (an oversized government) and *Taxes* (over taxation of the middle class). John and Bobby were not perfect men, but they believed a Government is supposed to serve its people and they died for that belief. But that is what happens when the people don't stand together and demand the truth. The *Warren Commission Report* was an attempt to appease the public and the *Mitchell Report* (investigation) of steroids in Major League Baseball is just as laughable. JFK, MLK, and RFK were assassinated by the "*Dragons of Power*". Why? It is simple, "The fear of unity". But never fear for God will punish them severely for their acts of treachery and they along with their aristocratic puppet masters shall suffer the fires of *Hell* for eternity.

The second and third apparatuses have a partnership with the Aristocratic Apparatus. These two are the *State* (or Government) *Apparatus* and the *Religious Apparatus.* The State Apparatus is the evil sword of the aristocrats. It controls law enforcement, the military, and the courts. The Aristocratic Apparatus use these governmental agencies to protect them from the masses. If the government agencies were not present, the people might rise up and slay the dragons. Thus justice has become a commodity for the rich and famous and the rest of us are at the mercy of twelve men and women who on many occasions ignore the evidence and the facts when rendering their verdict. I would prefer three honest judges that reviewed the credibility of the evidence rather then to let twelve strangers be manipulated by a persuasive argument that might send an innocent person to prison or let a guilty criminal go free. Only dishonest criminals and extremely liberal minded jackasses, along with the rich and famous, fear the repeal of double jeopardy.

A *Totalitarian Political Regime* exists where individuals are subordinates of the state through strict control of all aspects of life. If an individual actually believes America is a democracy then he or she is not paying attention. We are subservient to a corrupt government that is under the control of our *Capitalist Aristocracy.* To rectify the situation, we must stand together and be willing to make inconvenient sacrifices. First and foremost, we must demand more choices on the voting ballots so we can replace the ineffective Democrats and Republicans. Next, we must boycott irresponsible corporations. Arthur Blank was complicit in the Michael Vick scandal and he should endure a measure of penance for his involvement. And Ford filed bankruptcy and terminated thousands of employees yet somehow the bankruptcy didn't affect the family's ownership of their NFL Franchise Detroit Lions. They wasted billions of dollars on advertising while running the company into the ground, but the employees were the scapegoats for their sins. We as a nation of decent men and women should boycott *Ford, GM, AT&T,* and any other *American Corporation* that outsources American jobs. If the sports leagues and the NCAA continue to be defiant and merely enact cosmetic changes that do little to solve the corruption, then we must turn off the television, quit buying tickets, stop going to the sports bars, relinquish our consumption of jerseys and memorabilia, and boycott all their corporate sponsors. I am a huge fan of professional and amateur sports especially football, basketball, wrestling, and baseball, but if we don't become more active in a united response, nothing will change and the majority of us will continue to pay for our selfish ways.

The third apparatus is the Religious Apparatus which is a sickening commentary on the modern church. The Catholic Church is not alone in its rejection of God for a materialistic world. When the aristocrats moved in and took over the Church, God moved out. God is not present in most modern western churches of today. In the fourth century the Church partnered with the Aristocrats. During the *Inquisition* the religious institutions became so powerful the aristocrats created a more powerful State Apparatuses to reassert their status as the most powerful entity. Even though the three apparatuses have formed an unholy alliance, make no mistake, the wealthy elite are still the ringmasters. No wonder Mother Teresa questioned her faith-for she saw the Catholic Church for what it was, not the mythical illusions of what is supposed to be. And who amongst us doesn't question the unfair suffering throughout the world? I struggle with this on a daily basis and I haven't yet found any reasonable answers.

But the Catholic Church has become the wealthiest religious congregation in the world and their political and social influence is second to none. By doing so, they have forsaken God for materialism. Many Catholics are decent people who believe in God and serve their fellow man. Still, their unwillingness to admit or recognize their Church is out of touch with God is a serious mistake. Unless the Catholic Church relinquishes its wealth and power and returns to God's mission for all Churches, it will continue to deceive and sacrifice its followers for the same thirty-pieces of silver that Judas collected for betraying Jesus.

While the controlling alliance continues to raid the "apple tree of knowledge", they do so at the expense of our environment. And because of their control of law enforcement, the military, and the courts, we cannot overthrow them with violence even though that was the intent of our *2nd Amendment* "right to bear arms". Dr. King Jr. understood that peaceful resolution through unified boycotts and demonstrations was the primary key to positively affecting social change. Gandhi also used this method to unite India against British Imperialists. We don't have to reinvent the wheel, we only need to put the good of the whole before our selfish individualistic or group desires and make personal sacrifices for a worthwhile cause.

One might argue that politicians and the media are controlling apparatuses, but they are not apparatuses. Politicians and mediums are tools used by the controlling apparatuses to influence outcomes. By dividing the masses into subcategories, it is fairly easy for the wealthy to weld their power. Grouping us into stereotypical labels allows the aristocrats to crack the whip whenever they desire to illustrate their might. Without the partnerships, the Aristocratic Apparatus might crumble under its own corrupt foundation. It needs the State and Religious Apparatuses to protect it, not only from the masses, but from the greed and lust within.

As Democrats and Republicans debate semantics, taxpayer's dollars are wasted on useless earmarks. While these jackals constantly recycle the same old lies voters become more dissatisfied and repulsed by both parties. Meanwhile, agenda oriented groups are mimicking lobbyists to entice politicians into sponsoring poorly drafted legislation by using a few extreme cases to solicit empathy for their proposal. Washington has become the *Village of the Insane*-and California has become the *Capital of Crazyville* where the fruit trees of stupidity have produced an endless supply of nuts.

And finally we reach the bottom of the Western Totalitarian Social Order where the vast majority of the people reside. For without us who could the aristocrats besmirch or exploit? The only logical social discourse left is through a united political revolution, peaceful mass demonstrations and marches on Washington, boycotts of the corporate raiders, educative public forums, and individual sacrifice for the good of our nation. We can take our nation back by establishing new political parties that represent us and our beliefs. Conservative, moderate, liberal, and independent choices on voting ballots would represent the vast majority of citizens in America and as long as they stay away from the *Capitalist Corrupters*; we (the people) could regain our vision of democracy and rebuild our communities based on a caring nature. Yes, concern for others besides ourselves shows there is still hope for us.

Even though my goal is to facilitate a unified peaceful political revolution maybe we should start building a voluntary nationwide militia along side a new *Moderate Party*. For the truth is the Democrats and Republicans will use every resource available to hinder any attempt to reform Washington. And a voluntary militia (*American Militia*) of former service men and women, current or retired police officers and firefighters, and law-abiding citizens who believe in the 2nd Amendment working with new political reformers just might be what America needs to stop the hostel takeover of our nation by a few godless social elites on the far left. Currently most middle and lower class Americans are reaching a boiling point and if it occurs there will be a reckoning for those responsible. But we can avoid the oncoming disaster with a political revolution of conservative, moderate, independent, and some liberal reformers who replace the Democrat and Republican incumbents in 2010.

14

The Bureaucratic Machine

"He who puts his faith in Big Brother often pledges his allegiance to the dark forces of human nature"

"Join us or be labeled an outsider or troublemaker" seems to be the theme of western governments and their corporations in the *21st century*. The *Bureaucratic Machine* is a self-serving giant that answers to one authority; its aristocratic parents. And it will do anything to maintain the status quo at the expense of anyone. By screwing the taxpayers, blaming whitey, and pushing liberally divisive agendas while continuing expansion, the *American Government* has become an empire unto itself. At the same time, our government socially, racially, sexually, and economically divides Americans against one another while the "fat cats" get fatter. Many government bureaucracies are initiated by the rich and powerful who have controlled U.S. lawmakers for more than a century and a half.

However, Franklin Delano Roosevelt's expansion of the cancerous creature created an uncontrollable, unaccountable, and destructive menace that feeds upon the people it is supposed to serve and protect. It is a sad commentary on the decline of cultural values that our American government has become one of the most corrupt governments in the history of the world. But it is not alone in its secular movements for most of the world's western cultures have exchanged moral values for self-indulgence.

FDR's "*New Deal*" or "*Welfare for votes*" was and still is just a political ploy to get elected. He didn't give a damn about the American people for he was born with a silver spoon in his mouth and the political ambition of a jackal. FDR benefited greatly from and lavished in his aristocratic birth. Roosevelt was an ambitious politician who without his family's prominence would have never had the opportunity to serve in President Woodrow Wilson's administration. And the irony was Woodrow Wilson would have never been elected if Franklin's cousin

Teddy Roosevelt hadn't split the Republican Party in the 1912 Presidential Election. By doing so, Teddy expedited his cousin's Franklin's political career. But Abraham Lincoln was elected President in the same way with the Democratic Party split of 1860. And don't forget Bill Clinton benefited from Ross Perot's Reform Party candidacy in 1992. For it does not matter if there are three candidates when all three choices are the same old recycled hypocrites.

Another fact seldom discussed is FDR hid his physical disability contracted from polio in 1921 from the public and that tells me a lot about his true character. For I too wish I were not visually impaired, but I am not ashamed of it because it is what God intended. Though I do understand what it is like to be disabled in a world that views us as broken commodities that can't be fixed and how we are often forgotten or devalued. So I chose the title "*The Invisible Man*" because it represents people like me with disabilities who struggle to be included or accepted as equals-for we are the "elephant in the room" that everyone is desperately trying to ignore. But what FDR created is a *Bureaucratic Nightmare* with two missions, growth and survival by creating an illusion of dependency. And *Big Brother* devours anything that threatens its existence by endorsing popular myths as the truth.

It is common knowledge that FDR had sex with other women throughout his marriage and on the 12th of April 1945, one of these encounters in Warm Springs may have contributed to his death-for he was a wealthy playboy throughout his life despite his affliction. And many who seek the truth including myself are reasonably sure Eleanor Roosevelt and her Press Secretary had more than a casual friendship. Considering the fact that the vast majority of women and majority of men in America during this era were Christians, if they had known or even suspected Franklin Roosevelt's adultery and Eleanor's sexual orientation, FDR would never have been elected President of the United States even with the promise of the "New Deal". And the admiration by many women for Eleanor Roosevelt would have turned into hostile admonishment. Franklin Delano Roosevelt and Anna Eleanor Roosevelt's marriage was a necessity for an aristocratic family with political aspirations which a disingenuous media known for popular sensationalism refused to disclose to the public for they were aware of the consequences. Eleanor was Franklin's fifth cousin and they were from a wealthy aristocratic family that presided in New York, not the "deep south". Many authors and some liberal scholars worship Franklin Delano Roosevelt as though he were a Saint-but I suspect he is in Hell where most deceitful politicians dwell and those who worship false idols such as FDR, Abraham Lincoln, Lyndon Johnson, Bill Clinton, and the worst President in American history General Ulysses S. Grant will join them when "death" calls. As I have watched and observed Bill and Hillary Clinton over the past eighteen years, I see many similarities to Franklin and Eleanor's political union-and Hillary has often referred to Eleanor Roosevelt as an inspiration while Bill has "sexual relations" with every woman he has a chance to charm and dazzle with his devilish charisma.

Truthfully FDR's Social Security plan was never intended for the majority of Americans. Today many are angered over the Bernie Madoff "*Ponzi scheme*", but Social Security is the greatest Ponzi scheme in America rivaled only by the retirements of Federal and State employees. The age for receiving benefits was set at 65 years old because the average American didn't live long enough to collect. Do you think Roosevelt was unaware of the average life expectancy of the people? Most of the rural poor in the 1930's died before the age of 65. The Social Security Administration was the first of many bureaucratic government agencies created by FDR. And the people of the era were paying the government Social Security taxes and the majority would never see a *Return on Investment* (ROI) during their lifetimes. Though thanks to healthcare advancements, people starting living longer. But Congress, with its abundance of wisdom, forgot to go back and raise the age requirements for Social Security benefits. All of a sudden there were millions of people living beyond the age of 65 and they wanted their money, but the government had already spent their Social Security taxes. That's why we have a system of revenues collected, benefits paid out as a part of the annual Federal Budget. There is no true Social Security Trust Fund-for it is as allusive as the wind. And the Ponzi scheme eventually collapses when there is more money going out (owed) than there is coming in (taxes collected). Thus, we created a dependency on Big Brother for an invisible retirement system that is relying on current taxpayers to shoulder present and future burdens which is now on life support because of the coming retirements of the "baby boomers". Sure the obesity epidemic may ensure most American taxpayers in the 21st century will probably die before they collect their Social Security benefits, but their healthcare costs are going to cripple our economy and if they are eligible for disability benefits who will shoulder that burden?

There are some pieces of the "New Deal" that I actually agree with in principle. For society needs a facilitator to handle certain tasks that are too enormous for individuals to undertake alone or that cannot be entrusted to profit oriented industrialists such as employee's rights, work safety, healthcare, food and environmental protections, and so forth. And in theory, the National Labor Relations Act (NLRA) was monumental for it created a new system for employee's rights. However, corruption infiltrated labor negotiations and greed replaced sanity. Many of the ridiculous wages for unskilled labor and lower skilled labor gained through unethical tactics contributed to the demise of the American Auto Industry (especially GM). But both management and labor are complicit in the failures of most businesses. Many corporations that employed blue and white collared laborers have outsourced American jobs to favorable markets greatly aided by NAFTA.

Although the majority of western corporations throughout the world are taking advantage of foreign markets with minimal to no restrictions on labor, safety, health, or the environment. Most people are unaware that the Supreme Court originally declared the New Deal unconstitutional. Later their stand was softened and they eventually caved in to political pressure because they knew FDR and his henchmen of *Ivy League Lawyers* had devised a plan to remove many of the judges from the bench by enforcing a new retirement age of 70. This would have affected six U.S. Supreme Court judges and forty-four federal judges in the lower courts. Roosevelt planned to replace these judges with judges that supported his New Deal. And his appointees were from a new school of thought "legal realism" that believed law should adapt to changing conditions. Thanks too Franklin D. Roosevelt and his rich aristocratic lawyer friends our checks and balances of the Constitution designed by our forefathers are imbalanced. Our judicial system has run amok and its failures can be directly linked to FDR and his progressive ideology. That is why I often assert that Thomas Jefferson is the greatest President in American history because he recognized the potential for corruption of an oversized government. And at the same time, he realized that judicial activism would lessen the legislative and executive branches' authority and unconstitutionally shift the balance of power in favor of the judicial branch-which was not the intention of our Founding Fathers. Similarly, this same progressive thinking has been adopted by many western churches at the expense of morality, family values, and personal accountability.

And the United Nations, a creation of Roosevelt, Stalin, and Churchill is another bureaucratic nightmare that has outlived its usefulness. A spin off of the League of Nations, which was a liberal idea of Woodrow Wilson, the UN folly of today is sadly comical and depressing. Wilson employed FDR in his administration and thus began the secular movement of the *20th century* that seeks to form "a *Godless* nation" without the consent of the people. While during the same period (the early 1900's), atheism had become a popular movement throughout Europe. And the League of Nations is responsible for creating an environment where a sadist like Hitler could emerge. The economic demands on Germany after WWI by Russia, Great Britain, France, and the United States were as unlawful and unethical as the atrocities of the North during the *Reconstruction Period* in the South, after the Civil War.

Anytime people are oppressed by unsolicited tyranny and striped of their dignity an environment of hatred is naturally the end result. Even today there is a deep hidden hatred of the north by many white southerners that has never healed. For I have found myself fighting these impulses on occasions for I know the true history of the Civil War and the Reconstruction Period, but I remind myself that injustices of the past can't be fixed and I try to focus on a better tomorrow. Many blacks possess the same hidden hatred for whites but love cannot flourish where hate festers-for a nation united requires children of all races to come together as one loving family under God. And America should strive to serve as a beacon of hope for the world to see. Besides, Russia is the last nation on earth, other than China, that should ever point fingers when it comes to human rights violations and oppression of its people.

Thus, the UN is just another bureaucracy that has run amok. It just so happens that the UN is an international bureaucracy with more corruption, more red tape, and more deception. And for me the minimal amount of good does not outweigh the enormous amount of bad of the

UN. But again, with the assistance of a liberally biased media the UN advertises its good deeds as a redundant form of damage control used by every western bureaucracy. In theory the UN is a symbol of hope, but the reality is the United Nations ineffective policies and distribution systems are laden with inexcusable corruption at the highest levels, "*the true den of thieves*" in our postmodern era. Most of the financial aid, food, and medicine rarely reach those it was intended for while these crooked bureaucrats line their pockets.

What kind of human being steals from the poor? Well, I will tell you what kind, disgraceful bureaucrats like Kofi Annan. A political embarrassment, former Secretary General Kofi Annan of the United Nations should have been removed from his position many years ago. But empowering bureaucrats without the necessary credentials (merit) generally opens the door for potential scandals-for this political token used his position to improve his and his family's quality of life at the expense of the impoverished, yet he was given a free pass for his digressions. Just because a thieving bureaucrat is black doesn't excuse his unethical, immoral, or unlawful practices no more than it would if a white bureaucrat committed the same atrocities. Sometimes I throw my hands in the air and scream "What in the Hell is wrong with us?"

After all, what can we expect? Honest bureaucrats that actually work in the best interests of the people they are basically employed by. The UN is like 138 monkeys fighting over a bundle of six bananas. When one of these monkeys doesn't get a banana, he pouts like an undisciplined child who throws a tantrum when he doesn't get his way. At moments like this I almost believe Darwin's theory that the human race evolved from apes. When we put a 138 people in a room, we end up with a 138 opinions. Add in the fact that many are unqualified bureaucratic flunkies anointed by the aristocratic apparatus's political whores and we have total chaos, a natural disaster just waiting to happen. The only difference between a dishonest bureaucrat and a convicted felon is a 4 by 6 prison cell.

And the American taxpayers have carried the UN burden far too long. Not only does the United States provide twenty-five percent (25%) of all the United Nations program costs, we allow these freeloaders to party and live in New York and Washington which is also paid for by us. That right, all the expensive condos, offices, technological equipment, transportation, protection and security, expensive parties, all food and lodging, and just about anything these bureaucratic freeloaders request are funded by the *Good Old Government* of the USA courtesy of the American taxpayers. Hell don't be shocked, I said anything. Prostitutes and drugs are also a part of the partying decorum. It is time we told our politicians and government bureaucrats we've had enough of their dishonesty. Get the United States of America out of the corrupt United Nations fiasco.

It is no wonder that many Muslims view America and the West as *Satan's Village.* What our Muslim brothers and sisters need to understand is that the American people and other decent western commoners are also angered and offended by the corruption. Our American Government has become an entity of evil driven by the aristocratic nonbelievers due largely to one false idol; FDR. These privileged pagans will exploit anyone or any resource for profit. But the rich and powerful aristocrats dwell all over the world, not just in the United States, some live in the Middle East. And the American citizens are victims and have little to no control over our government corruption until we unite as a nation under God and hold the evildoers accountable.

I have taken on this devil in the past. Georgia Industries for the Blind was full of bureaucratic corruption. Governors from Jimmy Carter to Zell Miller were well aware of the abuses and exploitations of the blind and visually impaired by this state run agency and they did little to change it. But I am supposed to believe these former governors are Christians, yeah and I am Saint. People of faith who are in positions of authority (elected by the people) do not shy away from injustices. They are entrusted to hold corrupt bureaucrats accountable for their unlawful and unethical actions. And NIB (National Industries for the Blind) only cares about its own survival as well. It doesn't care if states exploit and abuse blind and visually impaired workers under false pretenses. NIB and all the state agencies under its control should be closed and the workers should be integrated into local workforces. Segregation was supposed to be outlawed in the 1960's. I guess politicians don't care about the blind and deaf because together we only represent a mere 2 % of the population which is the same percentage as the Jewish Community, but often their community is catered to by both Democrats and Republicans.

Georgia Academy for the Blind is another state run institution that has turned into a dumping ground for the multi-disabled. Personally I believe residential schools for the blind and hearing impaired, in every state, should be closed and the children should be integrated into their local schools under the inclusive education model. Why hasn't this happened? Because these Bureaucratic Dinosaurs are only concerned with survival and they could care less about what's in the best interests of the children.

Moreover, the Division of Rehabilitation Services (DRS) is supposed to assist people with disabilities. Employment, education, training, job placement, and assistive technological equipment are just a few of the responsibilities of DRS. Nationally there is a sixty-nine percent (69%) unemployment rate amongst all people with disabilities and people with disabilities consist of more than ten percent (10%) of our population. The blind and visually impaired national unemployment rate is around eighty percent (80%). According to our government these bureaucracies are doing one fine a job. Why doesn't this data show up nationally in the unemployment statistics? Well, our lawmakers decided if we the disabled receive supplemental incomes such as SSDI (Social Security Disability Income), then we don't count against the unemployment rate. If the disability community's unemployment rate was included it would change how many view the economy.

With the current growth rate of obese Americans, the number may double. Of course I believe overeating is a choice just like substance abuse or smoking and they should not be linked to people with disabilities. Trust me, no one wants or would choose to be disabled, but unfortunately we can't change our condition, we can only try and change the typical perceptions of being disabled. If people only knew the secrets that our governmental officials and politicians keep, the public might consider bringing back hanging.

In Georgia, DRS was placed under DOL (Department of Labor). Supposedly this would change DRS's inexcusable poor performance. Absolute nonsense, noting changed. These types of tricks are political gimmicks used to pacify the disenfranchised. When I was advocating for changed in Georgia Industries for the Blind, I had the IRS, SSA, and DFCS breathing down my neck. The Bureaucratic Machine uses any resource it can to discourage whistleblowers who advocate for change. You see the monster fears change and it will use every bureaucratic agency to oppose change, even when change is the right thing to do.

One must remember that the *Bureaucratic Monster* has connections at every level (local, state, and federal). It also has many friends in the judicial systems which it uses to its advantage. They are experts at using the media and have many friends working in the media. I was often asked, by DRS representatives "Jimmy what can we do for you?" "We'll help you, but screw the rest of the blind people was often implied." DRS never understood where I was coming from, it is their job and responsibility to try and assist all people with disabilities, not just a select few. The Divisions of Rehabilitation Services and Department of Human Resources (DHR), especially in Georgia, waste more money on Administrative costs than they spend on the clients and communities they are supposed to serve.

I went to several of the largest newspapers in Georgia and each time they ran from the story. One local reporter told me "You are right and I wish I could help, but I have to think about my career." I got similar responses from others who worked in many different state agencies. Many times I was told "I believe in what you are doing, but I am handcuffed by my position." They were saying the same thing the reporter said, speaking out could be detrimental to their careers. This is how the Bureaucratic Machine maintains loyalty. If anyone steps out of line, he or she could lose his or her job, and forget about advancement once one crosses that imaginary line of integrity.

One of the worst facts, especially at the state and federal levels, is the machine uses tax payers dollars to hire countless numbers of politically ambitious lawyers to defend the indefensible. The monster has become very proficient at politically spinning any situation. They call it "damage control". The truth is nowhere to be found. Only lies and deception exists when the Public Relations arm of the machine is pulled by these bureaucrats. A friend (a CPA) once told me when he went to work for the state as an accountant, he was so naïve. He actually thought he would be able to stop the embezzlers of state agencies. He was astonished when he reported these criminals to the appropriate authorities, and nothing was done. Most of the thieving executives were transferred to other state positions and allowed to finish out their careers with the state and receive their full retirement pensions. Yes Georgia is truly a "State of Shame" when it comes down to bureaucratic politics. And even though I love my home State; I will never support institutional corruption and cover-ups-for to do so is not only unjust; it is also un-American.

I suspect the reason why our state officials continually cover up corruption is because they fear public outrage and reprisal. There are many state officials who should be in prison, enjoying retirement sponsored by the taxpayers. Here is another dirty little secret; most of these lowlifes are members of their local churches. The state has two unwritten rules for employees or codes of conduct. First, employees must be involved with a religious institution. Secondly, employees must also be involved with at least one community serving organization. The illusion is to make their employees appear to be decent caring human beings. And some of the state employees of Georgia are good people, but they know their limitations. Most of their career advancements are not based on merit. For the majority of bureaucratic advancements are based on posterior kissing, affirmative action, turning a blind eye away from infrastructural corruption, having sex with one's boss, mistreating coworkers, and covering up all unlawful acts. If the black population of Georgia is less than twenty percent (about 18%), but black employees of the state are over fifty percent (50%), who, other than an irrational bureaucrat, can justify this disproportionate representation? For this is discrimination against every other race and minority. But state governments are not alone in their deceptive procedures our federal government operates in a similar fashion.

How is it that many of the people who could have criminally implicated Bill and Hillary Clinton mysterious met with death? Maybe that is why most of the others went to prison, they knew if they even thought about testifying, their life wasn't worth two cents. For the *Angel of Death*, Gabriel, was hovering over their heads waiting to blow his horn. While the theme "Doing whatever is necessary to protect the American way is life" is constantly reiterated in films. But if you don't believe our government has often murdered in the name of patriotism; then you probably don't believe the wealthy robber barons stole the lands from the Indians, then from the white settlers, murdered anyone who refused to sell, and exploited the Chinese to build their railroads. The corruption of our current government is worse than that of the Roman Empire. For we have taken corruption to the highest level in world history. The saddest part is that Satan has convinced many in western society that his or her existence is a myth, so people don't fear repercussions for their unremorseful actions. But on *Judgment Day* when all is revealed, billions of people are going to wish they had listen to the few voices that tried to warn them not to put their faith in man and materialism.

The Bureaucratic Monster is like *Cyrus* the three-headed-monster that guards the gates of Hell. It protects the unholy rich aristocrats from the masses. They fear our unity. This is why they continually divide the nation by using manipulative devices, such as the media. Our politicians hold tactical hearings to trigger emotional responses for similar results. Take the steroid outrage in baseball, all the politicians accomplished was to convince the owners of professional sports teams to come up with a bogus drug testing policy thereby appeasing the public. Even though a large majority of American citizens are against any amnesty for illegal immigrants, when all is said and done, there will be a watered down version of amnesty passed by a dishonest Congress made up of Democrats and Republicans.

Our political discourse must occur in the near future before it is too late. Our government continually fights the scientific evidence on global warming. They use their sleazy lawyers to edit and rewrite the truth. Anyone with common sense has noticed the changes in our weather over the last several decades. But doing the right thing would weaken the wealth, power, and influence of oil barons throughout the world. I guess Forty Billion Dollars in one quarter is not enough for these vermin. How much wealth can one man attain before he says "I've got enough?" Hanging might just be too good for these thieving bastards. Nonetheless the Bureaucratic Monster enables these pricks to constantly screw the people and the politicians only care about their piece of the profit. I know these irresponsible deceivers might not believe it, but I guarantee, one day these false leaders of flocks will answer for their crimes against humanity and they will receive no mercy.

In the spring of 1996, I tried to file discrimination charges under the

ADA (American with Disabilities Act) against GIB which is overseen by the DRS. On my way to Atlanta I thought someone would finally step in and help restructure the operating procedures of an organization that had been created to provide employment and advancement opportunities for the blind and visually impaired who wanted to work in 1939. But when I sat down with a case worker at the EEOC, he had no interests in providing assistance. From his prospective since I was not black or a female my concerns were irrelevant. He was hostile and rude and truthfully I was so angry I wanted to kick his unethical and unprofessional ass, but instead I sat there and listened to his anti-ADA rhetoric. At first he tried to discourage me from filing charges and when I said no he got angry and refused to assist me in filing charges.

Over ninety percent (90%) of all ADA cases are unsuccessful, but many more are never filed because of the EEOC's agenda. In GIB, jobs were given without posting them. Two Working Group Leader positions were given to two non-disabled black women who were not qualified and a Sales Representative was given to a non-disabled white male who had lost his job with another state agency that had closed (ARC), but these three positions were never posted. When a Production Manager position was posted and I applied for it the DRS Executive Director discarded the position until I left the agency three years later and then gave it to a black female who was also not qualified.

In a meeting with the Executive Director (DRS) he had made many discriminatory and prejudiced remarks about blind people. Again I guess when you question fairness some tend to get emotional because this jackass was scolding me as though I were an imbecile. While all this was going on, a state audit was performed that found many of the same violations I had alleged when I wrote to Governor Zell Miller. But the state auditor's silence was bought with a high paying position at Georgia's PBS (Public Broadcasting Systems). Under Georgia State Law, any time there is a dispute of this nature, a polygraph can be requested. And I requested a polygraph, but the state refused. If they had administer a polygraph the Executive Director of DRS, the EEOC case worker, the State Auditor, and some other state employees would have been in a lot of trouble. And Governor Zell Miller would have faced a number of questions about the ethics of state government.

We, a good friend and I, finally received interests from a lawyer that worked at ACB (American Council of the Blind). He was angered and startled be the abuses of Georgia Industries for the Blind and at the same time concerned with the National Industries for the Blind lack of intervention. But, unknowingly to him, NIB (National Industries for the Blind) executives were on the board of ACB and they fired him. For NIB was complicit in the atrocities and most were self-serving hypocrites that tried to shift blame to the states. However, they lied because they could have enforced equal access based on merit for all blind and visually impaired employees in every state run agency by denying contracts if these agencies violated equal opportunities for disabled workers. Today that is why I am for closing NIB and replacing the EEOC with a new less bureaucratic agency that investigates all employment discrimination based on the facts and merit of each case instead of political agendas of race and gender.

Resolutions

There was a time in our society when great leaders recognized that wealth and power tend to corrupt anyone, any system, or any institution. These secret organizations had many names, but their mission was the same. Any time an individual, a government, an institution, or class became so corrupt that they were beyond redemption. These secret orders emerged from the shadows and struck down the wicked. We, the current world especially in the western cultures, have become the most corrupt entity of history. We have exceeded all the inhuman exploitations of our past. Shame does not begin to describe our indiscretions. Our vanity has replaced common sense and our arrogance has become our faith.

The *Knights of the Templar* and the *Freemasons* were two of these secret orders that tried to protect man from himself. We are all born of good and evil and because we are mortal, many are consumed by the lustful temptations of evil. Wealth and power are the most alluring of all Satan's creations. Some might argue that sexual pleasure is another. But I say sexual pleasures are a benefit of the other two. Only death or institutional lockdown can suppress psychopaths and sociopaths because they are beyond redemption.

It seems the secret orders of our world have gone dormant, died off and become extinct, or they have crossed over to the dark side. If there was any time in history they were needed, the time is now. Though these organizations remain in name today, they traded *God, Country* and *Honor* for *Wealth, Power,* and *Immorality.* FDR was a *Freemason* and a *Knight of Templar* and so were many of his elitist inner circles, but the *Knights* and *Freemasons* in the United States began their unholy alliances in the 1820's and within twenty years their treason was complete. One expression often reiterated or paraphrased is "With great wealth and power comes great responsibility too much for any one person to handle." The *Globalization* of the *World* is a *Coalition of Evil.* The Antichrist will be a man or woman from these capitalistic thieves that will use the media to create an illusion of decency. Often I am very sarcastic, but anyone objectivity watching the rise of President Barack Obama from mediocrity has to wonder how his poison of persuasion has deceived many voters who refused to examine his merit, beliefs, associations, controversial remarks, and outlandish promises.

It has become easier for the status quo to manipulate any large group of people once they have been divided. Each group becomes so entrenched in what I call "idiotology" that they lose touch with common sense. As long as these capitalist swine keep the masses fighting amongst ourselves over trivial pursuits, they can continue their quests for greater power and wealth. As I will continually say, "We have the power of unity" to stop the madness.

Does our American law enforcement and our judicial systems need an overhaul? Hell yeah. All bureaucratic agencies need outside independent oversight, including our military. We can not trust any bureaucratic agency to police itself. History shows that these government bureaucracies will never do what is right. They act in their own best interests. Thus lies and cover ups, murders, corruption, protection of their own, and so forth are the end results of self preservation.

Therefore we need a new system-an *International Federation of Peace* with only 21 members total with representation from every continent. And the members must be of impeccable honesty and integrity that the wealthy elite cannot buy or sell (untouchable). Their priority should be the betterment of the world as a humane place-for Man and Nature must transition into a harmonic state.

I remember sitting in the local Social Security office (Griffin, GA) in 1996. I was asked, "Your educated, why don't you have a better paying job?" And I told her that I had sent my resume out for what seemed like hundreds of jobs, without even one interview opportunity. Then I made a comment "I will gladly trade you this SSDI check of five hundred dollars ($500.00) a month for your thirty-six thousand dollar ($36K) a year job." There was a silent pause and I could see the shock in her eyes. Next I asked "Are there any job openings in this Social Security office?" That really sent her fumbling; "Ah let me check with my supervisor. Hello Supervisor, this blind client wants to know if we have any employment opportunities." And her Supervisor replied "Why of course not." Case worker "Ok, I guess you are visually impaired. Your claim has been approved." Hurriedly she escorted me to the door, even though my mobility skills didn't require any assistance. "Goodbye" she exclaimed with a relieved expression "We'll check back in three years to see if you are still blind."

15

The Death of Courage

"Courage is shaped through our honesty, integrity, and personal sacrifice"

"When a man of character and good will gives all ten more must rise to the challenge and replace each lost soldier and continue his good deeds"

On June 6th, 1968 the last of three great leaders was stolen from the American people by the dark forces of evil. First, John Fitzgerald Kennedy was assassinated on November 22nd, 1963, then Dr. Martin Luther King Jr. was assassinated on April 4th, 1968, and finally Robert Francis Kennedy was assassinated on June 6th, 1968 after winning the California Democratic primary. Everyone was angered by the atrocities but no one stood up. There were a few good men and women who rejected the *Warren Commission Report*, but they were defamed by the aristocrat's propaganda forces. I was a mere child at this time and didn't understand the seriousness of the crimes. For we all know who did it and it wasn't the patsies paraded in front of us. This is the one time I would have condoned violence and every able bodied American should have stormed the palace and slain all the dragons (exception to the rule)- for no government bureaucrat, no member of organized crime, no military leader, no law enforcement agent, no member of the legislative, executive, or judicial branches, and no capitalist had the right to murder our *"Three Wise Men"*. Of all the tragedies in American history only abortion and slavery were more damaging to our society. Alas the ***devil*** had conquered America.

What separated John, Martin, and Bobby from the rest was their compassion and their courage. America and the world would be so much different today if these three beacons of hope had shined a while longer. While they were not perfect men, they were honest men and it saddens me to know I will never have the opportunity to meet them in this world. But no one picked up the torch and continued their mission.

Some retreated out of fear and many fell into the pit of depression while others sold out. A few even drank the poisoned red wine flooding the land with the aid of a disingenuous media. Still, I am troubled by the lack of courage of so many-for it was the duty of all good men and women to continue their dreams of equality, fairness, and the end of oppression. And the cost is irrelevant when the cause is just. But unfortunately the people surrendered and reform was replaced by the pernicious king's ultimatums.

On June 6th, 1968, America waved the white flag and surrendered its "*sword of promise*" to an "*evil empire*" whose foundation was laid by a false prophet named Franklin Delano Roosevelt in 1933. By using their flunky politicians, government bureaucrats, activist judges, and their corporate owned mediums the capitalist pagans redefined America's morals, values, and ethics. The "gray area" was established to distort right and wrong. Belief systems of "*self*" replaced value systems of the "*community*" and the crusade against God reached new heights. Drug usage, sex, and violence became more prominent and we lost focus on what was going on. It was not a "revolution", it was a shift in popular cultural underhandedly designed by the aristocrats and enforced by their totalitarian subordinates. Thus, an *"unholy war"* led by the diseased locusts of deception spread across western cultures unchallenged because our watchmen were asleep.

For any nation besieged with dirty secrets and drowning in evil deeds cannot claim a faith in God. Yes God is Love, but his decrees have always been grounded in the truth. And justice will never be served if we allow the truth to be buried along with the brave who stood up to the oppressors and said "Hell no". It is time for every honest and decent, man and woman, to reclaim our courage and reestablish our moral integrity so that those who gave all can rest in peace. None of us are unflawed, but most of us are good. These three soldiers of promise were murdered by the "*Emperors of Evil*". And even though I never had the honor to know them, it is as though they reach out from heaven and touch my heart and soul. Listen closely and you will hear the voices of the righteous whispering from beyond "Don't let God down".

Resolutions

A united political revolution is the seed of liberty and the foundation for change. Through unity we can take back all three branches of government and change the course of history. And we must not trust a biased media which is responsible for the liberal retardation that has mentally disabled around thirty percent of the American population. If we do not answer the call then many honorable men and women died for nothing.

While we bicker over insignificant nonsense the UN and WTO have become pawns of international corruption. At home, government agencies such as the FCC and DOT have become more powerful than Congress. For decades the CIA and FBI have ignored our Constitution while making up their own rules as they go. The FDA and CPA (Consumer Protection Agency) inspect about one percent (1%) of all imports so there is no way to accurately measure the actual toxic dumping of hazardous chemicals by China's government into corporate goods consumed by Americans. And bureaucrats such as Nancy Nord are corporate flunkies that shield their illegal acts. But if one wants to know where China stands then look toward its people for this communist government is standing on their throats. What do you think China would do if it ruled the world?

Many women of good intentions are responsible for the enormous bureaucratic messes in the Education Systems and DFCS-for without discipline there is no accountability and lowering standards doesn't bring people up it keeps them down. JFK, MLK, and RFK stood for equality that could be achieved through equal access. But few have shown the courage to speak out against the *Washington Establishment.* Thus, we must overcome our fear of standing alone for we are not alone. Reclaiming our moral integrity was a guarantee established by the architects of our Constitution who believed it was our God given right to do so.

Nevertheless, I believe there is courage and good in most men and women, but we have to find the will to search deep within our souls for the future depends on our selflessness. Even though tough choices sometimes sadden our hearts, we must remember true love is making difficult decisions when all reasonable options have been exhausted. For the majority of Americans must stand up and say "No more" and by doing so we can regain a measure of moral courage and reestablish America as the "Northern Star of Hope".

The only American asset left that China truly values is our military technological advantages. When China demands payment our economy will collapse because we have no realistic means of paying our debts. If President Obama and Congress outsource our military technology to China for debt relief, our limited freedoms will soon become very restricted. This economic crisis will affect our military, middle and lower classes including the underemployed, people depending on supplemental incomes, our elderly population, those with severe health problems, lower level employees of local, state, and federal bureaucracies, small businesses, healthcare, and education. Thus, President Obama and Congress are mortgaging our future by gambling with enormous deficits that we can't afford no matter how much they increase our taxes.

Therefore the progressive movement toward Socialism in America is very real. And if the Democratic Party is able to monopolize our political system, America will look more like a *Fascist Nation* of disobedient non-believers. Moreover, if this scenario happens, we the American people will have to eradicate every corrupt politician, every disingenuous media pundit, every dishonest bureaucrat, every wealthy supporter, and any fool who aligns themselves with these traitors. That is why I continually propose a peaceful political revolution of a new *Moderate Party* of reformers too hopefully avoid America's *2nd Great Depression* that will affect the entire world and our *2nd Civil War* between classes. For the price of our inaction today will ignite the violent reactions of tomorrow and many will drown in the blood of *Armageddon.*

Real Heroes

I once told a student of mine, who was a con artist and always looking for the easiest way of getting out of fulfilling his responsibilities, if you ever listen to anything I say, listen to me now. I said "You work hard and if that doesn't work, then you work harder." And this is the way I have always approached everything I do in life. I have had many disappointments, been treated unfairly, had to deal with depression, had my heart broken a few times, and I have fallen short of my own expectations on numerous occasions. There is no pill that will cure our shortcomings in life. Though, I feel each failure has made me stronger and more determined too succeed. Life is like a rollercoaster, full of ups and downs, twists and turns, but one should remember to enjoy the ride.

Athletes are not heroes. Movie stars are not heroes. Musicians or any other celebrities are not heroes. Their hype and popularity are created by the *Media* and the *Entertainment Industry* because they need us. They produce the commodities and we buy the products. We have been "defined" as "consumers" that purchase their prepackaged (subliminal and false advertising) bologna. Karl Marx believed that production dictated economics. But I say mass production and dishonest marketing drives capitalism in Western Societies. In Orson Welles "*Citizen Kane*" he used this idea to show how the power of the media could create an imagery of success that had nothing to do with the actual truth. An example would be Britney Spears. Some minimal dancing talent and no singing talent, yet she has made millions in the music industry. And her popularity was based on looks and clever advertising. Why do you think the Hurst and Kennedy families along with many other wealthy families invested in almost every media entity in the United States and the Western World? It sure isn't because they are interested in justice being served or the truth being told. Instead, it is about profit, maintaining control over the masses, marketing their products, creating false images, dividing the people, and yes if one believes in the "*Religious Scriptures*" it prophesizes how deception which is being used by our current media will bring forth the Antichrist. John and Robert Kennedy rebelled against the privileged wealth of their birth and that is why they were Heroes.

No, John and Robert were not perfect people, but they cared about the people. It is easy to find skeletons in every ones closet, yet it is the character of the individual that counts. Integrity can not be commodified, although the wealthy elite do their best. Personally I have always believed our government was behind the assassination of John Fitzgerald Kennedy. But those evildoers will find no mercy in God's court. If John F. Kennedy had not been murdered by the Judus's of the 20th century, he might have been considered one of the greatest Presidents since Thomas Jefferson. We will never be able to trust our government without independent oversight and a new political system. For the rich will sacrifice their own if he or she interferes with their attempt at world domination.

Everyone is imperfect, but there are lines none of us can cross or the penalty is *Eternal Damnation* and no Catholic Priest can exonerate a lying, thieving, drug dealing, and soulless mobster. Robert and John were two Heroes that had the courage and conviction to stand up against a corrupt system and say "HELL NO." How many of us would put our lives on the line? Thanks to FDR, our Government has become a malignant cancer that we must somehow find a cure for because it is slowly infecting everyone in the US and the Western World.

And didn't Dr. King once say "if a cause isn't worth dying for, then you are already dead"? Dr. Martin Luther King Jr. is another Hero who gave his life for his beliefs. Not many men have walked this earth with such dignity and humbleness since Jesus Christ and he was the son of God. But Dr. King's strength and courage, knowing one day he would be slain by the oppressors, should be an inspiration to every man, woman, or child who has faced the ugliness of our world. His non-violence message was a reflection of his faith. And Dr. King is already in the *Promised Land*, but his followers and other black leaders who sold out the black community and Dr. King's "*Dream*" will be voyaging to a different land.

Maybe one day Dr. Martin Luther King Jr. will look down upon the world and see us breaking bread together. But there is a river of sorrow in heaven flowing from Dr. King's tears because all of us have let him down. No one in America picked up the "*torch of hope*" after Dr. King's death. Every time the oppressor slays an honest leader, ten more must take his or her place-for we outnumber the oppressors sixty thousand to one.

Our Founding Fathers of the Constitution thought a democracy would stop a few from ruling over the masses. And they knew that too much power in the hands of so few would lead to the corruption of our society. While their idea of checks and balances, in theory, seemed the best route to go, they forgot that wealth and power will corrupt most decent people. And safeguards were lacking to stop the three branches (legislative, executive, and judicial) from a collusion of corruption. Thomas Jefferson, another Hero, took on the corruption. He removed all the dishonest judges (Federalists) from the bench. Jefferson was two hundred years ahead of his time. Today the American Courts are full of corrupt judges that legislate social discourse from the bench. For me, I believe this unconstitutional act is treason, punishable by death (exception to the rule). Other federal, state, and local judges are allowing guilty defendants to walk. While high profile celebrities and athletes are turning the *American Judicial System* into a *Three-Ring-Circus* with the assistance of bleeding heart liberal judges that are rewarded for their favoritism (bribes). There is no telling how many judges are on the payroll of organized crime and the ones that actually have to run for their judgeships depend on the wealthy for campaign contributions. Others are appointed by Governors and the President based on party loyalty and political ideology. What a freaking mess. There is an old saying about finding one honest cop; hell find me one honest judge or prosecutor-for the police where I live seem to be both honest and decent.

Many false Heroes are created by the "*Powers That Be.*" One is Abraham Lincoln. President Lincoln divided a country that to this day has not fully recovered from the atrocities during and after the Civil War. Do you think Vietnam is the first War where rich people sons and politician's sons didn't have to serve or were given non-combative assignments? Well this practice started in the Civil War with the Union Army. The poor, many who were Irish immigrants right off the boat were drafted into the Union Army. But the aristocrats could buy their way out of the draft for three hundred dollars ($300) and the majority of them did just that. And the truth is Lincoln was mentally unstable or what we label today as "mentally ill". His Union Army was run by drunken murderers without honor. President Grant's Administration was the most corrupt in the history of the United States. For they screwed the Indians, the Chinese, White Southerners; landowners in the Midwest and West, Mexico; they screwed anybody they could with the aid of a corrupt Congress and the force of the Union Army. However, I do believe if Lincoln had not been assassinated, the Reconstruction Period would have been less corrupt and more focused on healing a nation.

Another illusionary Hero is J. Edgar Hoover. Hoover was a degenerate with no moral fiber. Putting his name on any structure is an embarrassment to America and its people. And J. Edgar denied on many occasions the existence of the Mafia. Why, because they had him by the balls. Hoover was a cross-dressing homosexual and the Mafia used this knowledge to blackmail him. And I really don't care about his sexual orientation however he should have stepped down as the head of the FBI the moment his authority was compromised. But he didn't because he used his position of power to satisfy his lust.

While others in the FBI were doing all the dirty work, Hoover was taking all the credit. J. Edgar Hoover allowed organized crime to murder, deal drugs, traffic in stolen merchandise, rob, extort, blackmail, or whatever criminal activity they wanted while he was playing the fairy godmother to his choir boys. This was an abuse of power. And I do believe he was involved with the murders of John Fitzgerald Kennedy, Dr. Martin Luther King Jr., and Robert Francis Kennedy. But he also keep files on all political opposition which he used to blackmail them the same way organize crime did him. Mr. Hoover is no hero for he is a disgrace to the uniform and his name should be removed from the FBI Headquarters Building. Eventually, when history records the truth, J. Edgar Hoover will be known as one of the darkest governmental bureaucratic figures of all time. The only difference between J. Edgar Hoover and Hitler is where they lived.

Sometimes we forget the wealthy elite can create an imagery of decency because they control most forms of information dissemination. Heroes are vilified and jackasses are idolized. Franklin D. Roosevelt was an ambitious prick. The *New Deal* was a gimmick that won him the 1932 election. FDR created the Bureaucratic Cancer that is out of control today. Mary Shelley may have written *Frankenstein*, but FDR is the Creator of the Monster. Do you believe George Walker Bush is the first

President to manipulate information so he can get American support for military action? What do you think Franklin Delano Roosevelt did to change America's isolationist beliefs in gaining support for World War II? Well he allowed over two thousand people to die at Pearl Harbor because he and his military leaders knew this would change public opinion. The United States was already secretly shipping supplies to Great Britain on passenger liners such as the *Lusitania* and we were antagonizing Japan by cutting off their oil. We all have skeletons in our closets, though FDR's closet was an enormous graveyard full of lies, deception, and treachery.

But a lot of people think the New Deal saved America from the Depression. Thou art so wrong. For World War II revitalized the American economy. And the New Deal created a large bureaucratic mess that is filled with corruption and has become a backbreaking burden on the American taxpayers. The Hurst family (owners of the New York Times) had strong business ties with Germany before and during the War. Sound familiar, the Bush family has strong ties with Saudi Arabia where 15 of the 19 highjackers of 9/11 were from. FDR was no hero. Now, the jury is still out on President Bush, but one thing is for sure he was a *crazy cracker* that the rest of the world was not going to anger while his finger is on the trigger.

Jesus Christ is the world's greatest Hero because he gave his life so that all might have salvation. There are doubters among us, though I doubt they are singing the same tune on their death beds. Again, I am no saint, but I do believe in God and I do believe he sent his own son to redeem mankind. What I admire about Jesus is that he cared about the poor while he lived and traveled among them. His humility was exemplified through the way he lived his life. At times we become so fixated on acquiring wealth, we tend to forget we can't take it with us. Leaving wealth to your heirs is one of the most foolish acts a person can commit. Look at Parish Hilton. Could you image leaving an Empire to such an ignorant whore? Take James Dolan of MSG, how could his dad and uncle leave this moron in charge of anything? No one should be given enormous wealth. People should earn wealth through honest dealings and hard work. Then when one passes give you money to the less fortunate or respectable charities the same way Jesus gave all.

There are many Heroes throughout history. The prophet

Muhammad stood up against the pagan ways of the Middle East. It is a miracle that an illiterate man could recite the whole book of Islam (Qur'an) from memory. Though I disagree with the killing of non-believers, I do believe the Koran and the lifestyles practiced by Muslins today is the closest to how God wishes believers to conduct themselves. For Christianity and Judaism have become too entrenched in a *Secular World* that believes in wealth. As I said before, "We can not serve two masters." Muhammad faced many obstacles when he took on a corrupt society, yet he prevailed via "The will of Ali." For most of us it is hard to believe that God communicates to a chosen few. And there are many nut cases like David Currish that invoke doubt. But Joseph Smith and Brigham Young were also false prophets. However, where do our thoughts come from? For the chosen few, I believe their religious inspiration comes from divine intervention. Still we hath to recognize there are many quacks out there posing as religious leaders.

Mahatma Gandhi also stood up to be counted. He took on the Imperialists of Great Britain. Colonization of the world by England and France was the popular trend of the era. They not only wanted to dominate the world, England and France believed they were saving the world by forcing their cultural beliefs on everyone else. Isn't that what our Government (United States) is trying to do today? If you weren't of European birth, one was considered a Savage. Gandhi took on the oppressors. They tried their best to break him, but Gandhi's will was too strong. Could you go on a hungry strike for weeks at a time? Gandhi was a Hero because he was the face of a nation that revolted against the ruling imperial class from Europe.

Nelson Mandela took on the South Africa's occupation. And he went to jail for 25 years. Would you go to jail for you beliefs? Another occupied nation by rich European Aristocrats that believe the world is their oyster. There is enough wealth from the diamond mines in Africa to build hospitals and schools and to take care of the poor. So why are their diamonds exported to other countries and the African people rarely benefit from any of the riches? Mandela went to prison because he knew the imperialist occupation was not benefiting his people. Nelson Mandela is another Hero that spoke up for a cause he believed in his heart that he was right and eventually overcame.

Great men and women don't have to die or go to prison, but they must be willing to rise up and be heard. Sun Tzu's *The Art of War* philosophy is still used by every Western Government today. By categorizing people, preying on their emotional fears, and constantly bombarding them with "false truths;" Western Nations can maintain control over the masses. If we unite through new political processes, openly welcome our eastern brothers and sisters, and work together to found common ground, we can take back our world from the oppressors. But tragedies such as the assassination of heroes like Benazir Bhutto complicate the process. And for us to come together for the united purpose of ending western government corruption we must relinquish violent acts-by doing so we can unite the world and become ONE.

It is time for all of us to stand and be counted. We can no longer accept the crimes against humanity as our destiny. There is a little hero in all of us that just needs to be awakened. Each one of us can impact the world by changing our ways. Saying "no" to corruption is the first step in regaining our self respect. Life is not always as complicated as we sometimes make it. Most Heroes come from humble beginnings and others reject their silver spoons as a right to reign. Decency can be found in most that understand kindness is an act of love.

Many have given all so that you and I might experience a better quality of life. When individuals sell out their communities for the treasures of kings, they lose sight of the importance of faith. Their desires of wealth and power cast aside all reasoning and compassion for their fellow man. I have often said it is ok for a person to make an honest living, but people should not be out there trying to cheat people. You are not the only one, everybody's got to eat. A mechanic lying to and overcharging a woman for auto repairs should be ashamed. Just being an honest plumber or carpenter that does quality work for a fair price has a positive impact on society. When we all contribute a little, the social effect is enormous.

Being the best person you can be and treating people fairly in your daily business dealings makes you a hero. No, maybe you are not recognized on some grand stage, but your peers respect should be reward enough. Remember charity comes from the heart and Heroes are born of the heart. Sometimes I get angry and curse a little too much, but I still love people. And I do my best to try and treat others the same way I wish to be treated. It may not always turn out that way, and there are some people I just don't like, but I make an effort. How each one of us impacts someone else's life has a profound affect on how that individual's choices are shaped. Think of it as a "chain of love", each positive link makes the chain stronger.

I never was a fan of Mohammad Ali and probably never will be, but I am moved by his illness because everyone deserves compassion even though it is not always easy to give. However, many liberal idealists in the sports media are now trying to recreate his image and continually refer to Ali as a hero. He was a draft-dodging loudmouthed jackass that cared more about his boxing career than his country. His brash antics were repulsive and his flamboyant self-indulging lifestyle contradicted his self-proclaimed faith. As an athlete and skilled boxer he was one of the best and I respect his abilities as a competitor, but as a man I have very little respect for the Mohammad Ali of the 60's and 70's. Just because he was popular in the Black Community doesn't change the facts no matter what lies these jock sniffing journalists tell. For many great black athletes, scholars, and leaders such as Jackie Robinson, Dr. George Washington Carver, and Dr. Martin Luther King Jr. suffered unjustly, but they never allowed their class or dignity to dishonor the "cause" for their faith was in God. But legends are often created by hypocrites who worship the myth while burying the truth because it contradicts popular fiction. Mohammad Ali was an excellent boxer that fought too long and now is suffering because his foolish pride refused to recognize when to quit. And while it is truly a tragic ending, it doesn't transform him into a hero, but it appears his illness has humbled the former World Heavyweight Champions and that makes him a better man today.

16

The Law

"Truth is justice, morality is righteous, and sacrifice is love"

People need to understand that most law enforcement personnel are decent people. However, there are far too many bad apples. The code of silence amongst follow officers is absolutely ridiculous. If a follow officer is doing something that another officer knows is wrong and violates the oath, then he or she must report the offense. When an officer crosses this line, he or she is no longer an officer of the law. That's right the unlawful cannot represent "the law". And any officer that does not turn in a lawbreaker to the appropriate authorities is an accessory.

In films, we often see Internal Affairs (IA) going after the rotten apples, though real life is not imitated in Hollywood. The good guys don't always win and the bad guys don't always lose. Here, lies one of the biggest problems with bureaucracies, they can not be trusted to "police" themselves. Without independent oversight, damage control, cover ups, and abuses of power are all we can expect. And these corruptible behavioral patterns occur in all bureaucracies. Thus, independent oversight is needed in every facet of government as well as in the private sector of corporate businesses.

At one time, law enforcement actually protected and served the public. Today, they have become cleaners. Instead of trying to prevent crime, they intervene after the crime has been committed. When there is pressure to solve a case, the door is open for wrongfully charging an innocent person. Then the law enforcement agency and the prosecutor's office will use the media to create an image of guilt. But unfortunately poor defendants are at the mercy of ambitious prosecutors who rarely admit to mistakes even when they know the verdict is unjust. Before admitting they made a mistake, they will send an innocent person to prison with the assistance of crooked cops, unreliable witnesses, a jury that can't distinguish the facts from hypothetical fiction, and a judge who wants to get home in time for supper. Later, when a conviction is overturned by DNA or excluded evidence, these hypocrites go in front of the cameras and say the individual was convicted by a jury of his or her peers and justice was served. What justice, maybe if the judge, prosecutor, and detectives go to prison while the jurors are never allowed too serve on another jury.

With independent oversight, we could start prosecuting dirty law enforcement agents and politically overzealous prosecutors that are more concerned with conviction rates rather than the truth. As I said before most law enforcement agents are honest and they have a difficult job, but one bad officer is one too many. Take the Duke Lacrosse situation. The prosecutor was more concerned with getting reelected than he was about the truth. For the facts were clear, Nifong did not have enough evidence to prove a rape conviction. But he spun the case into a race issue for his own selfish ambitions. It didn't seem to matter that he might send three innocent young men to prison. Without hesitation he persisted to destroy their lives and their future careers. Besides going to Hell, what other consequences does the prosecutor face? He racially divided the community just to further his own political agenda. What a lousy piece of garbage, another self serving politician (democrat) with innocent blood on his hands. It is not enough to disbar Mike Nifong and remove him from office. He should be civilly liable and criminally charged for his unlawful acts. And the striper should also be criminally charged and prosecuted for it appears she is being given preferential treatment because of her race and gender.

Many black sports reporters jumped to conclusions before the facts every came in and half-hearted insincere apologies by ESPN and ABC sports reporters like John Saunders, while using the excuse of having two daughters, are unacceptable. Everyone has daughters, nieces, sisters, or mothers and we view rape as a cowardly act, but that doesn't give anyone the right to use their platform in the media to convict someone based on their prejudices rather than the facts. If roles had been reversed and a white striper had accused three black male students and a white sports reporter had jumped the gun, he or she would have been labeled a racist and probably lost their job. Instead of seeking the truth, most of the liberal white sports reporters followed suit and yet we are supposed to believe there is no biased agenda in the current sports media. And the President of Duke University along with many faculty members should be terminated for their unprofessional and unethical actions. Any student looking to attend Duke University should rethink their decision for there are many academic universities in the United States where the students actually have rights under the Constitution. Nevertheless, this never would have been a racially divisive issue if law enforcement had performed in a professional manner.

Our law enforcement needs to be restructured and those who violate their oath of trust have to be prosecuted based on the seriousness of the crime. And when convicted, they should be sent to a local prison, not a federal resort. We should consider closing all these federal institutions because prison is supposed to be a deterrent, not a vacation for the unlawful. And I don't agree with the witness protection program, rewarding criminals for turning on other criminals is unconstitutional and it affects the credibility of the outcome.

What a mess. Justice for all has become a disheartening joke. Justice is no longer about fairness and equality, it has become commodified. Just like marketing a product through representative imagery, justice can be twisted into a deceitful illusion. It can be bought by those who are guilty and excluded for those who are innocent. It has nothing to do with the truth. And California has become the laughing stock of the world for every celebrity is innocent even if the judge, prosecutor, and jury witnessed the crime.

Because many overzealous prosecutors are more concerned with their own political ambitions of becoming a

US Senator or the Governor of their state, they are unable to admit the wrongful persecution of an innocent person. At the same time, they continually cut deals with unscrupulous criminals and the guilty rich and famous. While high profile defensive attorneys will knowingly represent guilty clients and use every dishonest trick in the book to get these guilty degenerates out of trouble. Time after time, professional athletes, musicians, film stars, and spoiled rich brats receive preferential treatment by our judicial system. O.J. Simpson, Paris Hilton, Vince McMahon, Phil Specter, Ray Lewis, Michael Jackson, Barry Bonds, Robert Blake, and Alan Iverson are a few of the thousands of celebrities that have escaped justice. But the media is often complicit in influencing outcomes because it would be so unfair for these idols we adore to suffer the indignity of prison.

The whole judicial system of America is out of whack. Our media tries people in the court of public opinion every day. But the media has two purposes and neither has anything to do with truth and justice being served. First, the media is focused on network ratings. Getting the story out takes priority over waiting for the facts. Unbiased reporting and credibility don't count for much in today's media industry. Second, they are concerned with circulation. Sales of printed products are more important than ethics. The 1st amendment (Freedom of Speech) has been stretch beyond the original intent. Naturally the judicial system lent a hand in reshaping the "Freedom of Speech" amendment. The judicial system even allowed porn distributors to use the 1st amendment as a defense. One of the few decent pieces of legislation that President Clinton passed, internet pornography restrictions, was overturned by our corrupt judicial system.

One minute, our courts are legislating social discourse from the pulpit, the next minute they are quoting constitutional law. Not only do all judges, including Supreme Court justices, need to be elected by the people, but there needs to be independent oversight with the authority to change any unconstitutional ruling. We have got to clean up the judicial system because many judges are abusing their powers. The Constitution's intent for the Judicial Branch is to uphold the law, not to reinvent the law based on their biased interpretations or political agendas. "*Legal Activism*" is unconstitutional and any judge that ordains himself as the "Law" should be disbarred, removed from the bench, and prosecuted as a criminal.

Justice shouldn't be an exclusionary entity, justice should represent truth. Our judicial system is an important part of our culture. And its credibility must not be tainted by corruption. In every western culture, we have allowed the wealthy privileged to corrupt our systems of justices. They use the media, the politicians, the government bureaucracies, and every controllable mechanism to circumvent truth and justice when it interferes with their itinerary. But "justice for all" can only be served when the truth is more important than the result.

Chief Justice Earl Warren reserved his accommodations in Hell when he led the unconstitutional decision to remove prayer from public schools along with his assistance in the cover up of the assassination of JFK. But Warren's successors and former colleagues will suffer the worst of any pagan ever born in the deepest and darkest torture chambers of the eternal fire. John Joseph Cardinal Krol said;

> "It is hard to think of any decision in the two hundred years of our history which has had more disastrous implications for our stability as a civilized society."

I can't phrase it any better and though I have issues with the Catholic Church here they stood up and were counted and that I can respect. The reason why these Justices struggled with their opinions is because their legalization of abortion (Roe verses Wade) was unconstitutional. The American public was outraged but over the last thirty years with the help of an anti-religious media supporters have rephrased murder into a woman's right to choose. Justices Douglas, Blackmun, Brennan, Marshall, Rehnquist, Powell, Stewart, White, and Burger (Chief Justice) are responsible for more deaths than all the homicidal and genocidal maniacs in the history of the world combined. Just because some of their wives and daughters were liberal feminists, it did not give them the right to legislate from the bench. Disallowing prayer in public schools, legalizing abortion, and upholding affirmative action were all unconstitutional decisions by the Supreme Court which has overstepped it's boundaries of power for the last seventy-five years. It is asinine for the courts to replace personal responsibility with unconstitutional mandates. But if I don't make it into heaven, I will gladly oversee the torture of these disciples of darkness until the end of all time.

Most bureaucracies such as the Department of Education and the Department of Family and Children's Services are freaking nightmare. Losing kids, misplacing kids, leaving children in unsafe environments, and never accepting responsibility for their failures. Foster Homes have become a racquet for many trying to bilk the government for money. If a child is placed in a relative's or foster care home, all an irresponsible parent has to do is place an anonymous call making false accusations and DFCS will show up at your door like the SS Gestapo. No proof, no witnesses, no physical evidence; just a phone call from a piece of trash posing as a parent. Many of these children love their drug addicted and abusive parents and they will lie if coerced to do so. That is why there is a shortage in good Foster Homes because people don't want these bureaucrats coming into their neighborhoods like buzzards descending on a dead carcass. Now, if people could sue these idiots, it might make them do their job more professionally. When one of these morons wrongly accuses someone, she or he should be fired and civilly liable. DFCS needs independent oversight and constant reevaluation to improve its procedural operations. Many of the employees work at DFCS for short periods of time because it is just a stepping stone for their bureaucratic or political careers. How could any agency ever maintain consistency with ambitious personnel whose advancement up the state and federal bureaucratic ladder or getting elected to public office is more important than the children they serve? And "No child left behind" is as retarded as its architect because we are all different. Some children will be astronauts while some will be custodians.

All any educator can do is provide the proper tools to assist each child in reaching his or her potential.

Resolutions

Do you think we really need twenty-two to twenty-four law enforcement agencies? No! It seems the only new jobs being created in our current economy are either government service or fast food opportunities. Just what we need; more bureaucrats that foster anti-conservative views and unhealthy food that has spawn the obesity epidemic throughout the United States of America which is going to devastate our health care system over the next twenty years if we don't address it especially type two diabetes. All we need is four to five law enforcement agencies. Our Military (MI) Intelligence can replace the CIA (Central Intelligence Agency), NSA (National Security Administration), Secret Service, Homeland Security, and any other agency dealing with national security and international terrorism. One FBI (Federal Bureau of Investigations) agency can handle all domestic problems that don't fall under the MI's jurisdiction. And state and local police can assume the responsibility of the rest. But there must also be a network or sharing information when applicable. And we use our fifth agency the Coast Guard more efficiently to assist all other agencies in border security, drug trafficking, import and export security, and any other high seas crimes.

But if a law enforcement officer is living a lifestyle above his or her income, this is usually a good indicator that he or she may be on the take with organized crime or is involved in illegal activities. Therefore independent oversight of all law enforcement officers, financial records and behavioral patterns, has become necessary because of the bureaucratic corruption that is running roughshod throughout America. There is no doubt that law enforcement officers, military personnel, and firefighters should be compensated with higher salaries, better pensions and benefits for they sacrifice their lives for you and I every day, but we must also weed out the corrupted. And that includes law enforcement agents hanging out at the local "titty bar". Most of these stripe clubs are owned directly or indirectly by organized crime. Many of the stripers are involved in pornography and drug trafficking, so getting free blows is not a perk of an officer representing the law. To protect, serve, and uphold the law means a law enforcement agent cannot engage in or be associated with activities that may affect or damage their credibility.

Ross Perot was right in his belief that *American Politics* and *American Government* need to be reformed. And this vision of reform was also a belief of John and Bobby Kennedy as well. For if a society is not continually reevaluating its policies and procedures then it becomes as stagnant as an old fart with a lingering smell that drifts back and forth until it exasperates the entire room. Thus, there are many reforms that are needed and required to fix a system that only benefits the upper class.

First on the list is *Trade Reform* -repealing or dramatically revising NAFTA is a given for all trades with foreign nations must be reciprocal (no deficits). Any product produced outside the U.S. should be taxed proportionately based on the estimated costs to produce the same product inside the United States. And the WTO (World Trade Organization) is as useless as the UN-for without balance no trade-agreement between the US and any nation should ever exist. But we need to increase the size and authority of agencies such as the FDA (Food and Drug Administration), OSHA (Occupational Safety and Health Administration), and the EPA (Environment Protection Agency) with independent oversight especially when drug corporations such as MERCK or oil corporations such as EXXON are involved.

We must also downsize federal bureaucracies such as the Department of Agriculture and cut their subsidy programs or what many have coined as "*Corporate Welfare*" for the corporate owned farms. But we must also have more restrictions on pesticides and preservatives being used. When corporations operate without restrictions that is not a free market system, it is a system motivated by greed only and consumer protection is more times than not sacrificed as a statistical risk that "bean counters" weigh against profit.

An *Education Reform* bill is essential to improving our declining and dysfunctional education system. Women fuss all the time about have they don't have fair opportunities and if they were in charge how much better the world would be. Aren't over eighty percent (80%) of all teachers and administrators at the elementary, middle, and high school levels, including the State Departments of Education, made up of females? So, what does this prove? It proves that women are as good at screwing up as men. The reform must include reinstating discipline, competition in the classroom, and dress codes, reemphasizing *Math*, *Science*, and *Technology* raising the standards of all academics such as *English* and *Social Studies* that were lowered over the last thirty years while also teaching the true *History* of the United States of America. And physical education should be included every day for an hour, breakfasts and lunches should be nutritional, and all snack machines should be removed. But I also believe Art and Music are essential in developing well rounded students.

Therefore I believe there should be a three step inclusive program for all American public schools including a vocational track, a technical college track, and a college track based on a student's aptitude, skills, and abilities. But we have to be realistic in our assessments for there are always going to be children that excel while others do not as long as every educational option is explored-for what truly matters is assisting each child in reaching his or her potential. And pre-kindergarten programs for all high risks children should be coordinated with local schools systems. Early intervention is the first step to lowering risks and improving options. And one of the best options we can use for all behavioral disordered children that disrupt the learning environment of their peers is *Military* run schools instead of the ineffective alternative schools.

Another part of the education reform must be higher salaries for teachers and increases in pay based on job performance not tenure. Because this is America and every immigrant who came here had to learn English, Hispanic students must learn English, but we should provide before and after school programs that assist Spanish speaking students and parents that are here legally in assimilation. While I believe in "English First", we must encourage and nurture every student. And it is true teachers definitely deserve better pay, but paraprofessionals should also have higher standard requirements and receive more compensation for their contributions. But I also believe all post-secondary education should be free to Americans that met the academic requirements of the institution or at least pay for the education of teachers, nurses, scientists, and doctors that agree to work in areas where there is a need for the first five years after graduation.

Reforming our tax system is a must. Under a less complex system, I believe a combination of a *Flat Tax* and a *Fair Tax* would be the best solution. A ten percent (10%) flat tax for those at the lower end (under $50K) and a thirty percent (30%) flat tax for those at the higher end (over $1 million) for everyone must share the burden. At the same time, a fifteen percent (15%) national fair tax on all purchases excluding homes is also a part of the solution in which five percent (5%) stays in the local community, five percent (5%) is allocated to that state, and the remaining five percent (5%) is sent to Washington. But sadly the Welfare Reform Bill of President William Jefferson Clinton was a scheme because the federal government redistributed the supplemental income to welfare recipients under the Earned Income Credit legislation. For he wasn't called "Slick Willie" for nothing, he earned this nickname because he is a hustler on "*The Highway to Hell*'. Here the entitlement client might pay up to a thousand dollars ($1K) in federal taxes if the individual works fulltime and in return receives six-thousand dollars ($6K) if he or she has dependents. Any first-grade math student can comprehend the eventually outcome if an individual pays one-thousand dollars and receives six-thousand dollars in return the Federal Government would eventually go bankrupt.

Moreover, irresponsible American Corporations that outsource American jobs, imports foreign produced products and materials, or operate without an environmental friendly business model should pay a higher tax rate of up to fifty percent (50%). But American Corporations that act in a more responsible manner would have the Corporate Tax rate reduced from thirty-five percent (35%) to twenty-five percent (25%). And all offshore accounts where corporate executives hide taxable incomes would be subject to a fifty percent penalty tax and the individuals involved would face a minimum of twenty years in an American State Prison. However, American workers must also make sacrifices and that includes ousting all of the current corrupt union leadership for no partnership can survive without reasonable concessions from both sides. And if GM and Chrysler are really interested in revitalizing their company brand and the American Auto-Industry, they would move their entire operations to "right to work states" such as Georgia.

There are millions who believe taxation is unconstitutional. But actually taxation is not unconstitutional. The original intent of taxation was to support an army and a small government. What is unconstitutional is the disproportionate collection of our taxes. People in the middle class who achieve success are penalized the most while people in the lower class who do the least are rewarded. But the upper class uses tax exemption laws designed for their benefit to avoid paying their fair share and they wonder why we loathe them so. Maybe we need the IRS to enforce the codes, but we could greatly downsize (at least 95%) this bureaucratic tyrant with independent monitoring to ensure fairness. And truthfully I don't mind paying taxes, but I do mind the wasteful spending of our taxes.

Next, *Judicial Reform* has become necessary to rebalance the power between our three branches (legislative, executive, and judicial). All judges formally appointed by Presidents and Governors must be approved individually by National and State voters. A mandatory retirement age of eighty and service at each or any level should not exceed eight years. Also an independent oversight committee must be established with the authority to remove or criminally charge any judge that operates beyond his oath (outlaws social discourse from the bench). And repealing double jeopardy to actually ensure everyone receives a fair trial and to stop the lunacy in states such as the "*California courts of idol worshipers*". Making the rules up as they go is not and was not the intent of establishing the judicial branch under the constitution.

If we want to address "global warming" then *Environmental Reform* is needed. But we must be willing to invest in clean alternative energy sources such as solar power. Nuclear power is not clean or safe because of its dangerous radioactive waste and our dependency on oil must be lessened or the fight for oil will eventually start WWIII. And I believe former Senator Bill Bradley is correct with his suggestions of more fuel efficient vehicles and a $1 gas tax to reduce Americans dependency on oil-for as Americans we must be willing to make individual sacrifices that benefit our country as a whole. But I also believe all auto-manufactures should be required to developed energy efficient vehicles with mileage standards that exceed 50 miles per gallon. Ethanol if we can produce it more cost efficiently without reducing our food resources must be available nationally and we must stop the water pollution and extinction of species. More than likely pesticides are the culprits, but if cellphones or wireless communications had been a part of the problem for the decline in the bee population that is a serious situation we must be willing to address. At some point Americans must be willing to make sacrifices for the good of our country and the world.

There are many legal reforms that can be achieved through an honest effort of a reformed Congress. *Illegal Immigration Reform* that allows work visas for around two million agricultural workers, but criminally charges and financially penalizes employers for hiring illegal aliens is necessary. This legislation must also criminally charge and financially penalize realtors and landlords who sale or rent to illegal immigrants. And all welfare benefits must be cut off including medical assistance except in the case of a severe emergency. By requiring legitimate documentation which almost every American citizen has to submit for all employment, housing, education, or assistance programs, the immigration problem would slowly began to resolve itself through a standard verification process (example the E-verify some employers currently use). But at the same time children of illegal immigrants must not be allowed to attend our schools. And it is not a question of caring because most of us do care, but sometimes tough choices have to be made to solve difficult problems. Thus, we must pass strict legislation that also includes compassionate provisions such as leaving at the end of the calendar school year (June 1st) or giving illegal immigrants six months to get their affairs in order. And employers and landlords would have ninety days to verify legal status, but government bureaucrats would immediately be held accountable for any violations. Furthermore, any criminal activity should be met with severe penalties such as twenty years to life with immediate deportation after the sentence has been completed.

Every American citizen should be entitled to free quality healthcare which could be achieved under *Universal Healthcare Reform.* But choice, prevention, and oversight must be included as well. Nevertheless, there are many other reforms that need to take place to change the bureaucratic nightmares and political corruption in Washington. An *Equal Access Act* that guarantees employment opportunities and advancement are solely based on merit for everyone would be more effective than all the other *legislative acts* combined. *Prison Reform* that actually works toward transitioning inmates back into society with the skills and abilities they need to become productive law abiding citizens. Unfortunately many Departments of Correction such as California are so corrupt they need immediate federal intervention and oversight. One of the most important reforms that is often debated but never adjudicated is a *Livable Minimum Wage.* Such a wage could be adjusted based on the cost of living in a particular area or region of the U.S., but a baseline of at least ten dollars and eighty cents ($10.80) an hour must be established. And *Social Security Reform* must be achieved to meet the needs of future generations thereby ending our dependency on Big Brother. But *Political Reforms* such as term limits and financial restrictions are also necessary to clean Washington's "*house of horrors*". And *Government Accountability* is essential to reestablishing public trust.

All the costs of said *Reforms* can be met. First, we must stop the wasteful spending of Congress (Pork Barrel Projects and Earmarks). Then we must downsize (at least two thirds) and eliminate stagnant bureaucracies. And if our Government operated on a legitimate balanced yearly budget we could seriously diminish our nine trillion dollar deficit by 2013. Though I believe in maintaining the strongest military in the world; it has to be done more cost efficiently and any excessive corporate charges would be considered treason and the executives would be held accountable. And all foreign trades must be reciprocal (equal) and by doing so we eliminate our trade deficits. But we must also consider revisiting the *Gold Standard* as an option for our declining American currency. Furthermore, we must invest in new opportunities to replace the tens of millions of outsourced middle class jobs (hybrid auto manufacturing, solar and clean renewable energy sources, new American infrastructure-a solar powered mass transit system-a vastly improved highway system with standard upgrades for bridges, organic foods (a part of any Universal Healthcare Plan must be prevention and that includes eliminating steroids and harmful preservatives in our food supply), continued technological developments, healthcare advancements, new green ideas, etc.) if we are going to meet our future challenges. But it is time for every American to quit being speculators and become more active in the determination of our destiny-for the game is not over until we say it is and the majority of Americans have always been compassionate, resourceful, and innovative and that is what it is going to take to meet our economic challenges over the next five years.

Without personal sacrifices and legitimate reforms, "change" is a deceptive concept used for emotional responses that forget to question "the how". So when anyone talks about our foreign challenges such as Russia, China, or terrorism, many liberals refer to it as "fear mongering". But the truth is these dangers are "real" and the world better start paying more attention. And that is why I believe we need an *International Federation of Peace* (IFP) to replace the UN and an international army, the *World Peace Keepers* (WPK), to replace NATO. Most liberals swear they stand behind the *American Flag*, but many are more than willing to wave the *White Flag*. For I too am upset about the Iraqi situation, though I also believe we have to find reasonable solutions that allow our soldiers to come home with their dignity-for many soldiers have given all and if America folds the tent; it would dishonor their sacrifices and doesn't say much for us. And even though I am visually impaired and I don't approve of violence, I will bear arms and fight for "our lady" (America) before I allow the liberal cowards to surrender her to China and Russia. Maybe we should reconsider deporting illegal immigrants and consider deporting liberals without a spine.

For years China and Russia have been sending "software spies" to America to figure out how to disable our defense systems. However, the real world is not a video game for there are real problems and real dangers. Therefore, it is imperative that we seek peaceful international solutions while maintaining our "watch" for America is last *Shepard* guarding the flock from the *Wolf Pack* of Russia and China. And I believe World War III is inevitable if the world community doesn't start investing in space exploration, if we don't begin to address global warming with real solutions, if we don't reverse the over-population growths of many nations especially in China, India, and Africa, if the international community doesn't agree to nuclear disarmament, if we don't kick our addiction to oil, and if America continues to move away from God and toward the secular progressive ideology of liberals that emphasizes "self-importance" and "self-indulgence" while disregarding morals, ethics, and values. So I am saying "Humanity must come first and the needs of our world communities are more important than the selfish desires of an individual." And changing our direction is the key to changing our destination otherwise we are complicit in the disasters that befall America and the rest of the world. For I actually believe the 2008 Congressional and Presidential Election is the most important event in American history since our Declaration of Independence in 1776. But if voters submit to emotional choices based on popularity and discount the experience needed to meet our challenges; then *Middle America* might finally reach its boiling point-for there comes a time when all decent men and women who have been pushed too far answer the call and those responsible will be held accountable.

Unfortunately the Stock Market collapse, the media's bias for Barack Obama, John McCain's mistakes, and angry voters maybe remembered as the beginning of America's downfall. When the unemployment rate continually rises every day the stock market should be on a steady daily decline as well. Therefore I am very suspicious of the gains during late March of 2009 especially when I continue to see a great number of stores in large malls and local shopping centers closing and I am reasonably sure it is more than just short trading (betting on a corporation's success or failure). But the primary reasons why con-artists like Bernie Madoff find success are a lot of people rarely learn from their mistakes, often refuse to believe they are gullible and naïve, or sometimes material greed blinds their judgment. And when the Commercial Restate Market is in a serious flux why isn't this crisis a national story?

Moreover, the numbers projected by President Obama's Administration just don't add up. First, AIG has received close to $200 billion that the American taxpayers will never recover. Secondly, the Wall Street Bailout in October (2008) that then Senator Obama supported was over $800 billion (over $100 billion in pork and $700 billion in TARP One) which I doubt we (taxpayers) will ever fully recover especially when we add the $400 billion in interests. Next we had an $800 billion Stimulus Package with billions wasted in pet-democratic projects and a $400 billion Omnibus Bill with over 8500 earmarks for both parties. And the Obama Administration is planning to buy $1 trillion in toxic assets from irresponsible lenders or the same institutions responsible for the Stock Market Crash last fall. Well that is great news for these unapologetic banks and mortgage corporations, but bad news for the American taxpayers and the ninety-four percent (94%) of responsible homebuyers.

But let's not forget President Obama's Budget Proposal for 2010 of $3.6 trillion that will increase each year of Obama's Presidency with a shortfall (deficit) of around $1.8 trillion plus a deficit in 2009 of around $1.2 trillion. And we must also add the costs of two military operations (Afghanistan and Iraq) for 2009-10 of at least $400 billion. Now factor in another $600 billion per year for increases in healthcare costs and we end up with a $7.8 trillion deficit before interests in President Obama's first two years. If we borrow the money add one-third of the total ($2.6 trillion) and our National Debt is doubled by the end of 2010.

And if the treasury continues to print more money because China will not or can't afford to back anymore of our "*eight trillion dollar extravaganza*" the inflation rate will far exceed the twenty percent (20%) projections of the most conservative economists. Furthermore, the United States GDP cannot grow at a 2.6% rate (President Obama's projections) when record numbers of small and large businesses are closing and unemployment is rising every month with no end in sight. Based on the facts our GDP will decrease from 2.2% to less than 2% which is a bad sign for our economy. But the insanity doesn't stop here for there are more wasteful spending bills (a Second Stimulus Package, TARP Two, the UN, more Corporate Bailouts especially companies with Unions that contributed tens of millions of dollars to Obama's campaign, increases in Education without any accountability, Infrastructure projects that are generally awarded to the supporters of the Democratic Party, and all the pork barrel projects and earmarks that both Democrats and Republicans can add in to every bill) of a few trillion more in the Democratically controlled Congressional pipeline. So I ask "How can any member of Congress look their constituents in the face without shame?"

If President Obama continues down this path of unprincipled, unchecked, and out-of-control spending, Americans will soon wish they could change their votes for John McCain. For the path that President Obama has chosen will lead to Governmental Bankruptcy and Economic Collapse. And President Obama's plan of reducing our missal defenses while China and Russia continue to build up their military forces and missal capacities borders on treason. But don't expect the Media to inform the American Public of the facts because they have vowed to go down with the ship.

And I am weary of liberals, democrats, and their media pundits accusing realists (pragmatists), moderates, conservatives, independents, and republicans of scare-tactics because we disagree with their out-of-control spending during a national economic crisis. Often they reference racism, bigotry, anti-Semitism, or McCarthyism against anyone who disagrees. Or their media cohorts besmirch, defame, or attack individuals like Sarah Palin who dare challenge their *Democratic Establishment* with lies, innuendoes, or misleading propaganda. Not even a fool would propose increases in spending during an economic downturn. But President Obama's Administration is full of fools and corrupt appointees. Why does the mainstream media refuse to challenge President Obama's incompetent and corrupt partisan cabinet appointments? Nowhere is it written or implied in the *1st Amendment* (Free Speech) of our *US Constitution* that any media representative has the right to endanger America's sovereignty, but treason is punishable by death.

The Presidential Election of 2008

First and foremost, I know the Republicans and the Democrats do not represent *Middle America.* And the popular trend now being enforced by the *Thought Police* in the media is to "reject" or "renounce" anyone who doesn't follow their politically correct nonsense especially criticism of religious organizations. I got news for the *Republican Party* and the *Democratic Party*; I rejected and renounced them both many years ago. It is true I am registered as a Republican, but I am a moderately conservative independent. Therefore, I say what I believe and I stand by what I say and if a Presidential Candidate disapproves of my honestly; so what. And the media's (a branch of the *thought police*) policing religious, racial, and gender etiquette is unequivocal hypocrisy, so why would any candidate submit to their "rules of engagement"? Here's a suggestion; a candidate could say "People have a constitutional right to their opinions even though I sometimes disagree with their opinions."

It is foolish to think either party represents the majority. And though I am dissatisfied with both parties, I voted for John McCain because he has been *battletested.* Moreover, from my point of view, the goodness of a person is more important than the disagreements I have with that person. For to change Washington, we need a new inclusive *Moderate Party* and a genuine *Conservative Party* that represent their constituents while soliciting small campaign contributions from individuals and small businesses to stop the financial influence in Washington. And I have no delusions that John McCain can fix all the problems in America because the Democrats and Republicans in Congress are not of the people, nor do they represent the people. But I am reasonably sure Barack Obama can't handle the difficult challenges "because words without substance are just words", "rhetoric of hope and change doesn't happen without real solutions", and "making promises that are popular is politics as usual" which Bill and Hillary Clinton have been trying adamantly to point out.

How are we going to pay for Barack Hussein Obama's "trillion dollar promises"? Maybe he should consider changing his middle name to

Insane because these *Democratic Government Programs* are going to be paid for by raising taxes on the middle class and cutting the military's defense budget. Rich people don't pay taxes; they pay their accountants. In 2007, Barack sponsored over $90 million and Hillary sponsored over $300 million in earmarks. On the other hand, John McCain has refused to sponsor earmarks for over twenty years. Most of these earmarks go directly to campaign contributors. Are we really this stupid? It shows his inexperience and lack of understanding both domestic and foreign policy. His "promises of hope" should be change to "false promises for votes". And how can he portray himself as an anti-establishment candidate when the *wealthiest most influential Aristocrats* and the *Hollywood's elite* are supporting him? Truly, the greatest hustle since the *Trojan Horse.* And Obama's record is as far to the left of fiscal conservativeness as any liberal dare go. But lawyers are very skilled in deception.

Most white males, especially in the South, a small percentage of blacks, Hispanics, Asians, and some white females realized during the late 1970's that the Democratic Party no longer represented their values, but many white females and a few in other minorities in 2008 are beginning to understand the hypocrisy of the Democratic Party and their media surrogates. Nonetheless, if they stay in this abusive relationship; the domestic and foreign disasters that are going to rain down on America over the next several years if voters are persuaded by illegitimate hype will burden their souls forever. For any fair-minded person would put the best interests of America before their own self-interests and if you don't recognize that every candidate in both parties except for Barack Obama has been held to a higher standard of political and personal scrutiny by an irresponsible media that is endorsing the least qualified candidate (Obama), then you are not paying attention.

Furthermore, Dr. King, Gandhi and Jesus were men of peace. And Dr. King was a disciple of God, a civil rights leader, and an inspirational speaker with substance. Barack Obama is an eloquent speaker that lacks substance, experience, or any significant achievements as a member of Congress. He served eight years in the Illinois State Legislature and four years in Congress (two of these years were spent running for President). Comparing Obama to JFK or RFK, who both had far more experience and had accomplished much more during their political service, is disgraceful. Thus, the comparison is a deceitful attempt by a less than credible media to persuade moderate and independent voters to back their fictional candidate.

Even though I am disappointed with both parties, the main reason I supported John McCain is because he has always put America's interests first and he has served her with pride and humility. But while Senator McCain like most Americans would prefer a civil debate, the media surrogates of the Democratic Party will dug his grave and buried him in it. And if people don't believe then I suggest you ask Bob Dole (Republican Presidential nominee in 1996). Our character assassins (liberal media) defamed the former Senator by framing him as "the senile old rich white guy". That is why I believed Secretary of State Dr. Condoleezza Rice would have been the best choice for Vice-president. She would have brought credibility and character that no other potential choice could while neutralizing the media's vicious racial and gender attacks. And the truth is we are all individually flawed and we have all made mistakes along the way for there are no perfect candidates, but there was one honorable and experienced candidate for President in 2008 and that person is Senator John McCain.

Here's the *Hustle*. Drug corporations, oil corporations, software corporations, and most large American and foreign (operating in the US) corporations have tens of thousands of employees. Our larger unions some of which are still tied to *Organized Crime* also have millions of members as well. These corporate employees and union members give smaller donations in increments over a period of time. Since each individual can contribute up to twenty-three hundred dollars ($2300) annually, he or she can contribute smaller donations throughout the year. Now the candidate claims transparency and brags of not taking donations from those who have run Washington for the last one-hundred and seventy years. But if one-hundred thousand employees contribute just five-hundred dollars ($500) each that adds up to fifty-million dollars. And if a million union members each give one-hundred dollars ($100) that is another one-hundred million added to the till.

Truthfully this underhanded methodology circumvents campaign finance reform. And the corporations and unions can contribute hundreds of millions in this manner to maintain their status in Washington while their candidate (Obama) swears he is against them. The majority of these campaign contributions are then used for advertising blitzes throughout the United States in an effort to influence voters by bombarding us with three continuous messages; "change", "hope", and "yes we can". At the same time, some of America's wealthiest families who are financially vested in the largest media corporate conglomerates in America use their media surrogates to endorse their candidate while attacking his opponent with innuendos and unsubstantiated accusations. Generally corporate donations are given to both parties in an attempt to hedge their bets, but the Democrats are in bed with *Organized Crime*, the vast majority of the *Media*, *Hollywood*, *Unions*, and the *Wealthiest Families* and *Individuals* in America. While the Republicans bath in *Oil*, break bread with

Gun Runners, and solicit *Capitalist Prostitutes* while living on *Wall Street.*

Therefore, it is true that deception is a very useful tool in political campaigns. And Barack Obama has mastered the "art of deception". So I understand why Hillary was upset because she was more qualified. But in the Democratic Party, *Race* trumps *Gender* and *Preference* has replaced *Merit.* Nevertheless, those who choose to swim in shark infested waters will eventually be shredded by these same sharks for that is what sharks do. I actually felt sorry for Hillary, but these same arrogant assholes attacked Sarah Palin in the same manner and these Obama flunkies also besmirched John Sidney McCain one of America's finest.

Many in the media floated the idea that "It is so wonderful to have a woman and African American competing for the Democratic nomination. If Hillary wasn't so polarizing and Barack was actually qualified this concept would have made sense. For I believed when Hillary ran for the Senate (NY) in 2000; she would run for the Presidency in 2008. And that is why I have often said the Clinton marriage is a political union. On the other hand, besides not being qualified, Barack Obama and his wife belonged to a black segregated Church for 20 years that preached *Black Liberation Theology* an ideology founded in racism and hate. Dr. King fought against segregation and racism. Therefore, segregated racist Churches do not represent God or what Dr. King stood for. But if a white male candidate belonged to a segregated Church with a racist agenda, he would be crucified in the media every day. And Senator Obama's candidacy was not held to any reasonable standards.

Thus it is not so wonderful, but it is damn right shameful.

Since the Democrats have placed more importance on promoting minority candidates while rejecting the quality and merit of a candidate; then Ralph Nader would have been a more logical choice for liberal voters. I have tremendous respect for Dr. Nader. Moreover, if Dr. Condoleezza Rice were on the ballot, I would have voted for her not because of her race or gender, but because she was qualified and I have no doubts about her "content of character" which Dr. Martin Luther King Jr. hoped an integrated nation would one day have the courage to do. Thus for me, the merit of the candidate is more important than the minority status of the candidate.

Some are going to say I have been unfair to President Obama, but I will gladly debate them anytime and anywhere. And I have been more than fair because I have been very critical of both the Republican and the Democratic Parties. The truth is if any white male or female of any race ran for the Presidency of the United States on Barack Obama's resume they would be ridiculed by the public, mocked by members of both parties, and persecuted by the *American Press Core.* Actually, I could have written an entire book on *How Obama Mania Conned America.* It is time Americans started examining the facts and stopped drinking *the kool-aid of deceptive persuasion.* Moreover, genuine movements or causes are led by credible selfless leaders who put aside personal agendas and personal ambitions for the good of our country. Barack Obama, as of the spring of 08 was the only Presidential Candidate that had not been held to any reasonable standards or practical qualifications that should have been required for the Oval Office and if that represents "change" then I guess I will abstain.

It has become fashionable to ridicule President George Walker Bush. And truthfully I have been very critical as well. But though I disagree with his view that Iraq is central to future peace in the Middle East, I respect him for standing by his beliefs even though it is an unpopular stance. Truthfully, he has not been given enough credit for keeping America safe since 9/11 and that indicates to me the bias of a disingenuous media that detests conservative white men. Didn't George W. Bush and Barack H. Obama both graduate from Harvard, so how are they different since they are both *Harvard Men*? Maybe an amendment to our Constitution that excludes Ivy League graduates from becoming President is something we should consider. Nonetheless, how history defines George Walker Bush doesn't' matter. For Bush's successor, President Obama has inherited domestic and foreign challenges that could ruin the United States of America if common sense is replaced by popular rhetoric and far left agendas.

And honestly the reason why I did not vote for Hillary has nothing to do with her intelligence. Truthfully she is bright, experienced, and compassionate in her beliefs, but I believe Al Gore would have been the best qualified Democratic candidate. However, the disrespectful treatment by the *Obama Networks* (NBC and CNN) and the unprincipled behaviors of many in the *Democratic Party* was uncalled for and very upsetting too me. Maybe when women stepped into the voting booth in November of 08; they should have asked "Who really represents the voice of women?" Hopefully in the near future there will be an inclusive *Moderate Party* that represents the voices of the middle class, but there was a moderate choice and John Sidney McCain has always been supportive and respectful of women.

Truthfully I don't dislike Hillary or Barack, but that doesn't change the questions of credibility and merit. And personally, I believe former Governor Mike Huckabee (R) is a decent man of faith, but the vast majority of the media loves to lynch or burn Christians at the stake. Furthermore, anyone who really believes in the Almighty and at least tries to live right would never support the Democratic Party Agenda. But the Republican Party Agenda isn't anything to boast about either. All that remains is the character and integrity of the candidate. Therefore, when you are looking down the "barrel of hard times", I prefer sound judgment that comes from years of experience and John McCain personified wisdom and courage under fire.

Now that the election is over, even though my candidate lost I have had time to reflect on the outcome. And I will admit the idea of electing a minority candidate is a "grand" concept for America, but the future will determine whether our idealism trumpeted our pragmatism. For as I have continually said "There are consequences for our choices".

Furthermore, there are four reasons why Senator McCain lost in November:

(1) Senator John McCain failed to recognize he had two political opponents: Barack Obama and the Mainstream Media.
(2) The choice of Sarah Palin was not the problem; it was the handling of Governor Palin by McCain's campaign advisors.
(3) McCain's support for the Wall Street Bailout was the most critical error of judgment in his entire political career.
(4) Barack Obama out spent John McCain over 7 to 1 ($600 Million to $84 Million) in political advertisements.

Thus to say the fix was in is an understatement for the 2008 Presidential Election was manipulated by the "Powers that Be". And if the 2nd Great Depression cometh then it is our right and duty as Free Men and Women to hold the Democratic Party and any Republicans involved, members of the Media, the Wealthy Elite, Barack Obama's staff, and President Obama himself accountable for no where is it written in the United States Constitution that a select few have the right to alter or subjugate the outcome of any election.

Therefore I find myself in a state of confliction; on one hand I would really like for President Obama to succeed because he represents the hopes and aspirations of all minorities including myself, but on the other hand I despise the political corruption and underhandedness that was used to ensure his victory. If political elections in America are now determined by a wealthy few who can use their propaganda machine (the media) to influence unjustifiable outcomes eventually public outrage will turned into organized violence. And the approaching Depression (2nd Great Depression) will have serious global ramifications that will be the catalyst for America's 2nd Civil War.

President Obama has an opportunity that few men or women will ever have especially minorities. But from what I have seen in the early stages of President Obama's Administration, his actions don't reflect the change or transparency he promised so I am very skeptical. And adding $5 Trillion to our national debt in the President's first year in office will accelerate our economic collapse. Now is not the time to panic, now is the time to lead for if President Obama keeps on shoveling the same old manure eventually the American people will complain about the stench.

Thus the duality remains. As most Americans are, I am pulling for President Obama. But the facts that Barack Obama has almost no history of bipartisanship, his voting record and ideology are far to the left of center, and he rarely challenges his own party's leadership (Democrats) as again demonstrated in the monstrosity piece of legislation (1100 pages that no one read before voting on it) labeled as a Stimulus Package. At the same time, the majority of the media refuses to ask President Obama any tough questions or follow up on his vague answers just as they did over 18 months leading up to the Presidential Election and many of the cabinet appointees have considerable baggage that most pundits in the media have decided not to disclose to the American public. Moreover President Obama's inexperience is starting to show with his misunderstanding of how to fix our economy and his misinterpretation of the electoral outcome in November.

On President Obama's first 100 days in office, I graded him with an F- which is a fair analysis based on the facts. But naturally a biased media failed to examine his corrupt partisan appointees in his cabinet, refused to acknowledge his apologetic European and Middle Eastern tour accomplished nothing though it confirmed his weak leadership to Russia and China while guaranteeing Israel stands alone, and unequivocally defended President Obama's massive increases in our national debt and continued bailouts. If there is no longer an unbiased media, then these jackals have no rights under the 1st Amendment (Freedom of Speech) for they have betrayed the public's trust.

It is not enough to look and sound Presidential for eventually a President must formulate policies that actually work. Truthfully we are all in this together, but those leaders who make poor judgments must eventually face the "Reaper" for the "on the job training" or "learning curb" rhetoric is unacceptable. And while I wish President Obama the best of luck my internal extinct say we are in grave trouble because President Obama and his inner circle of social elitists seemed to be paralyzed by America's challenges. However, their arrogance discounts people like me because we don't exist in their world and how could anyone not of their class know more than they, but eventually "*Chicken Little*" will find himself in the fryer because no one will believe anything he says no matter how elegant it sounds. Therefore, I can only hope that President Obama will began to listen to the voices of reason and think outside the "Washington Political Box" otherwise he will be historical defined as the worst President in American History since Hoover.

What Americans must be aware of is that if the Dow goes from 8000 (eight thousand) in April of 2009 to 10000 (ten thousand) by the end of 2010, they did not gain twenty-five percent (25%) on their portfolios as politicians will triumphantly proclaim. Instead, investors (especially 401K plans) will actually lose seventy-five percent (75%) because the NPV (Net Present Value) of the dollar will decrease one-hundred percent (100%). And this rapid decline in the dollar is a direct result of President Obama and the Democratically Controlled House and Senate doubling our National Debt to around $22 trillion in just two years. Moreover, the Dow would have to reach 16000 (sixteen thousand) for investors to break even because of the massive inflation caused by the Democratic Party's lack of fiscal restraint. Literally the Democratic Party is bankrupting America with the assistance of the American Press for they have decided what President Obama represents is more important than the truth. Therefore Democrats, their media pundits, and liberal judges are trying desperately to repeal the 2nd Amendment (Right to Bare Arms) for they fear a national revolt by angry citizens.

Cutting $200 billion out of a $3.6 trillion dollar budget for 2010 is insignificant. Even if President Obama's and the Democrats over-spending eventually brought the American economy out of a deep recession the question should be "at what cost". For the truth is the mainstream media has deliberately ignored President Obama's lack of fiscal restraint and by doing so has insured massive inflation, higher taxes, and enormous debt. At the same time the dollar is devalued, everyone's taxes will increase dramatically no matter which political party controls Congress. Thus President Barack Obama and the Democratic Party with the aid of over eighty percent (80%) of the American Press have enslaved at least ten generations of future taxpayers while at the same time these fools have endangered our national security and our sovereignty.

Let us not forget President James Buchanan laid the track for the "*Civil War*", President Woodrow Wilson's *Treaty of Versailles* planted the seeds for "*World War II*", and President Obama's increases in our national debt and cuts in our military's budget are setting the stage for "*Nuclear Armageddon*". Thus, I can only hope that President Obama shifts directions, stops the out-of-control spending, overhauls his administration, and governs more pragmatically in regards to domestic and foreign policies because that is the only change I can believe in. For *We the People of these United States of One America* have the power to stop the madness and the *Founding Fathers* guaranteed us the right to do so.

17

Race

"There are racists in all races and prejudices exist in all men and women"

Where should I start? Victimology, racism, woe is me, just shut up. Black people and white women think they are the only groups in America that have suffered unfairly. You want to know about discrimination, the blind and visually impaired community, have an eighty percent (80%) unemployment rate along with American Indians. Of the twenty percent (20%) working blind and visually impaired, over fifty percent (50%) are underemployed. Having to depend on a supplemental income most of one's life because we can't even get an interview for a decent job is not so wonderful. Hell, the entire disability community has close to a seventy percent (70%) unemployment rate. Do you think that we don't want access to a better quality of life?

I am going to briefly summarize some historical facts. If young blacks would stay in school, they might learn more than the fictional history often taught by lazy teachers or some civic leaders with a racist agenda. Too many young blacks, especially males, are dropping out of school to chase unattainable dreams. Unfortunately a lot of self anointed *Black Leaders* lack the courage or don't have the intestinal fortitude to tell the black youths this is a path of failure. "*Your education is the most important asset you ever earn in life other than your salvation. It is more important than any amount of money you make or possessions you obtain.*" I too, found this out the hard way. When leaders in the *Black Community* don't preach the importance of education, they are doing the community a disservice. And saying what is popular instead of what needs to be said is a selfish act that benefits no one.

The truth is not always taught in school, sometimes one has to do his or her homework. Always remember, history is written by those in power. Native Americans, Mexican Americans, Chinese Americans, Japanese Americans, Cuban Americans, Irish Americans, German

Americans, Italian Americans, People with Disabilities, Women, Gays, Jews, and yes African Americans have all dealt with injustice in America. It would be difficult to name a group that hasn't suffered. Let's go one step further. Subcategories such as height, weight, dress, physically appearance, age, and education just to name a few. How many dwarfs work with you? Do you think employers are not turned off by obesity? Have you ever seen someone dressed like a hip hop star working in your local bank and if you did, would you be comfortable with it? How many ugly secretaries have you seen in local area businesses unless it is the boss's wife? How many short FBI agents or local detectives have you witnessed? What do you think the percentage of workers, without a high school education, is in management of major companies? Would you want someone without a college education managing your business? Why do you think some businesses will not hire older Americans with education and work experience? What about corporations that layoff experienced workers and then hire foreigners on government issued *Visas* (H-1B) for salaries far below the position's pay grade? And take a good look at the majority of *American Corporations* that are constantly merging or reorganizing as a way of cheating loyal employees out of their retirement pensions? You see, to be an American, for the majority of us, is to face adversity and strive to rise above it.

"Oh but we were slaves and we deserve our 40 acres and a mule that was promised"-let it go. For I and the vast majority of whites agree that slavery is one of America's saddest tragedies in our brief history. And many of the atrocities committed by our *Federal Government* are shameful and repulsive, but none of us can change what has happened. *Affirmative Action* is not going to fix anything. If blacks accept that the only way they can get ahead is through affirmative action and preference programs, then you are admitting inferiority. Thus, you are the *Uncle Toms* of selling out if you buy into this dependency rhetoric. Liberals are actually demeaning African Americans by suggesting you can't do it without their assistance. One of the best writers, I believe, on race and culture is Shelby Steele. He says "*I, too, am strained to defend racial quotas and any affirmative action that supersedes merit.*"

Every time a white person speaks out against affirmative action, he or she is labeled a racist. I am not a racist, but fairness can't be imposed it must be achieved through hard work that rewards an individual on the merit of his accomplishments. There are racists in all races, not just whites. Take a good like in that mirror because that is the person who is responsible for your success or failure. It takes courage to stand up and be counted and that has nothing to do with racism.

Do you know that slaves were sold by their own people? That's right. Many of your African ancestors were sold into slavery by other Africans. During the tribal wars of Africa, the losers were either killed or enslaved. This was not a new practice by any means. Throughout history the Egyptians, the Romans, the Grecians, the Chinese, the Babylonians, and so forth enslaved their conquered victims. White merchants didn't just sail up to the coast of Africa and yell "all aboard." They purchased many of the African slaves from ruling tribes and then resold them in slave markets throughout the world.

Another fact is that the Civil War was not fought over slavery. It started because the southern states seceded from the union. From the southern states point of view it was an issue of "state rights" that were guaranteed in the Constitution. However, Lincoln viewed it differently. He felt it was a rebellion; an "act of war". In the election of 1860, Republican candidate Abraham Lincoln won with less than forty percent (40%) of the popular vote. This was attributed to a split in the Democratic Party which allowed Lincoln the victory as a Republican. It happened again in 1912 when the Republican Party split allowed Woodrow Wilson to steal the election. Again, in 1992, Ross Perot's Presidential candidacy assisted Bill Clinton in his Presidential victory.

President elect Lincoln received close too 60% of the electoral votes because Northern Democrats sided with the Republicans and the Southern Democrats were furious. So they decided to form their own government called the *Confederacy*, where they elected Jefferson Davis as their President. If the southern states had not seceded from the union there would not have been a Civil War or if the Southern Democrats had supported Stephen Douglas (the Northern Democratic nominee) then Abraham Lincoln would not have become President. Another fact, Lincoln wasn't the Republican Party's first choice, William Seward was but he was suspected of backing abolition violence. And *The Emancipation Proclamation* was declared by President Lincoln 17 months after the attack of Fort Sumter. Also, the decree was intended to weaken the South's economy thereby weakening its army. And Lincoln actually stole the idea from one of his own Generals. The Confederates were trying to fight two wars, the Northern Army and the Rebellion in the south. And Amendment XIII which abolished slavery in the United States was ratified on the 6th of December 1865. But, as often happens, legends are more popular than the actual truth.

General William Sherman's army raped women, murdered women and children, robbed and pillaged, burned cities to the ground, and this psychopathic son of a bitch was considered a hero. In today's world, this sick bastard would be on trial for war crimes along with Grant. After the Civil War, white men were stripped of their dignity. Southerners who served in the Confederacy could not vote or run for public office. All their lands and businesses were stolen by *Carpetbaggers.* Most local, state, and federal elected officials were either white male Carpetbaggers or black males. The majority, of the newly elected blacks, were illiterate. And they were often taken advantage of by their white male colleagues. While it is true that many newly elected black politicians may have been more concerned with improving their quality of life, they voted with the corrupt northern politicians and thieving *Carpetbaggers* for unethical legislation which focused on *revenge* and *reparations.* By dehumanizing veterans of the Confederacy, an environment of hatred was created for groups like the *Klu Klutz Klan* to spawn. This same unethical abuse of power occurred at the *Treaty of Versailles,* where Germany was raped and pillaged. Again an environment of hatred was created by stripping people of their dignity. Thus, the monster Hitler emerges as the leader of the *Nazi Party.* Everyone knows of the atrocities committed against the Jews, but many don't know that this sick monster killed all the men, women and children with disabilities first. Quite often the fact that Hitler murdered people with disabilities is left out of the historical discussions.

What blacks and other oppressed groups should be working toward is equal access which can be achieved through social awareness, not governmental intrusion. No, employer owes me a job because I am visually impaired, but I do expect equal access to opportunity based on merit. And the most qualified person should get the job. My idea of affirmative action is "If there are two candidates for a position of equal qualifications, then the minority candidate should be given greater consideration." When a company selects a less qualified minority candidate over a more qualified candidate, this is also discrimination. Every employee that is passed over for a promotion that is given to a less qualified minority employee should be in court filing a lawsuit against that company (exception to the rule). Even though I detest lawyers and I am feed up with the social trend of suing, it might require people standing up and saying "we have had enough of this nonsense" through the legal process. I might be in the minority, but I actually believe black people can achieve great things by depending upon themselves, not divisive tools such as affirmative action. If a black person buys into the liberal propaganda that opportunity can only be accomplished with preferential treatment, then he or she has already lost. An individual has to take the responsibility of preparing himself for an opportunity when the door opens.

As I grew older and learned more about Dr. Martin Luther King Jr., I have become a great admirer. He seemed to really care about all the poor and disenfranchised, it didn't seem to be limited to just race. Where many had failed, Dr. King was able to bring all oppressed groups together for a common cause. His non-violence philosophy took more courage than any mortal man had ever shown. Only Jesus's life was more impressive and he was the son of God. And Dr. King gave his life trying to build a better America.

Dr. King believed a man's character was more important than the color of his skin. Unfortunately, many of Dr. Martin Luther King Jr. followers sold out for government jobs and preferential treatment programs. Just another example of how the allure of wealth and power can tempt anyone. Many leaders such as Jessie Jackson and Al Sharpton are letting down the Black Community. Al Sharpton is nothing but another religious hustler, but I actually believe there was a time when Reverend Jessie Jackson was a decent human being that really cared about the Cause. Today he has lowered himself to blackmailing corporations for millions of dollars disguised as donations to the Rainbow Coalition. Though I too believe in boycotting corporations that act irresponsibly that doesn't mean compromising our integrity for monetary bribes. When Jessie is not blackmailing corporations, he is going into communities and racially dividing blacks against whites. It saddens me to see a recognized leader sellout. And I still want to believe Jessie can redeem himself, but Al Sharpton hasn't shown me that he gets it.

There are many great *Black Leaders* such as General Colin Powell and Secretary of State, Dr. Condoleezza Rice. Individuals like comedian Bill Cosby and English professor and author Shelby Steele are a few more positive role models. But Colin Powell's endorsement of Barack Obama appeared to be racially motivated and if so was a racist act. And besmirching Sarah Palin as the reason for not supporting John McCain is a cowardly excuse. Still there are many black executives in fortune 500 companies that the Black Community should be more aware of for these individuals and leaders are role models for any community. They exemplify what an individual can achieve through hard work and dedication. So why does the Black Community often not embrace credible Black Leaders? Many of the successful blacks are viewed as Uncle Toms or "losing there blackness" because they don't believe in government entitlement programs that have consumed the Black Community. If your pastor is preaching "Vote for the Democrats or Republicans" instead of the holy word, then he is no good. And if he is not serving God, then he is probably serving himself. A preacher's responsibilities are to explain the word, speak out against unrighteous behaviors (sins) of his members and community, and lead by example. For no credible minister can woe every woman in a skirt and then stand up and preach on adultery. When there is a "just cause", ministers should help organize peaceful movements that enlist people of all races. It is the responsibility of every community to stand together against any injustice, but we should always wait until the facts are in before we jump to conclusions because emotional responses without justification generally add to the conflict.

There are many problems in the Black Community. A seventy percent (70%) rate of children born out of wedlock is absolutely disgraceful. Many of these women are having multiple kids with different absentee fathers who have no intention of paying child support. If one makes a baby, then he is responsible for taking care of that child. All children need a positive male role model in the home or present somewhere in their lives. And gangbanging and selling drugs is not a positive role model-for there are only two outcomes for this behavior, death or prison. But many self-serving black leaders and some black college professors keep reiterating the same old fictional theme "slavery and whitey are responsible". Absolute bull-malarkey for each person is responsible for his or her actions. Yes FDR hooked America on government entitlement programs which Lyndon Johnson further expanded, but we must decrease our dependency on Big Brother and take responsibility for our own choices.

A liberal feminist friend, yes I actually have friends, once told me she didn't blame black youths for selling drugs. She said they can make more money in a day than most can in a month. My first reaction was "That is taking the easy way out. And life is difficult for the poor in every race, but I have the utmost respect for a man or woman who makes an honest living and absolutely no respect for a drug dealer who poison or pimps his own people." There was a time when Malcolm X and the Black Panthers would have never allowed these criminal activities to infiltrate their neighborhoods. I might not agree with their violent methods, but the results were more effective than any written laws.

In November of 2004, I was talking too, two friends after George Bush defeated John Kerry in the Presidential election and they were whining about the outcome. They both said "We liberals are Christians too." I replied, "But only the conservative Christians are going to heaven." Obviously, they were not amused. Truthfully though, Liberalism is in direct opposition of Christianity. One cannot believe in the Doctrine of Liberalism and at the same time be a Christian-for no one can serve two masters although many of us try too. This doesn't mean Republicans are Conservative Christians. Republicans just panhandle for the Christian Right's vote. Christianity is not present in either party. Religious Leaders of the Black Community are supposed to be leaders in the community. Well, it is time they became leaders instead of enablers. For they must stand up and shout from the pulpit "Put down your weapons and walk away from the gang lifestyle, stop using and selling drugs, cease all unlawful behaviors, stay in school, respect your elders, , be responsible for your sexual escapades, be a father to your children and a role model for other children, stop blaming whitey for your failures and rise above the stereotypical hype, love everyone, live every day as though it were your last, and if you are successful in your life give something back so that others can improve their quality of life-for the joy of giving is the greatest pleasure anyone will ever experience in this life.

Living from paycheck to paycheck where it just becomes a struggle to pay for food, housing, and some needed accessories is the modern form of slavery. It is tough, but not impossible to rise above one's Socio Economical Condition. It takes focus, effort, and hard work. And people first must understand that not everyone is going to be a millionaire-for "*The American Dream*" is a myth. However, the goal should be to improve one's quality of life for this is the "*attainable dream*". If a worker wants access to better opportunities, the worker must increase his or her training, experience, or education. You can believe this "No one is going to give you anything, you have to earn it."

Another fact, not everyone is cut out for or capable of going to college. Though, one should remember a plumber, electrician, mechanic, carpenter, welder, computer technician, medical technician, and so forth can make a quality living. There are hundreds of opportunities for high school graduates that don't go to college. The responsibility fails upon each one of us to identify our talents and work on enhancing these abilities for many of our career guidance counselors are just sociology majors (a soft degree) looking for a steady government job with decent benefits and a retirement package.

But I am not talking about football, basketball, baseball, singing or rapping, or some other impossible dream. One has to understand the chances of making it to the highest levels are almost impossible. For every one that succeeds, there are one million that failed. It is ok to chase your dreams, but not at the expense of your education. If one has nothing to fall back on, then the fall is quite tragic. First, one must have the talent. Next, one must have the dream. And finally, one must have the opportunity. Without all three elements in place, you are destined to fail.

I had the talent and I had the dream to be a professional wrestler, but the Wrestling Corporations, WCW and WWF (now called the WWE), did not give me the opportunity to realize my dream. I have friends, one who died a couple years ago (2003) that have the talent and the dream of being successful musicians. Some are more talented than many of today's successful musicians, but without the opportunity, they just like myself, are invisible.

And the entertainment industries along with the sea of unscrupulous agents make fortunes off of talented people. Yet for most, it is same old story over and over. A successful entertainer that made tens of millions of dollars is broke and using drugs. Constantly getting preferential treatment by a sympathetic judicial system only makes the situations worse.

That is part of the problem, no one has every told them "no." Many of these self-centered jerks have received hundreds of second chances and I find it hard to feel any compassion for them. Just because the Entertainment Industry exploits their ignorance doesn't mean they are not responsible for their actions. Unfortunately, too many youths idolize these pitiful examples as role models. If former stars had an education to fall back on, they probably would have invested some of their financial gains. Instead, they flush their livelihoods down the toilet on drugs, gambling, sleeping with every groupie in a dress or marrying these gold digging sluts. Sometimes they fall for investment scams and sometimes they revert back to the street life. But victims they are not, because anyone who has every opportunity imaginable and blows it doesn't deserve my sympathy. Today's falls from grace, by these arrogant jackasses, are the modern form of Shakespearian Tragedies. And I, like most intelligent human beings, have grown weary of the constant special treatment of these prima donnas.

But the *Entertainment Industry* is a controlling entity that runs its *Plantation* through slick marketing and in many cases unfair contracts. They will do anything to protect their commodities (entertainers) as long as they are profitable. This includes protecting criminals by twisting the law, using the media to spin the truth, and manipulating outcomes until their clients no longer serve their bottom lines. When billions of dollars are riding on their products (entertainers), the Entertainment Industry which includes amateur and professional sports can never be trusted to do the right thing. It always starts with "allegedly" and ends up with some insignificant penalty like probation or community service. One can not actively participate in a double homicide and receive one year probation. And naturally they all have miraculously found Jesus. But if our judicial system doesn't correct the current trends vigilante justice is going to spread like an unstoppable wildfire throughout America-for there comes a time when the people can no longer support the injustices and that time is near.

Clever marketing of alcohol and cigarettes is one way the wealthy elite exploit the disadvantaged for profit. Pushing products with higher contents of alcohol and carcinogens to the poorer communities is more than unethical it is inhumane. But these greedy capitalists also target the poor with products higher in sugars and fats as well. When we have very restrictive choices and are living from paycheck to paycheck; this is a form of *Organized Slavery.* Still as bad as it is in America, it is worse in a lot of other countries where *Globalization* has began. Imagine working 14 to18 hours a day, 7 days a week, for twenty (.20) to .fifty (.50) cents an hour. In many places young children are being used or sold into slavery by these Corrupt Industries which are largely owned by Western Corporations around the world.

At times we are so caught up in our own problems that we tend to forget about our other brothers and sisters throughout the world. Look at the American Corporate Conglomerates, they are moving American jobs (outsourcing) to cheaper foreign markets. Then these bastards bring the products back into the United States and sale them to the American people. But how can we address these important issues if we are racially divided?

The cost of living in the United States is approximately 3 times higher than our minimum wage. *Corporate Lobbyists* are in Washington making sure Congress doesn't change the minimum wage standards, or at least not enough to affect their quarterly profits. Thus, what we have is a more organized form of slavery in the world today. Most people can't get ahead, and it becomes a means of survival for our daily bread. *We live, we struggle, and then we die.* But the time has come for every community to rise up and say "Damn you greedy bastards, we have had enough." Maybe in the hereafter these capitalist pagans will feel God's wrath, but it is time the dishonest *Aristocrats* felt the people's wrath.

Resolutions

One resolution is to stop practicing segregation. Races and political oriented groups must work together to radically affect "real change". Great leaders like Dr. King fought so hard to end segregation, yet people preach integration and practice segregation. And the blind and visually impaired, the hearing impaired, Mexicans, Cubans, Christians, Muslims, Blacks, Jews, the Disabled, and Seniors are all guilty. Don't think for one second that I don't tell blind and visually impaired family members and friends that it is ok to socialize with others in our community, but at the same time we need to integrate into the real world with others who are different. For I became adamant with organizations, like ACB (American Council of the Blind) and NFB (National Federation of the Blind) that are supposed to advocate on issues concerning the blind, when I found them to be more social and less active. Though I understand it is only natural that we tend to levitate toward those like ourselves, however we must strive for inclusion and diversity which sometimes means stepping outside of our comfort zones.

What better way is there than to educate others about *Black Culture* than attending a black college or university? I do believe the majority of students should always remain black, but a forty-five percent (45%) enrollment of other races could go a long way in improving racial relations in America. Non-denominational Churches that encourage racial and religious diversity is something that appeals to me. Using Town Hall meetings and Forums to openly and respectfully discuss difference in races and cultures will benefit our communities so we can work together in a more trusting relationship-for segregation in Churches, Colleges, and Communities inhibits effective communication.

When the two segregated residential schools for the blind (Georgia Academy for the Blind) integrated partially in the late 1960's and fully in 1972, it was an eye opening experience. We roomed together, broke bread together three times a day, we played ball together (yes blind people play basketball, football, kickball, softball, bowling, volleyball, and so forth), participated in team sports together such as wrestling, swimming, and track & field, we got into trouble together, we studied together, we socialized together, and we did everything together that most families do; 7 days a week, almost 9 months a year. To this day, my schoolmates are more than friends, they are my family. Even though I am a strong inclusive education advocate and I believe these residential schools should be closed, I have always been thankful for the knowledge I gained and the experiences I was fortunate enough to have with my extended family. Everything wasn't always perfect, sometimes we argued and fought over silly stuff, but at the end of the day, we loved one another just like a family is supposed to do.

Many in Black Caucuses are the true *Uncle Toms* and Hispanic Caucuses are just as corrupt as the crooked ass White Politicians. For I thought I might one day enter politics so I could make a difference, but I remembered what Civil Rights Leader, Jose Williams, said about our current system. Every time a decent piece of legislation, that would have helped the poor, was on the floor, the dishonest white politicians convinced the black politicians to sell out. And Jose became so frustrated, he quit. Now, I know Jose Williams drank too much and he had other problems, but I believe he really cared about the less fortunate. And we all have problems, so there will be no stoning today. Jose Williams's character and heart are what count and that is why I admired him and some of the current self proclaimed Black Leaders could use some character for they damn sure seem to have forgotten where they came from. Though a politician's race doesn't matter for if he is a Democrat or Republican there is a high probability he or she sold out their communities a long time ago. But we can't change the corruption without a new inclusive and diverse political system where character matters most.

There has to be changes in leadership and policies if we are going to break the cycles of dependency. The more we depend on our self-serving bureaucratic system, the harder it becomes to break the chains of our masters. And we need real welfare to work programs, we need real prison reform, we need more prevention and intervention before problems escalate, we need stronger emphasis on academic standards for education and improvements in career orientation, we need higher wages, we need legitimate programs that assist people in home ownership, and all programs must be void of bureaucratic nonsense. Approving a mortgage of seven-hundred thousand dollars (700K) for someone whose gross income is thirty-eight thousand (38K) a year is more than unethical; it is criminal. These abuses in lending are directly responsible for our housing crisis. Community leaders must work together to protect the people from financial scams that ruin lives. And communities must also assist one another in ending their dependency on the *Evil Empire* that FDR created in 1933.

And Abraham Lincoln is not the great savior either. He was against the expansion of slavery which the majority of whites in the Midwest, West, North, and South supported. Less than one in four owned slaves in the South and though many disapproved of slavery the *Southern Agricultural Economy* had grown to depend upon the free labor even though most Southerners knew slavery was inhumane. But the blacks in the North were also exploited as cheat labor and many Northern Whites looked down upon them with hostile contempt. Lincoln said "The Negro was inferior to the White Man." And he also said "If the Southern States had not seceded there would have been no cause for war." For the truth is slavery would have eventually been abolished without the "Civil War" because it had become unacceptable throughout the civilized world, not just in America.

But black jurors can't acquit guilty black defendants and expect the White Community not to be upset. The acquittals of Marion Berry and O.J. Simpson defy any logic and these irresponsible acts make the Black Community look foolish while disrupting racial relations. But the white jurors in California seem to be incompetent or high on "celebrity crack" for many of their decisions undermine what little integrity is left in our judicial process. And in accordance with the large majority of Americans, I am against any amnesty legislation for illegal immigrants. Though I am not without compassion for I understand most are seeking to improve their quality of life, but bypassing established laws or passing legislation that goes against the majority's will is another deceptive way of dividing communities racially. And even though it is true America is a nation of immigrants except for Native Americans, it doesn't justify illegal immigration for our ancestors came here legally. It is also a myth that America needs cheap labor for these so-called jobs numbering around 2 million not 20 million. Thus, the illegal immigration in America puts a strain on our economy for it affects wages of American workers, it inhibits our public school systems ability to function properly, it impacts welfare and medicare programs negatively, about ten percent of these illegal immigrants are involved in criminal activities so it burdens our legal system, and it undermines national security, but no one in Congress will take a stand on illegal immigrations for Democrats see votes and Republicans see exploitable labor. Wouldn't it be more cost-effective if America invested in the infrastructure of Mexico so its people wouldn't have to migrate to America in search of a better life?

Angry Black Women are the most difficult people to deal with on the entire planet. But *selfish white women* run a close second. And these women are easy to identify for they are usually professing their *Christianity* or screaming *Sexual Harassment.* Yet they wonder why men would rather work with other men. And it has gotten to the point a man can't even speak to a woman on the job. Complimenting a woman on their clothing or appearance is not "sexual harassment" it is what gentlemen do. But these SUV driving, cellphone gabbing prima donnas think everyone is suppose to bow down and kiss their royal ass. Too much *Oprah* and *The View* could lead to unhealthy relationships for no man but a pussy will put up with the "extremely liberal feminists" whose mission is to emasculate every male on earth.

Though the Latino and Asian women seem to have a better understanding of men-for most good men do not want to dominate women. Men want to be loved by women. And men are not perfect and neither are women. Some cultures allow promiscuity while others view it as an unforgivable sin. There has to be open and honest dialogue about cultural differences before we can build our diverse village. But "gender preference" is a divisive tool used to pit men against women. For if hiring and promotions aren't based on merit then the end results do not represent equality. And "respect" is a two way street and it can't be enforced for it has to be earned.

However, if the poor in the Black Community, White Community, and Hispanic Community put more emphasis on a quality education we could drastically decrease the poverty levels in the United States and by doing so we could lessen our dependency on Big Brother who is the largest pimp and pusher in America. And Casinos can not fix the social inequalities of my Native American brothers either. For a united community must build bridges of cultural diversity and the only race that matters is the *Human Race.*

18

America's Sports Culture

"Admiration is earned respect, but Idolization is artificial worship"

America. Land of the free, where anyone can realize the "*American Dream*". Yeah right, maybe if the dream is to watch a baseball game, eat a hotdog, and then enjoy a slice of apple pie. Sports in America, has become big business. At the amateur level, there are corporations creeping at every turn. *McDonalds, Nike, Gatorade, Coca Cola, Pepsi, Reebok,* just to name a few of these leeches capitalizing on sporting events. They have corrupted the integrity of the game all in the name of the almighty dollar. Vince Lombardi was wrong when he said "Winning isn't everything, it is the only thing." For I say "Winning with integrity is more important than winning at any costs."

No matter how severe the violations are in college sports today, the NCAA generally hands out a few lost scholarships and a couple years probation, while still allowing these universities to participate in post-season play. No one has paid the piper since SMU (Southern Methodist University) received the death penalty in the mid 1980's. That's what happens when the NCAA partners with corporations; it's like allowing convicted criminals to sentence themselves. But the NCAA has become so corrupted, I am not even sure an act by Congress can fix this bureaucratic toilet.

American corporations and the television industry (especially ESPN) are running the NCAA sports programs. And the majority of the universities are breaking every rule they can get away with in recruiting and maintaining academic eligibility for athletes. Auburn, Georgia, Ohio State, Virginia Tech, Nebraska, Florida State, along with a number of other Universities emphasizes sports more than academics. Even the Christian Universities (Notre Dame) are cheating to compete. In God's name, will someone please tell me when cheating became an acceptable behavior?

I remember over 25 years ago when I was at a small college (Georgia Southwestern College now State University), how several basketball players were kept in easy classes just long enough to play out their eligibility. One particular, all conference, (NAIA) player was working as a janitor on the night shift in the P.E. department after his playing days were over. It left a lasting impression on me for I always felt this kind of exploitation was disgraceful. And we are not doing any young athlete a favor by cheating. For I have heard college coaches preach that "sermon" that it benefits these young athletes to experience college campus life while they are playing ball. No it does not. It benefits the coaches and Athletic Department.

If a student can't meet the academic standards that a university requires of all its non-scholarship students, then that athlete doesn't deserve special treatment (Georgia Tech). The fact that any University admits athletes who do not meet the same academic standards of the general student body is unconstitutional and discriminatory. Every student who was denied admission with better scores and academic achievements should file lawsuits against these institutions (exception to the rule). The academic fraud and covering up of the unlawful activities of star athletes, warrants independent oversight with the authority to hand out severe penalties and end the corrupt reign of the NCAA. For I have heard all the arguments and none have every convinced me that cheating is ok. Sure a lot of these kids would not even be in college if it wasn't for their athletic ability. But that is their own fault along with many of our lousy high school teachers, counselors, and coaches who do not put enough emphasis on academics. Any teacher or coach, that doesn't try to assist these young athletes in the understanding of how important education is to their future are performing a disservice to their young pupils. Every young athlete is responsible for putting as much time and effort as they do in improving their athletic skills, into their academic development. It is a shame and disgrace when an athlete graduates from college and can't even read. How far will these son-of-a-bitches go? Well, until we drop the hammer on these corrupt universities, they will continue their path of shame because of the pot of gold at the end of the rainbow.

Jane Kemp was right when she didn't allow Coach Vince Dooley and the rest of the University of Georgia Staff to intimidate her into passing a dumbass football player that didn't belong in college in the first place. Even though she won her lawsuit, she paid a heavy price for standing up against the corruption in college athletics. Former graduates of UGA (lawyers, journalists, and politicians) attacked Jane's personal life and tried to destroy her credibility. But all these bastards earned a one way ticket straight to hell.

The irony is most of these crooked ass coaches portray themselves as Christians. But Christians don't cheat and they don't burn *whistle blowers* at the stake. Lying hypocrites is all most of these coaches are and Jesus is a crutch to be used in case they decide to run for public office. One thing that really angered me was where were the feminists, when this woman was being crucified? For feminist are more than willing to protest the Augusta Masters but leave a courageous woman standing alone. Personally I could care less about those rich arrogant pricks in Augusta. But Jane Kemp is a *Hero* because she stood for something just look Rosa Parks. Sometimes heroes are ordinary people that have the courage to say "no". The truth is Dr. Adams and Vince Dooley should have both been fired along with Jim Herrick for his basketball follies. Many have even pushed for Saint Vince to run for Senator. Well he is not qualified to be a US Senator for he is a dumbass football coach with a degree in P.E. that ran a crooked athletic department at UGA.

It is not humorous that when Hershal Walker was recruited to Georgia, his family mysteriously moved from an outhouse to a very nice house without any visible financial means to make this leap. I want people to be able to own their own homes, but not this way. Approved loans for family members, cars for the athletes, coaching positions for the fathers, homes, and any other monetary benefit for the amateur athletes is supposed to be illegal, but the NCAA turns its head until someone is outed. Danny Manning's father was given a coaching position at Kansas. If Danny wasn't the top player in the nation would his dad have been hired by Kansas? Hell no. What about Reggie Bush's family living in a palace? Does anyone actually believe the USC coaching staff was unaware of what was going on?

Coaches caught on fast. They know if players are driving new flashy vehicles, it draws too much attention, so they assist some of these athletes in getting used cars. Many of the wealthy alumni of these universities give the players cash, help them acquire cars, and give them bogus jobs in the summer. Most of these athletes get paid for jobs in the summer that they never even show up for or they are given jobs they are unqualified for and receive ridiculous salaries. The section 8 housing scams by Virginia Tech and Nebraska is an underhanded way of paying college athletes. These Universities are breaking and bending every rule, and if an alumni member gets caught, naturally the university had no knowledge of what transpired. What messages are we sending our youth? Well we are saying that cheating is ok as long as you don't get caught, and don't worry about academics if you're a great athlete.

Do you think Ricky Williams started smoking marijuana after he entered the NFL? Do you think the Texas coaching staff was unaware of Ricky's drug use? As long as Ricky could carry the rock and score touchdowns, he could have used any drug he wanted too. Yes I smoked marijuana too when I was young and I drank too much as well. But there comes a time in every person's life when we have to grow up and put away foolish behaviors. It seems most coaches, family members, friends, teachers, religious leaders, and mentors have never told great athletes "no" this behavior is unacceptable. And most of us believe every man or woman desires a second chance, but amateur and professional athletes have received hundreds of second chances.

When Nebraska recruited Lawrence Philips and Colorado recruited Ray Carruth, both universities were well aware of their ties to gangs. They didn't care, just like the Rams and Panthers ignored their history. As long as they could help in winning football games, that is all that mattered. What 18 or 19 year old guy wouldn't sign up to play for a university (Colorado) that provided alcohol and women for them? How many criminals does Bobby Bowden have to recruit before he exceeds his limit? Well I guess as many as he can as long as Florida State stays competitive.

Robert Smith realized his grades were more important than football practice at Ohio State. Maurice Clarett did not understand the game he was involved in. He outed some of the corruption going on at Ohio State and he was vilified. Just because he is not the brightest athlete in the world, doesn't mean he wasn't telling the truth. Former players at Alabama exposed their illegal recruiting tactics and the NCAA begrudgingly intervened because of outside pressure. Jose Canseco is a moron, but he was telling the truth about the usage of steroids and HGH (Human Growth Hormone) in baseball. Every time someone exposes the corruption in college athletics, instead of addressing the illegal activities, these universities, with the aid of former graduates that are lawyers, judges, journalists, and politicians attack the person who told the truth. No one can stand up to their character assassinations because we are all imperfect. Watered down degrees and corruption in athletics is ruining American Institutions that are supposed to represent honor and integrity at the highest academic levels.

Charles Barkley, Brent Fullwood, and many of Auburn's ex-athletes have never attended a class. Charles was a junior in Communications and he probably could not tell you what a classroom, at Auburn, looked liked. Hell he probably couldn't even name one professor at Auburn. The corruption isn't funny, it is ridiculously tragic. It is a poor reflection of an American system out of control and the NCAA is the *Keystone Cops* allowing the violators to run amok.

I loved Nolan Richardson's coaching style, but not graduating players is inexcusable. No winning basketball games is not a coach's only responsibility; you were supposed to be a leader of young men and you let them down when you didn't emphasize the importance of academics. I would like to see Coach Richardson get another chance at a large University as long as his recruits meet the admission standards and most of them graduate with a legitimate degree, not a degree in basket weaving. Playing the race card seems to be a disgusting trend today, but people make mistakes. And I believe Nolan Richardson is a great coach and he deserves an opportunity to redeem his legacy.

John Thompson is another great coach. Though he may think most white people hated him he is wrong. His teams played great defense and hustled for forty minutes and I loved his coaching philosophy. However, I disagree with his intervention with Allen Iverson. A.I. was a thug and a criminal in high school, and his preferential treatment received from a sympathetic judicial system was unjustifiable. And Randy Moss received similar special treatment by the same corrupted judicial system and it was also indefensible. For John Thompson didn't save Allen Iverson he became an enabler for AI's problems. Thus, John Thompson is responsible for his own demise, but not to worry for a very liberal media always provides an analyst opportunity for an ex-player or coach even when most lack the necessary qualifications.

And I lost some of my respect for Coach Mike Krzyzewski at Duke when I found his players were graduating with soft degrees in Sociology, Philosophy, and Religious Studies which are about one step above basket weaving or finger painting. His players are getting preferential treatment such as freshman and sophomore players registering before Duke's juniors and seniors (regular students), taking the easiest professors, getting to write papers instead of taking tests that their classmates have to take, and receiving favoritism from professors who are Duke University basketball fans. Who can even verify these jocks even wrote their own papers? A legitimate Academic Institution would never allow such corruption. Coach K has nothing to be proud of and he is as dishonest as a lot of his colleagues. Just because some former graduates and players at Duke University appear on ESPN and try to defend the indefensible doesn't make it right. What in God's name do you think these losers are going to say? Have you ever seen any of these dumbasses not making excuses? Is Mike Krzyzewski a good coach? If the measurement is in wins and losses, then the answer is yes. However, if the measurement is integrity, then the answer becomes more complicated. For I do believe Coach K is a decent person, but I can not respect cheating or what some might refer to as bending the rules.

Another coaching situation involves Coach John Chaney (recently retired) at Temple. I am not talking about his record. As far as I know, John ran a clean program and he graduated his players. It was not right to send in a thug to hurt another team's player because he got upset with bad officiating, but we all make mistakes in the heat of a moment. And I respect his record and I loved his idea of practicing early in the morning, but what he said to Coach John Calipari went beyond professionalism. However, it was an excusable mistake when he said "I'll kill you" during an after game press conference. But what I am really talking about is a double standard. If a white coach had said something close to this statement, he or she would have been fired by the university and ostracized by a liberal sports media. It would have been headlined in every news outlet for months. There would have been a call for the white coach's head on a platter. Do I think John Chaney should have been fired? No, we are all venerable when we are angry and upset and sometimes we lash out without thinking. But when the media says it is impartial, it generally depends on who said or did what.

Dan Issel, former coach of the Denver Nuggets is just another example of the bias in the media (double standard). He responded to a drunken obnoxious fan that probably should have been thrown out of the arena before the confrontation, in a moment of angry. That could have easily been any one of us. What he said was not right, but is understandable. However, Issel lost his job because the Hispanic Community protested and a disingenuous media fanned the flames of the fire. It seems the only race that can be offended without recourse is the White Community.

Let's explore the *Double Standard* even further. Russ Limbaugh was hired by ESPN to boost their NFL ratings. When he said the sports media was liberally biased, he was telling the truth. Then Russ implied that sports mediums like ESPN were trying to force the next great black quarterback down the America's throat. How he articulated his point wasn't politically correct but some of his assertions were true. And the poster child of their bias was Michael Vick. For Warren Moon slay the dragon of ignorance many lunar eclipses ago. And I don't care what color the quarterback is on the field, he could be green and that would not matter. But I critique quarterbacks on their performances and I don't need the media to constantly remind me that the quarterback is African American; my vision is not that bad. But the media continually makes references to race through code words and phrases such as instinct (black) verses intelligence (white) or athletic (black) verses uncoordinated (white). And how many times has the media referred to a white boxer as "the next great white hope" which is a prejudice remark. In 2006, Bryant Gumbel of HBO's REAL SPORTS compared the Republican Party (GOP) to a KKK rally. Personally I don't care for either party, but this was a politically biased and racist comment. Nevertheless, Bryant Gumbel suffered no ill effects for his unprofessional behavior. However, if a white sports journalist had referred to the Democratic Party as a *Black Panther* or *Black Muslin* rally, that journalist would have been charged with a "*Hate Crime*". What Bryant Gumbel did is unacceptable and I quit watching REAL SPORSTS because society can't have it both ways-everyone has to be accountable.

Today, if a college recruiter goes to scout a running back, when he finds the running is white, the recruiter leaves before halftime. If the running back is black, he is given an athletic scholarship before halftime. The same thing happens in basketball unless the all-knowing McDonalds "*Knights*" the player as an All-American. The irony of this ridiculous behavior is that it is committed by mostly white coaches. A player's race should not matter; his or her performance in the classroom, involvement in extracurricular activities, individual abilities and teamwork on the field, court, mat, etc., and involvement with the local community should determine whether a university offers a young athlete a scholarship. If a college education was as universal as a high school education, it might go a long way into cleaning up some of the recruiting atrocities. And I am all for sending crooked coaches and administrators to prison, but it might backfire because they would probably recruit felons for their next job just like the NFL.

Most Academic Institutions of today have bought into the theory "*Cheat to Compete.*" Because supposedly everyone else is doing it, they too must eat the poison apple. Of course this is absurd, but it is their way of the ends justifying the means. Unfortunately, justice has absolutely nothing to do with it. It centers on greed and a thirst for winning. People in Hell want ice water, and these leaders of culture will one day understand this concept. No one is without sin, but those who lead falsely will suffer a thousand times more.

I have often heard nonsense like "its different today". No it is not. *Character* and *Integrity* have never changed, people have changed. We are too busy trying to fit into western society, so we sometimes forget our actions define our society. If our tolerance for cheating has reached its apex and it no longer matters to our culture, then maybe the Eastern view of *American Culture* is right. When morals and manmade laws become obsolete, lawlessness reigns.

Today's American society worships high profile individuals as though they were Gods. Most of these jackasses might be *demons*, but they dang sure ain't Gods. Our worship of these fictitious heroes is the same as worshiping false idols. There is only one God, and most of these ignorant bastards may use God when they get in trouble, however, God is not present in most of their worlds. Many cultures in history such as the Greeks, the Egyptians, the Romans, have all worshiped false idols. Eventually each Empire crumbled under its own corrupt foundation. Godless societies will never flourish because they believe in nothing and intend on corrupting all. Every great scientist has known there is a higher force in our universe at work. For every mystery we unlocked, there are a billion more to be explored.

But I am not saying every professional athlete, film star, musician, etc. are Godless. There are Christians, Muslins, and Judean believers in the midst of these high profile celebrities. But using Jesus and God's name doesn't mean much if one is living in opposition of the word. If you are not a fan of Dwayne Wade and Lebron James, then you are not a basketball fan. For I believe both of these young men are not only great athletes, but they are also decent human beings and I enjoy watching them perform. However, the difference is I don't worship them and think they can do no wrong. Being a great athlete or entertainer does not entitle them to a "*Free get out of jail card*" although in the American Courtroom this seems to be the current unconstitutional pattern.

And I understand what Bill Russell was saying about not wanting to sign autographs. For he didn't view himself as special, basketball was a job. And Bill wanted to talk to people and listen to their thoughts and ideas. Moreover, he wanted people to see "the man" not the professional athlete. I admire Bill Russell because his character defined who he is and basketball is just a sport he excelled in. And we have to be able to separate enjoyment from worship. For I love football, amateur wrestling, basketball, and baseball, but they do not control my life, they are a small part of my life. And I am not sure about up north, but down in the south high school football is a religion. More people go to high school football games on Friday and Saturday nights than to Church on Sunday mornings. And unfortunately here in the *Bible-belt.*; winning football coaches are placed on pedestals. One might think that a place so deeply rooted in Religion would have more moral fiber. However, winning has replaced all logic and decent folk are consumed by vanity.

Changing dress codes doesn't change the character of an individual. The *Thug Basketball Association* (NBA) is filled with overpaid spoiled selfish brats. And David Stern, the God of this profane regime, is skilled in deception and has an answer for every outbreak. Why of course only one referee was gambling, only one player was shooting it out at a club, and the 2006-07 NBA Western Conference Finals were not influenced by suspending two of the Phoenix Suns star players in Game six. And I guess the Portland and Sacramento Conference Finals against the Lakers in their 2000-02 Championship three-peat were not influenced by poor officiating either. But when the truth comes out that more than half the NBA officials were involved in gambling which violated League rules, the answer was to legalize gambling by officials. The reason for the gambling restrictions of any professional or amateur official is too maintain the integrity of the game. Now the *Genie* has been released and because of this unethical irrational decision knowledgeable fans will continue to have doubts about controversial outcomes in NBA games. So what does the Almighty Stern do, with the coercion of NBA executives and team owners the NBA has made the Boston Celtics relevant again. With the theft of Kevin Garnett and a favorable schedule at the beginning of the 2007-08 season; the NBA deflected the gambling scandal with the assistance of the sports media. But in the 2008-09 playoffs Celtics point guard Rajon Rondo committed two flagrant fouls in consecutive games against the Chicago Bulls and received preferential treatment instead of being suspended for two games. Yet the NBA, MLB, and NFL constantly deny allegations of east and west coast bias for higher ratings in the Finals or Championship game or maybe Commissioner Stern and the Players Association Executive Director Billy Hunter were not concerned about the vicious assaults because both victims were white players. Congratulations Mr. Stern your one way ticket to Hell has been confirmed.

Most of the youth today think they are somehow entitled to everything and don't have to answer for anything. And the Thug Basketball Association (NBA) can keep handing out one game suspension for flagrant fouls, though the penalties rarely fit the crime. What is it going to take, paralyzing a player before the NBA actually does something? But the NBA knows that the majority of the viewers and ticket purchasers are white, so they cleverly market the NBA as family entertainment, and "*The Almighty*" David Stern knows that the majority of these fans are fed up with the unnecessary violence. What if the NBA actually tested players for illegal drug use? If it was done by a credible independent lab, the NBA would have a PR (Public Relations) nightmare worse than its gambling scandal.

Most of the players walk, double dribble, palm or carry the ball, grab jerseys, elbow, hand check, push in the back, go over the back, travel, lead with the forearm, impale defenders with the off hand or arm, camp in the lane for more than 3 seconds, flagrantly foul a driver, grab the net or rim, or flop on almost every freaking play. And when I am trying to enjoy a basketball game, I don't care to see a football game break out. I was watching ESPN one night when they showed a player never dribbled the ball from half court before slam dunking the ball. Three officials and not a single one of them blow their whistle.

Basketball just like football and baseball has become more about individual athletic talent and less about team fundamentals. But one of the most corrupt professional Sports Leagues today is the NFL or what I label as the *Criminal Football League.* Full of current felons and former players that are felons allegedly, the NFL is a poor reflection of what our Western Civilization has become. As long as these sorry excuses for human beings can contribute to an NFL franchise, teams and dishonest lawyers will continue to twist the judicial system in their favor. Most Americans except for some ignorant local fans have grown weary of the constant deals being made by prosecutors and defense attorneys that allow criminals to play pro football.

Every time they get in trouble, someone comes to the rescue, so many of these amateur and professional athletes never learn because they have never been held accountable for their unlawful behaviors. There is no one with intelligence that can objectively look at the criminal cases of NFL players without having serious cause for concern about the *American Justice System.* Where are the Thomas Jefferson's of the world when we need them most? But some fans do not want to believe the players they admire are two bit hoodlums. It is the same way a mother doesn't want to believe her child could do anything wrong. But wishful thinking has nothing to do with social deviance.

And the steroids and HGH usage only adds to the aggressive behavior of the players. Without independent testing and oversight, the Professional Leagues are going to continue thumbing their noses in the face of the American public because their bogus drug testing procedures are laughable. And who says there is not an agenda in the NFL tied to the sports media (ESPN) for a questionable offensive pass interference penalty in the 2007 AFC Championship game late in the first half cost the New England Patriots a Superbowl Championship and the year before (2006) the Seattle Seahawks got jobbed by the officials in the Superbowl against the Pittsburg Steelers. Maybe the Criminal Football League (NFL) should consider holding its annual draft at Rikers that way their lawbreakers can get a firsthand look at their future home.

Often I refer to MLB as the *Martian League* because these aliens are from another planet. Out of touch with fans and the American public, baseball has been operating above the law for far too long. It doesn't matter that there was no steroid policy in baseball. Steroids were outlawed in 1988. Do you want to know why people despise the Players Union? Well, I'll tell you. The Players Union is ran by greedy lawyers and former players that actually believe they have the constitutional right to violate any Congressional legislation they choose because it is not in their CBA (Collective Bargaining Agreement). Thus, they feel immune to any law that interferes with their *Standard Operating Procedures.* Every intelligent sports fan knew these bulked up *Herculeans* were on the juice. All Congress did was put on a show for the public and then MLB instituted a phony policy to appease the masses. The *Mitchell Report* is as disingenuous as the *Warren Commission Report.* While former Senator Mitchell's intent may have been honorable, Major League Baseball's intent was not. Only one current player insignificantly cooperated with George Mitchell. Accusations and probabilities with no penalties is the central theme of a report designed to cover up Baseball's unlawful conduct for almost two decades. And a few more appearances in front of Congress in which MLB brags about its current testing and promises to do more is as effective as throwing a drowning man an anchor. If players in the last two decades are inducted to the Hall of Fame, then Pete Rose should also be inducted.

What would these greedy bastards do if we turned off our televisions and quit going to the games? These extraterrestrials are so far out of it, they probably wouldn't even notice. If we bring back hanging for crooked judges, prosecutors, and lawyers, Donald Ferr and David Stern should be the first creeps in line. The Martian League (MLB) will never change without being forced to do so. Their anti-trust exemption needs to be lifted. If fans could sue all Professional Leagues for fraud, it might encourage the Professional Sports Leagues to change their current unlawful behaviors. Society can't exist with two sets of rules. Rules that benefit the rich and famous while abusing the poor are going to change. And the majority of Americans are fed up with the injustices and double standards and the day of reckoning is coming. Still I long for the days when athletes played for the love of the game and money was just an added bonus.

It seems more important to appear in one highlight on ESPN rather than doing what is required by team efforts to win. Style points and large contracts mean more than moving a runner over into scoring position or taking a base on balls. And pitchers are too busy trying to pitch like Greg Maddux instead of throwing strikes or overthrowing trying to get a K (strikeout) instead of trusting the defense behind them. It does take athletic ability to compete at the highest levels. However, current players don't understand fundamentals and playing as a team, otherwise they are selfish pricks concerned only with their personal stats that are used to fleece their employers for outlandish contracts.

Resolutions

It is ok to enjoy entertainers as form of escape from our mundane daily routines as long as we keep it in perspective. Although, athletes and entertainers may possess talent that most do not have, they are still human. They are not special, they are not above the law, and the majority are awful role models. Most are as bright as a flashlight without batteries and that's why they need to keep their political views to themselves. But sports can bring communities together. They show commonality of people from different walks of life. Men of all races are able to bond and sports also provide emotional outlets for expression. And not all sports are bad, but some of the people involved in sports have no moral integrity. So we should all remember that our passion should not exceed our reason because that is when we tend to place sports and athletes above everything else.

Moreover charity comes from the heart and I am always suspicious when Professional Leagues market their good deeds-for you can dress a wolf in a sheep's skin, but he is still a wolf. While I do believe some of the players in all professional leagues do actually care about those less fortunate, I feel the large majority are greedy self centered assholes and if they do make a charity appearance, you can bet a camera is near by. For good deeds are done without recognition.

There are so many things that need to be addressed in amateur and professional sports which are not going to change without a new political system. We can no longer trust the NCAA, Democrats or Republicans, the Courts, the Owners, Coaches, Players, Leagues, Educational Institutions, the Media, and Bureaucrats to represent the best interests of the public. They are all embroiled in the corruption of the current system. And we may have to turn off our viewership, stop buying tickets, and quit purchasing any product that aligns itself (sponsors) with the offenders-for we need three new incorruptible political parties. And we should always require and demand independent oversight. Moreover, if we prosecute the violators of the public's trust, we can hold these institutions and individuals accountable for their actions.

The American Professional Sports Leagues, along with the

professional leagues throughout the world, are out of touch with the public. And the greed of the American Professional Athlete is very troubling. Most don't care about anyone except for themselves. They are not team oriented, they are selfish pricks and their bottom line is getting paid. Their Unions are full of crooked ass lawyers and former players that seem to live on another planet. No matter how much they get paid, they always want more. I am astonished that the owners have never stuck together and said damn the Players Unions. If the owners run their businesses the same way they run their professional teams, most of these idiots would have gone bankrupt.

Paying any player, in any sports, twenty ($20) million dollars a year to play a game is the most absurd nonsense I have ever witnessed in my lifetime. And the only thing that remotely compares to this ludicrous behavior is paying an actor or actress twenty ($20) million dollar to pretend in a film. Truthfully the majority of the people will never make one ($1) million dollars in their lifetime. Thus there is no justification for these UNGODLY salaries and there never will be. And the Owners should all unite and say "Enough, we will no longer pay extortion." For that's what it is "extortion." *Blackmail* and *Extortion* are crimes in America and it is time we start holding players and their unions accountable.

Today's professional players live in fantasy worlds. All they do is play video games, chase women, get drunk or high, and every once and a while show up to play a game. They are treated like Gods by the Media unless it is Barry Bonds, and most of them have been given hundreds of second chances in their lives for things the average person would have been incarcerated for doing. Then after their playing careers are over, these same Media Conglomerates hire these inarticulate prima donnas as analysts. Where does it end? Most of the time, these Sports Media Corporations pay the ex-jocks more money than their educated journalists. Instead of trying to rub shoulders with these unqualified clowns, the real journalists should go out of their way to show the public how goofy these ex-players and coaches really are because it is dang right shameful. If our society doesn't care anymore about the enormous amount of corruption in *American Sports*, then we truly are unsalvageable.

Action speaks louder than words, so it is time for us to act. We cannot continue on this current path of disintegration. Every great

Empire has fallen because of its failure to recognize the erosion of society. The American foundation is on the brink of collapse because the inmates are running the asylum. The majority of corporations, our legislative branch, our judicial branch, government bureaucrats, and the media are not worried about the American people. Their focus is on manipulation and control via profit and we are their guinea pigs. Our non-violent insurrection by the people may be our last hope because those who hath made Unholy PACS are unlikely to recognize the errors of their ways.

And networks hiring ex-athletes that can't even put two intelligent syllables together is unequivocally unethical. Holy moly, next Michael Vick will be the Commissioner of the NFL; for some compared him to Jesus, but that's after his short vocation in the *Big House.* And John Daly (I actually like John Daly; I guess because he is down to earth) will be the President of the PGA; the alcohol and tobacco industries would be elated. Next, Queen Latifah will be running NASCAR because she drove a taxi in a movie, and Barbara Boxer will be in charge of immigration because we all know how unbiased she is. Hell, why not let Bobby Brown head the FBI's *Drug Task Force*, he definitely has the experience. And we could put Ronnie Milsap in charge of NASA and Stevie Wonder in charge of FAA. Why stop here, let's make "*P-Daddy*" Bill the Executive Director of Porn for Viacom and Hillary the President of the AMA (American Medical Association). But wait, Oprah could run Microsoft and Jennifer Lopez could be the Queen of England: for isn't *J Lo* already the fairy princess with the magical ass.

Next, Pee Wee Herman could head up DFCS and Terry Bradshaw could run the Department of Education. And Lewis Black could be the new Pope of the *Catholic Dynasty*; for he is an honest Jew. Barney Frank could become President because he would not drop the Football for a piece of ass, at least female ass. Maybe Willie Nelson and Toby Keith could run our correctional facilities; for it might be time to start hanging violent criminals. Surely Rosie O'Donnell could chair the RNC and Pat Robertson could chair the DNC. And Tom Cruise could run the WWE because he is a man's man. And Anna Nicole Smith could have been the director of our US Treasury Department; after all she was the best *Gold Digger* in America before her tragic ending.

But the media's blitz in our homes with constant images of Anna

Nicole's death while disregarding important issues like global warming was asinine, though this is the way of an out of control entity that has lost all credibility. Truthfully Anna's death is sad, but when one plays with fire one often gets burned. And my sympathy is for the homeless, people with malignant cancer, women and children who are abused, people that have little to eat or wear, people that have lost their jobs, people that can't afford medical care, the elderly that have been swindled out of their life savings, and the impoverished throughout the world. Dying doesn't cleanse our sins, nor can it change our past even though the entertainment media attempts to create illusionary icons out of dead celebrities.

The same way the Celtics were given an easy early scheduled in the 07-08 season, the New York Mets were given the same favoritism in 2006. For the best ratings, the NFL, NBA, and MLB prefer the large market teams such as Los Angeles, Boston, New York, or Chicago in the Finals or Championship Game. Bud Selig and David Stern should resign, but I doubt their delusions of self importance will allow it unless the owners force them out. Roger Goodell began his tenure with a tough on crime approach, but that was just a PR move to deflect the fans outrage over the NFL players conduct on and off the field. He has already begun to soften his sentences and I am reasonably sure the owners had something to do with it. The NFL needs a retired judge with an impeccable reputation and a history of being tough on crime as its commissioner with unquestionable authority to clean up the NFL's lawlessness. It is not a right to participate in professional sports just because someone is athletically gifted. It is an opportunity and a privilege that few will ever have, so fans do have the right to expect owners, coaches, and professional athletes to abide by a strict code of conduct.

Still the *Kingdom of Retardedville* in pro sports is very difficult to fathom. The fact that Charles Barkley has three published books and probably didn't even write one sentence is an example of the failure of our academic institutions. And I know T.O. didn't write his book either, but one has to be able to read and understand the meaning of words first. If Charles becomes the Governor of Alabama then the south will never rise again. Being popular never made anyone qualified for public office. And a Governor doesn't just play poker and video games, chase women, and golf all day, he actually has to perform some civic duties or maybe it's different in Alabama.

I remember Sparky Anderson (one of the greatest baseball managers in the history of MLB) once said his dad (a painter) told him (paraphrasing) "It does not cost anything to be nice to people." So I have tried to live my life with this idea in mind. Sometimes I get upset or agitated, but I do my best to live by this creed. For we have all done things in our lives we regret and most of us would change some of them if we could, I know I would. Excuses for poor behaviors will never satisfy our hungry for redemption. As I have grown, I have come to understand that life isn't always wonderful. But just because Jose Canseco, Maurice Clarett, and Tim Donaghy are never going to win *Mr. Congeniality*, it doesn't discount their stories. If anything, it is a testament to the unaccountable corruption defiling professional and amateur sports in America.

In 1983, Georgia Southwestern College started up an NAIA football program. Back in the day I was a fairly decent athlete, I could slam dunk a volleyball, I could hit line drives all day in slow pitch softball, and in high school I ran a five minute mile and was also the second leg of our four-forty relay team. At the residential school for the blind I attended team sports were wrestling, track and field, and swimming, but we played football and basketball recreationally all the time. I was a State Champion in wrestling and a heck of a volleyball player. And honestly I was not the guy you wanted to fight unless you wanted your ass kicked. So I tried out for the football team.

Naturally, since I hadn't played organized football in high school I looked awkward in some of the drills. From the first day the defensive coordinator tried everything he could to make me quit. He and the offensive line coach cursed me every day at practice. It had nothing to do with performance because during our live scrimmages I was relentless making play after play in the backfield. I was only five foot ten inches (5-10) one hundred and seventy-five pounds (175lbs.) playing defensive tackle. And I was unstoppable rushing kicks and in goal line defense. Now the defensive coordinator said I ran a four-nine forty (4.9) however, when I ran against the supposedly four-six forty (4.6) guys I bet them. One of our drills was rushing the quarterback which I also excelled in.

On many occasions the offensive line coach chastised his lineman saying "You let that blind MF beat you." For the entire fall I dealt with this nonsense.

The next fall we had more tryouts and cuts before the team began its first scheduled season. When I was moved to outside linebacker, I was reasonably sure the defensive coordinator was going to finally get his wish and his animosity was only because I was blind. I could have played fullback or wide receiver because I was an excellent blocker and I could run with power. And I had always be able to catch a football every since I was a small boy. I had one of the best vertical jumps on the team and I had a second gear when a ball was in the air. The only reason I was cut is because a few coaches could not overcome their prejudices. And it is true I could have probably pitched for our baseball team if I had tried out because I had a canon, but I was worried about the speed of the ball off the aluminum bats, so that was my choice.

After I was cut, I was offered an opportunity to assist the offensive line coach and equipment manager by the head football coach who I considered a decent person. And I tried for a few months, but I was not comfortable with appeasing their guilt for their sins. A similar situation happened at the WCW Power Plant (professional wrestling school) in 1990. I was the best athlete there and many of the trainees acknowledged this fact. Now I was around one hundred and ninety-five pounds (195lbs.) and I could fly or mat wrestle with anyone. Many times I wrestled five or six matches in a row without rest and could remember all the spots. No one could run the ropes like I could and I was used to break in the new guys. The only thing I could not do was give myself a contract with WCW or the WWF (now the WWE). Thus, on many occasions when I am listening to someone complaining, in my mind I have often thought "If you only knew?"

First and foremost, we are going to have to raise the academic standards in all K through 12 programs. Competition in the classroom especially in Math, Science, English, and Technology is the first step. And Physical Education should be mandatory every school day along with nutritious breakfast and lunch programs. For President Obama's throwing (wasting) taxpayer dollars at every social program has been a failing Democratic Party philosophy for almost 80 years. Without accountability, discipline, higher standards (that include a college track, a technical college track, and a vocational track focused on assisting every student in reaching his or her potential), and pay scales based on job performance; no amount of money will fix our failing educational institutions.

Next, we must create an independent oversight committee that has the authority to institute severe penalties for academic fraud, recruiting violations, and pay to play schemes for all colleges. And we must also establish new laws (more severe) that send bankers, corporate executives, sports agents, sports network executives, journalists, professional league executives, and alumni to prison for violating these new policies. Moreover, coaches, athletic department directors, college professors, and college presidents should be terminated and prosecuted if their involvement warrants legal action. It is time we restore the academic integrity of our colleges and universities if we are going to compete in a global economy during the 21st century.

Truthfully, we must all make sacrifices to improve our communities and if that means boycotting professional and amateur teams and their sponsors, turning off the game, not purchasing their tickets and merchandise; then that is what we must do for united we stand. But Congress must also remove all professional leagues anti-trust exemption statuses and because of the betting (legal and illegal) there must be independent oversight to ensure outcomes are not rigged or wrongfully influenced. And when outcomes are fixed, then those responsible whether it is an owner, promoter, commissioner, official, organized crime associate, corporate executive, aristocrat, or media pundit with an agenda, they must be held legally accountable. Thus by creating and enforcing more punitive legislation, we can salvage the integrity of the amateur and professional games we love and enjoy.

Moreover, MLB should have five teams in every division. In the AL and NL east, each should have one team in Canada. In the AL and NL central, each should have one team in South America (Mexico being one of the two). And in the AL and NL west, each division should have a team in Japan. Traveling on Mondays and Thursdays is the best way of accommodating MLB teams and realignment ensures two inner league series per week which fans really enjoy watching. But reducing the 162 games schedule to 138 games makes even more sense for the baseball season is painstakingly too long. It is very simple, play teams in your division 12 times (48 games), play the rest of the teams in your league (AL or NL) 6 times (60 games), and play one division of the opposing league rotating every year 6 times (30 games).

On the other hand the NHL and MLS should go international. The NHL should have 8 teams in Canada and 8 teams in the United States with 4 teams in each division where they actually play hockey. In the NHL East it would be New York, Boston, Philadelphia, and Washington. And in the NHL Central it would be Detroit, Minnesota, Chicago, and Colorado. Now the other 16 NHL teams would be based in Europe also where they play hockey. There should be only 8 playoff teams (each division winner) and the winner between Canada's two division winners would play the winner between the two American division winners for the Grey Cup. That winner would then play the European winner (out of the 4 division winners) for the World Hockey Championship Cup. But the MLS should have only 4 American teams (New York, Chicago, Los Angeles, and Atlanta), 4 Canadian teams, 8 South American teams, and 48 more teams throughout the world again with 4 teams in each division. That means there would be 16 playoff teams battling for the World Soccer Championship. And the winner between America and Canada would play the winner of South America and that winner would advance to the next round.

Eventually I believe the NBA should move into the global market (around 2020), but for now a thirty team market works. Also very simple 5 teams in each division with 6 division winners and two wild cards just like MLB (only 8 playoff teams; 16 teams in a 30 team league is too many and the playoffs drag on forever). And the NBA should consider moving some of its franchises like the Warriors to Boise, the Clippers to Seattle, the Raptors to Cincinnati, and the Hornets to Birmingham, the Kings to St. Louis, and the Timberwolves to Jacksonville. But I would really appreciate it if every Professional Team in every Professional League and every Professional Athlete would stop using charity for marketing PR campaigns for true charity is done quietly without any recognition.

On the other hand the NFL is a corrupt power unto itself. No CBA agreement can operate above and outside our federal, state, and local laws. Until we have independent drug testing where the science is ahead of the cheaters, there can be no confidence in any the current League systems. And there is no such thing as privacy when any professional or amateur athlete is violating our laws. But until we ban injury reports, points spreads, and betting on games there will always be corruption in every professional league as well as college. Without an independent amateur and professional oversight committee or body with the authority to administer severe penalties and investigate the influence of organized crime or other influential entities that violate the integrity of an outcome whereby this governing agency can prosecute every offender, the corruption will continue to go unchallenged.

Though the main reason many NFL games suck on Sunday is because over half the teams don't have a *Franchise Quarterback*, so we are treated to that boring 1930's run, punt, and play defense outdated brand of football. And part of the problem is Universities are not preparing College Quarterbacks for the next level. Many colleges are running a spread offense that doesn't allow a quarterback to develop as a passer. Therefore, the NFL should communicate to every high school quarterback "if a quarterback desires to play at the professional level, he should only sign with a university that runs a pro-style offense".

But every professional league should have a three incident rule. First offense a player is suspended for one year without pay. Second offense a player is suspended for two years without pay. And on the third offense a player is suspended for life. For playing professional sports is not a guaranteed right, it is a privilege that millions dream of, but only a few experience.

Moreover the salaries of athletes, coaches, and executives must also be brought under control and corporate tampering most end. While the spirit of the Union was grand, the corruption in Union Leadership is still influenced largely today by Organized Crime. There comes a time in every society when crime and chaos can no longer be tolerated and extreme measures are taken to restore a balance. That time in America is today-for the Unions in Professional Sports have ruined the games-manship and integrity of every Pro-League. But every corporation (GM, Chrysler, Caterpillar, GE (General Electric), Apple-Mac, Delphi, etc) that has to deal with corrupt Union Leadership (UAW, AFL-CIO, SEIU, etc) should move their entire operations to "right to work states" such as Georgia where they can compete in a global economy. And maybe three strikes equals life metamorphoses to three violent acts and that criminal gets the needle (exception to the rule) or maybe we should also consider deporting anti-American fascist groups like the ACLU and their unapologetic members -for our "Freedom of Speech" has been stretched far beyond its original intent. Even more troubling is liberals support free speech as long as one agrees with them, but let one disagree and liberals either begin their character assassinations or deny an individual's right to speak. For America, just like its citizens is flawed and imperfect, but if one doesn't like our country then he or she is free to leave. If our mainstream media's Democratic Party pundits spent a few years in China and Russia, they might better understand and appreciate living in America.

Unfortunately unions, organized crime, and the majority of the mainstream media have formed an alliance with the Democratic Party and until we eradicate this problem along with corporate hedging of both the Democratic and Republican Parties; Washington will not change. However, a legitimate third party such as a Moderate Party would give voters another choice thereby holding Democrats and Republicans accountable. For there is no such rule that says any amount of crime is tolerable and it is our responsibility as a society to ensure all criminal acts have an appreciate punishment for those who choose to violate the rules.

The Antagonist (Media)

For some unknown reason the media has become the "antagonist" of the people. What ever the majority is for the media is against. The vast majority of Americans are against amnesty legislation so the media supports illegal immigration, the majority were against abortion so the media changed the language to "a woman's right to choose", the large majority of Americans are against affirmative action so the media supports preferential treatment and quota programs based on race and gender, and since over ninety percent of us to some degree are conservative the media is anti-religious. And when legislation is passed that reflects the majority of the public's wishes (beliefs and values) the media and their liberal (minority) posse seek out the assistance of the courts. Thus, credible journalism has become a lost art while personal agendas dominate the day.

Just because we have five major Media Conglomerates does not mean there are not coconspirators. All five are basically one big monopoly. Fox News is conservatively slanted but that is just taking advantage of an underserved market. Their partnerships are primarily concerned with marketing products and propaganda to the American public, one of which is Sports. And the idea of "focusing on the positive" is their way of covering up or utilizing spin as a form of damage control. Often the Media will mention a negative story and then all of a sudden it vanishes. This is a clever way of trying to convince the public that they are unbiased. The actual truth is the Media is liberally biased especially the Sports Media.

ESPN (Extremely Shallow Predictable Nonsense) or "Same Old Crap" is part of the problem in today's *Sports Culture.* Sports networks like ESPN and FSN (Fox Sports Network) should be ashamed of their conduct. They are not credible sports journalists anymore, they are ratings chasing, ass kissing, corporate cock sucking, bias whores. The truth is no longer the driving force of a story. How the story will affect their corporate and league (College and Pro) partnerships influences the telling of the story. Defending the indefensible has become the "norm".

"Allegedly" means wait until I retain my lawyer so he can spin the truth and get my lying crooked ass off.

What ESPN covers in an hour and a half program, I can get in five minutes from my local news affiliates. ESPN has become so predictable and so boring that I can't stand to watch. And they show the same old reruns over and over again all throughout the day. Jesus, give me a break. If it wasn't for their coverage of college football and basketball, I probably would not watch ESPN. I do admit I like PTI, I also like the College Baseball World Series, and a few other programs such as the NCAA Wrestling Championships. Though for me, ESPN has become so boring, it's nauseating.

And as usual, ESPN is always pushing their liberal agenda because controversy sells. It offends me and I am so tired of some of the black journalists and ex-players defending black athletes when they get involved in criminal activities. Report the facts and stop using the race card as an excuse. When a white athlete is involved in unlawful conduct the media tears him a new asshole and I am cool with that. It is the *Double Standard* that constantly keeps rearing its ugliness. And I am equally dissatisfied with Barry Bonds and Roger Clemens in regards too the steroid follies of Major League Baseball. There was a time when ESPN actually employed credible sports journalists. Now the only dinosaur left is that brown nosing Chris Berman (graduate from Brown) and his nose is so far up these unqualified ex-pro athlete's asses that he should have been a proctologist. For I agree that all minorities deserves more opportunities in coaching, but I don't want to hear a political oriented sermon while I am trying to watch the game.

Many of the white color analysts today are walking a politically correct tightrope. They are afraid to call it like it is and so we get a watered down version of play-by-play. Quit making excuses for these pricks that have never paid the price for anything, they have ever done, just the facts please. And Howard Cosell was absolutely correct when chastised networks about hiring dumbass ex-jocks. If an ex-pro or college athlete doesn't have a degree in Journalism, Communications, or a related Media Field, the Networks should not hire these buffoons. And no, a degree in Sociology, Philosophy, Psychology, or Religious Studies does not qualify an ex-athlete to be a journalist or sports analyst.

There are differences in cultures and Michael Vick and Barry Bonds are just two examples of how communities react differently. But it is not the media's job to fan the flames of racial division. Unfortunately for the public an antagonistic media is what sells. And it is true the media of the past was often sensationalistic or served as the *Fiction Department (1984)* of *Big Brother.* But with the advances in communications and technology of today the truth is out there for the people to find.

Furthermore, the guilt complex of liberals lacks merit. Insinuating that if voters didn't vote for Barack Obama they were racists was a manipulative way of trying to influence a political outcome. The fact that Barack lacked the experience to run the Oval Office which has been evident with his many poor decisions in his early and current administration was hidden under landslides of propaganda. Maybe not being qualified has more to do with the decision of knowledgeable voters not supporting Barack Hussein Obama. Just look at how the media jumped ship and abandoned Hillary. Next *The Obama Times* (The New York Times) and *The Obama Post* (The Washington Post) began their character assassination of John Sidney McCain one of the few honorable politicians in Washington which intensified with the nomination of Sarah Palin. However, Obama's inexperience or lack of legislative achievements never received the same scrutiny from the media because it enjoyed playing the race card as a guilt mechanism and that is why it has no credibility. While at the same time the media was viciously attacking Governor Palin, Joe Biden was given a special needs pass for his false assertions (lies) and continuous gaffs that if exposed nationally would have probably changed the election. There will come a time when the public will no longer stand for the propaganda and hate rhetoric of the *Antagonist.* And then the *Hero* will exterminate the *Villain* for that is the way the story goes.

19

Gay in the USA

"A Humane Society cannot exist without the inclusion of all people"

Just like feminists, Gays represent a small portion of our population with a large voice in the Media. And I really don't care about an adult's lawful sexual orientation. For I know a few gays I consider friends and they are some of the nicest people I have encountered during my life. Character and integrity, for me, are the most important elements of the individual. And often I have wondered how people can hate someone they don't even know, it makes no sense. Unfortunately, people who are different are seldom embraced by our society. But life itself is a constant struggle for us to let go of our prejudices and fears so we can become better human beings. Thus, by evolving into a more understanding culture, we transform into a more diverse society.

Gay (homosexuals and lesbians) is not a disease. And you are not going to catch it if you come into contact with Gay people. But I fully understand the crazy phobias of the ignorant and uninformed-for the *Blind* and *Hearing Impaired Communities* are treated like a plague by a lot of people in the other Communities that buy into social stereotypes. And to intelligent minds it seems silly, but people fear what they do not understand. I have been offended on many occasions when people find out I am blind and the first thing out of their mouth is "I'm sorry." And I usually reply "Why, it isn't your fault."

Some say "You don't look blind" and I usually comment how are blind people supposed to look? I guess dark sunglasses and a cane are requirements for being blind but I never got that memo. When I find out someone is gay, it doesn't matter because a person that is comfortable with his or her own sexuality is not afraid of others who are not heterosexual. And the most important thing to remember is we are all human beings that have the right to dignity.

Right now, our American Culture is in a quandary over gay marriage.

Our *Media* and *Courts* are battling our *Legislators* over this issue. Of course this is just another divisive tactic of the controlling *Aristocratic Apparatus.* Our politicians only appear to act when their political careers are in question. For me it is simple; let Marriage remain a religious ceremony controlled by our *Religious Apparatus* while letting our *State Apparatus* sponsor *Civil Unions* for Gay couples. Problem solved, right? No because common sense is lacking in our American political arena. While politicians refer to this nonsense as debating, I prefer bickering old farts. But a boot in the ass of a politician a day might remind them the people have something to say.

Now I can not say I understand homosexuality because I am heterosexual. For me, once a man has experience great sex with a woman, there is not much that compares. Only the satisfaction of good food comes close, but it is not quite the same. And the only thing I have found more pleasurable is giving and that is why Christmas is my favorite Holiday. So I say Santa Claus does exist for he is the joy in every child's eyes on Christmas morning.

But I have experienced discrimination and I think that is why I am an advocate for equality in the workplace. No one has the right to mistreat anyone because they disagree with their lifestyle. As I have continually said, we have a right to voice our opinions, but that does not give us the right to force our beliefs on others.

If America is a representation of the melting pot of cultures, we are not a very good example. There is so much hatred and jealousy in our country that we appear more like a "train wreck". And there is no doubt I don't like the corruption in our current culture, but I do love people. So I find the Nazi mentality of superiority quite humorous. There are no perfect races for we are all imperfect creations. Some people are intelligent, others are artistically gifted, some are mechanically inclined, and the majority of us are ordinary people with similar problems. But we become so focused on our differences that we forget our commonalities; although we should openly and civilly discuss both to better understand one another. Besides life is too short to hate or fear people that remind us that "*our worlds*" are just a small part of "*The World*".

Moreover, I do not understand how youths can get caught up in hate groups. Five guys beating up a gay person doesn't make you a man. It makes you a cowardly criminal, and in prison you will become an inmate's bitch. And I understand that most people have a need to belong, but joining gangs and hate groups is not going to fix your life. As I have said on many occasions, everybody has a story. It is what we do in life that defines the positive or negative outcomes. For it defies logic to beat or shoot another human being. Maybe gays should start forming their own gangs and begin whipping your punk asses.

Whether people like it or not, the *Gay Community* has always existed. So, get use to it because they are not going anywhere. We, as a society, need to respect the Gay Community and embrace them as a part of our growing diversity. That doesn't mean you don't have the right to disagree with their lifestyle, yet if we are to achieve a harmonious state, we must love all. For I disagree with the feminist liberal agenda, but that doesn't mean I dislike feminists. And morally I disagree with the gay lifestyle, however, I still believe they are my brothers and sisters and God is their judge, not some *Georgia Cracker* like me.

Scientifically, there is no proof that someone is born gay. I am visually impaired because of congenital cataracts; that is a biological fact. But I am also part Native American (Cherokee), part Irish, part British, and there ain't no telling what else; that is also genetic. The *Gay Lifestyle* is a choice. Is it right or wrong? From a religious stand point, homosexuality and lesbian lifestyles are sinful. From a legal stand point, both are permissible in our Western Cultures. Personally I don't have a problem with the Gay lifestyle because I am not the one that has to answer for it. And I have more than enough sins to answer for on *Judgment Day*, so as far as I am concerned, it is a personal decision.

If our church goers are without sin then let them throw the first stones. But of coarse we know that everyone has faults. No one is saying that you have to hang out at the local gay tavern. Just treat people the same way you wish to be treated. Most of our Western Churches are filled with members that are hypocrites. At times I am not sure who is moral and immoral. Are ministers supposed to preach on the allure of sins and the penalty for disobeying God? Why of coarse and they are also supposed to tell the worshipers to "*Love thy neighbors as one loves thy self.*" Which means; we are supposed to love everyone, not just certain ones.

But I have heard the new liberal label "human condition". Hell I don't know what that means. And the more people make excuses, the less trusting I become. Choose to be Gay and let it go. But the idea that if a teenager is different he or she is Gay is somewhat silly however. What teenager hasn't felt awkward or different at one time or another? Damn that would mean everyone is Gay. Since I love women, am I a lesbian?

Our Gay Community has had more representation than most people realize. In America, James Buckhannon was the first known Gay President. Living with another male in an apartment for many years and his niece planned the White House parties. If that isn't gay, what the hell is then? And Eleanor Roosevelt was the first gay First Lady. That right I said it. FDR had a whore in Warm Springs and Eleanor had her lesbian lover parading around as her press secretary. It is somewhat ridiculous, but in America, marriage can aid or destroy a politician's career.

And Rock Hudson hid his homosexuality for years. Gays even have their own religion "*Scientology*" and the prophet Tom Cruise. They (gays) are represented in professional wrestling, football, basketball, and baseball. Hell, if Shane-O-Mack isn't gay who is? And Congressman Barney Frank, the Village People, Ellen, and Star Trek's Mr. Sulu are a few famous gays. So Star Trek really was going where no man had gone before. But the GOP is where many gays hide in the closet. Is there a Political Party gayer than the Republicans? And I also suspect the Roman Catholic Church was probably filled with gays in every century. If the former Prime Ministers of France and Canada are not gay, then they must just be pussies. But King George (during the fight for Independence), William Shakespeare, Joan of Arch, and Helen of Troy could have been gay. For the point I making is whether someone is gay or not is irrelevant.

There is however, one element of the Gay lifestyle that I struggle with and that is the adoption of children. On one hand, I believe the primary concern should be a loving home. But, I am also well aware of the numerous studies that show children with a male and female role model in the home generally are more successful in life. Maybe it has something to do with my religious roots, but Gay couples adoption of children is where I draw my line in the sand. At this point Gay becomes relevant.

Now I will stand up for Gay Rights on almost any other issue, however I just don't feel children, especially high risk children, should be adopted in Gay homes. And Rosie O'Donnell is not the voice of the Gay community. But she is an obnoxiously rude bitch that most of us can't stand and should be the last person the Gay Community would ever want as a viable voice. Since I do believe the Gay lifestyle is a choice, I feel we, as a society, have an obligation to protect children. And it is true I am a sinner, though the adoption of children by gay couples is one moral issue I hath to stand up for and say "no."

My stand on adoption might angry some in the Gay Community, yet I feel I am right on this one. As I continually reiterate, there are consequences for choices. What do I think should be taught in schools about homosexuals and lesbians? Actually, I don't think the Gay lifestyle has anything to do with educating children. Simply teach children that we are all different and they should treat everyone with respect. And our educational systems need to refocus on the fundaments of reading, writing, arithmetic, along with science and technology and leave the political ideology for family discussions.

However, I am not saying children should not be around gay people. For I said adoption in a home is where I can't agree with liberals. But I don't believe a gay Scout Master is a threat to children. I was a Boy Scout and we had a lot of fun. Though, I don't believe we would have known or cared if our Scout Master was gay or not, he was an adult and we were taught to respect our elders in my day. Scouting provides a foundation of how young man should carry themselves throughout life. And Gay people have morals just like heterosexuals. Most in the religious community feel the gay lifestyle is a sin and I agree. But what about drinking and smoking, and don't forget gambling (the lottery is gambling) and cursing. What about the business people in churches that cheat their customers. And let's not forget that the majority of religious universities allow corruption to run ramped in their athletic departments. For we all commit sins. It is much easier to see other people's immorality than it is to admit we all have vices that violate God's laws as well. And a gay Scout Master would have other adult male chaperones at every function, so what is the big deal? Quit worrying about gay Scout Masters and worry more about *Child Molesting Priests.* For I would be more trusting of children supervised by gay adults than Catholic Priests any day. Though it is my contention that children need a male and female role model in the home, but the village should be more diverse.

Resolutions

First, quit parading around in court jester's costumes. Hell, I will fight for your rights (except for adoption). But you don't need a parade to let us know you are gay. Wearing an earring in the right ear, cigarette in the left hand, limp wrist, squeaky voice, tight pants, cutting hair, wearing makeup, calling women bitches, bringing me the big slice of pie, are just a few subtle indications. But wearing sandals, especially with whites socks, is gayer than gay, And black guys wearing earrings in both ears means they are confused about their sexuality-left ear means cool brother while both ears means "woman".

But no employer has the right to discriminate against a worker based on her or his sexual orientation. However, if he or she is incompetent, then fire his or her sorry ass. Though most of the Gays I have met throughout my life seem to be hard working individuals. And gay people "got to eat" just like everybody else. Since I have been treated differently most of my life by employers, I know how it cuts when a person is looked down upon. Heterosexuals are not superior to Gays, so it makes no sense to think like a jackass. But physically, men on average are stronger than women (there are exceptions), however, genetics doesn't make heterosexual males more intelligent or stronger than their homosexual male counterparts. Hell, a lot of the couch potato, out of shape sports junkies put the dumb in dumbass. Some are the same "*kissing cousins*" from the trailer park on televisions shows like "*Jerry Springer.* And the cultural popularity of the reality shows makes Americans look foolish. But the decline in our educational system has contributed greatly to the dumbing down of our culture.

Gays in the military or law enforcement shouldn't be an issue. But personally I still don't approve of women in active ground combat or on the gang infested streets because I grieve more when a woman is killed. However, homosexuals are just as competent as heterosexuals and the macho BS of most heterosexuals is ignorant fear. Unfortunately, peer pressure exacerbates stereotypical behaviors of stupid assholes. As I said I believe the gay lifestyle is a choice, but I didn't say they aren't people too. Living the gay lifestyle doesn't affect a homosexual's job performance. And a homosexual just might save your life one day.

But I will admit that I don't approve of the gay lifestyle invading my living room on every television series. *Will and Grace* I can handle, but *Queer as Folks* is going far beyond my idea of decency. All television programming in Western Cultures have gone far beyond the boundaries of morality and corrupt television executives are responsible. However, an inclusive society has the right to choose its acceptable standards while rejecting the Emperor's unlawful decrees.

Therefore Gays are entitled to equal access based on merit just like everybody else. Again, most groups have suffered unfairly in western cultures, but to build a new village that is more inclusive and diverse than our current society, we hath to overcome our prejudices. And we are all God's children and that includes gays and the atheists. For there is a little gay in all of us-my favorite color is purple, I like musicals (not opera), I am artistic, and I am a good cook. So I say "my brother's problems are my problems and my sister's sorrows are my sorrows". Nevertheless the *Gay Community* has come along way for you have your own city (San Francisco), your own country (India), and your own continent (Europe) so relax and enjoy the day.

20

Feminism

"Hatred, envy, and foolish pride incarcerates the soul and damages the heart"

"The blood shall flow through the Valley of Death and the creatures that legalized abortion will fear the wrath of God and the punishment shall be far worse than any of the eternally damned"

The most amazing creation that God hath made is a beautiful woman. So why do Feminists want to rule the World? Is the reason penis envy? Or do feminists think they can do a better job? It doesn't really matter because feminists represent less than five percent (5%) of all women throughout the world. Most women are hard working believers that do not support the majority of the Feminist's Agenda. Unfortunately they have a disruptive voice in our *Western Liberal Media* that sole intent is to divide genders, races, cultures, and so forth because we are powerless when we do not stand together.

And feminists have used their forum (Media) to convince decent women that men are literally screwing them over. Most women, especially women of God, are being manipulated by *Power Grubbing Bitches* that want to dominate just like their *Rich Male Asshole* counterparts. If you are a striper, a prostitute, or a porn star, you deserve to be treated like a whore. For I believe in equality for everyone based on merit. And a whore is unqualified, so she uses men's lust against them. Jesus forgave Mary Magdalene, but she had to repentant and leave her sinful ways behind.

Do not think for one second that I am saying men should dominate women. But I am saying we need to work together on fundamental issues that are ripping apart our society. And yes I am offended when a woman says she voted for a candidate based on his looks. For I heard this illogical nonsense about Bill Clinton and the women in the early 1900's that fought so hard for the "right to vote" are ashamed of this irresponsible behavior. To think that some white women voted for President Clinton because they thought he was handsome and charming and some blacks voted for Clinton because he was considered "a player" (sleeps with every woman he can) is a dysfunction in culture. How ignorant can we become before America descends into the Abyss?

In a gender studies class, I argued about how surveys can be manipulated to quantify an argument based on a political agenda. The survey compared salaries of men and women undergraduates. It left out type of degrees, years of experience, and institutions. First, if a male has a degree in Finance and a female or another minority has a degree in Sociology, he should make more money. Secondly, if a male has fifteen years experience and the female or other minority has five years experience with the same degree, he deserves to make more money. If the male graduates from an Ivy League School and the female or other minority graduate from a public University or College with the same degree, he is suppose to make more money at least for the first five years. After five years, job performance factors into the equation. But this is how feminists manipulate data to get legislators or liberal judges to twist the system in their favor. If the female or other minority had the most reputable degree, most years of experience, or graduated from the more prestigious institution; then they would deserve the higher salary. But fairness doesn't seem to be a part of the *Feminist Movement.*

My mom has said for as long as I can remember "Two wrongs don't make one right." Affirmative Action is never going to fix the past and giving unqualified or less qualified people jobs over more qualified candidates is culturally divisive. But feminists want their bread buttered on both sides and they don't care about the damage they are inflicting upon society. When a woman uses sex to gain an advantage, she has lost touch with God's purpose. For I have listen too and read much of the history regarding women. And rich women rarely suffered and many women throughout history have ruled over nations of men. Cleopatra and Queen Elizabeth I were two devious, seductive, and vicious rulers. And their reigns were as corrupt as any men that ruled in our past or present.

But the poor and uneducated women are the ones that have always suffered. This is still apart of our cultural today, but some of the suffering is self inflicted. For dropping out of school, getting pregnant, and marrying or living with abusive men has serious consequences. What about women smoking, drinking alcohol, or using drugs when they are pregnant. In these cases, the child is the one that pays the price. And the lucky ones are born with LD (learning disabilities) or ADHD (attention deficit hyper disorder). But they will struggle in school because of the sins of the mother. Meanwhile the unlucky ones are born retarded, without limbs (arms or legs), or addicts. Many of the mildly retarded children will eventually be serving time in our correction systems because they can't adjust to normalcy.

But I am not making excuses for their anti-social behaviors because I believe, once a person knows the difference between right and wrong, that person has a choice. Ninety percent of us grow up poor and everyone has a story. Most of us choose to abide by our laws whether we agree with them or not. What I am saying is this is a predictable outcome that might have been prevented with better choices by the mother or intervention of healthcare professionals.

And women not having the right to vote or own land in America was an injustice. Though I said earlier, America is a nation full of injustices. Pick any group or segment of the US populous, except for a wealthy few, and one will find troubling unfairness and struggles for equality. But the feminist's desire to control through any means necessary is a disheartening sight. And I will never believe that it is an insult to women for being caring souls. For the insult is for some women to desire to be like the rich capitalist pricks that can never have enough power and money-for you are trading your souls for materialism and that is a heavy price to pay.

But I believe the majority of women have strong roots in faith and many are the glue of a family. And my mother has always been the backbone of our family and has given all with little in return. However, some good women are being deceived by feminists to act in unwomanly ways and I am not talking about that "In the kitchen, barefoot and pregnant bullshit" of ignorant ass men. I am talking about control of a relationship and when they don't get their way, everyone in the home suffers. Eventually when a relationship becomes a battle for dominance, divorce is the out. And a majority of marriages (over 50%) are ending in divorce in the Western Culture today. Why? One of the reasons is a war for control over finances by men and women. Once this begins, everything else in the relationship is affected. Most feminists have poor relationships with men because they can't compromise on any issue. Therefore, they want all the other women to be as miserable as they are except for the few that find that wus of a husband or boyfriend they can just run all over "Yes dear, whatever you say dear." But this is the same abusive behavior of cowardly men with low self-esteem.

Often I am amazed how many women can't get along in the workplace. Constant bickering, bitching, and complaining and no not just at that time of the month, it is every freaking day of the week. Hell, every employer should give women the week of their period off with pay every month, so the rest of us can have some peace. But men can bond at a bar, a ballgame, at work, at church, in their neighborhoods, or almost anywhere we go. And the only time trouble starts is when a woman causes it.

I taught for a couple of years and the comments I heard from women about one another was shocking. And naturally being a compassionate mediator, I use to tease some of my friends with comments like "Why can't ya'll get along" and then crack a smile. But I have also seen it with nurses, the jealousy is astonishing. For the irony is women want to work, but they can't seem to get along with one another at work. And one minute they are the best of friends and the next minute they are screwing their friend's husband or boyfriend.

Most feminists rarely get laid or the sex doesn't meet their expectations. Therefore they hate the world and everyone in it. And many of their male counterparts (aristocrats) would never get "the girl" if they didn't have money. While the rich males are off making money, their wives are screwing the gardener, the pool boy, the mail man (that is why our mail is always late), and any man that pays them a little attention. But this is nothing new; throughout history spoiled rich women have committed adultery with any man with a penis when their husbands were away. And Professional athletes think they are slick leaving their wives at home while they are out prowling after midnight. But their wives are also having sex with other men and they cover for one another too. For working at a charity event is a code for many of these gold diggers meaning they are getting their grove on or they are trolling for future prospects. But one of the humorous ideas of infidelity is *Guys* screwing around are viewed as unfaithful husbands having sex with whores, while

Gals screwing around are viewed as lonely sympathetic wives making love to their lovers. Stop it for your marriages are unholy alliances. For the men married the gold diggers to bare their children and decorate their mansions. And the women (gold diggers) married their husbands for their money and fame; knowing it can open doors for most of them that they never could have achieved on their own merit.

Now, I am not condoning violence against women, but I do understand how a good man can be provoked. And the athletes with a history of violence against women are felons and should be incarcerated. Most of these assholes are protected by the NFL and NBA, but there are some in the MLB too. Being a gifted college or professional athlete doesn't give any man the right to abuse women. And the NFL's Cincinnati Bengals crime spree over the last six years plus is a disgrace to the League. However they are not an exception to the rule. For they represent what the NFL has become. If the feminists start protesting the unacceptable behaviors of Professional Sports Leagues I might be inclined to join them.

However, there are complications. Right now, all a woman has to do is claim she is a victim of rape without any supporting evidence. And some feminists twisted statistics and paraded a few extreme cases before our idiots in Washington and got the fools to pass new laws that lack common sense. An innocent man can easily be imprisoned by an overzealous prosecutor for having consensual sex. And the rape shield law is ridiculous for the character of a witness must always be an issue in any court case because credibility depends on it for a just outcome. But ambitious prosecutors will knowingly prosecute a high profile case of rape to advance their political careers. One need look no further than the Duke Lacrosse incident or Kobe Bryant-for a woman that had sex with three men without bathing or changing her panties is not credible in my view. So we need independent oversight to ensure fairness in all rape cases. If not, pretty soon the feminists will have every man in prison, except for the actual guilty *Neanderthals* in the NFL.

And we have to find a medium for protecting women and children without violating a man's right to defend himself. Some women and children lie. Once accusations are made, a man's career, life, and reputation in the community will never be the same. Even if he is found innocent, he is scarred for life. So, for me there has to be real evidence not circumstantial allegations. But feminists seem to be on a *witch hunt* or should I say *warlock*.

Today's feminists seem to be the vigilantes of the 21st century. And they don't care who they hurt or whose lives they destroy, their mission is a selfish march of hate and angry. "F men" is their creed, but not sexually. God have mercy on their tortured souls because these sheep are not coming home to the flock. Yet our media vilifies white racist groups, and rightfully so, but hate groups like feminists are spun into victims with a just cause. Your fight for equality in all non-physical occupations I gladly support, however, your hatred of men is intolerable prejudice. And it makes you no different than the chauvinistic pigs you despise.

Why can't we get along? Hell I love women. My mother is one of the most decent human beings I have ever known. Do I think women in the Western Cultures have gone too far? Yes, but that doesn't mean I think a woman's place is in the home. There are certain things women can't do as well as men; it is genetic and has nothing to do with men wanting to suppress women. For I would have loved to serve in the military, I might have been a police officer, or maybe even a professional baseball player if my vision were better. But I don't look at it as anyone's fault, it is the hand I was dealt and nothing is going to change that. And I am thankful for my mind and the new advances in technology that at least offer me and others some realistic hope. Do I get angry about employment discrimination? You damn right I do. If I am qualified and can do the job with reasonable accommodation, then I deserve equal access. If a woman is qualified and can do the job, then she too deserves equal access.

If feminist's main objectives are to destroy society, well they are doing a damn good job. Unfortunately, when chaos returns, it will set women back two hundred years. For most of these women are so entrapped in their liberal political ideology, they can't acknowledge the errors of their ways. There is a middle ground where we treat women with respect and guarantee equal access on merit, but that doesn't seem to be enough for most feminists. Just because the Antichrist might be Hillary or Oprah, doesn't mean you are going to rule the world. It means you will eventually reap what you have sewed and all women may suffer for a few selfish feminists' mistakes.

Abortion the dreaded topic that most have an opinion on. First off, if I hear one more *Candy Ass Liberal* male say "It is her body and she has a right to do what she wants with it," Hell I just might slap the bitch out of your pussy ass. These liberal males have been pussified by women. And they have no backbone and that is why they can't stand for anything except for legalizing all drugs. Or they will agree to anything a woman says just to get laid. Most women don't desire a wussy, for they want real men that will stand up for what they believe in. Besides most ball-less liberals are too fat, too drunk, or too high to get laid. Before we can ever get liberal men to recognize the errors of their ways, they must first undergo a spine transplant or otherwise they must be relocated to Vermont. It is hard for me to fathom that the people of Vermont elected a liberal extremist like Howard Dean.

Feminists with the aid of their media friends spun abortion into "*The right to choose*" nonsense that has divided a country. That was the intent all along, to twist the facts and push an emotional button of women. First and foremost, there are many choices. A woman has the right to abstain from sex or choose who she will have sex with. And a woman can use birth control or require her partner to use a condom. Moreover a woman knows when she is ovulating and can avoid sex during this time. There are many choices for a woman. So this false idea that men are taking away a woman's right to choose is insane.

For I believe we all have a soul and conception is the beginning of consciousness. If over ninety percent (90%) of all women believe in God, then how can they fall for these liberal tricks? If you have an abortion, make no mistake, it is murder. Now, it may not be considered murder in the Western Courts, but it will be judged as murder in *God's Court*. Though I can empathize with exceptions in the cases of rape, incest, life of the mother, or a severe disability, but the act rips at my heart for I believe by legalizing abortion we have let God down.

But even though I am against abortion because I believe it is morally wrong, you will not see me on a protest line. I continue to say "We have a right to voice our opinions, not force our opinions." If legalized abortion is repealed, it must be done through a new Congress (new political system) as the will of the majority. Again, that is why I say Republicans and Democrats are full of bull-dung. One is either *pro-life* or *pro-death*, one can't be both.

Another argument is that if a woman aborts a fetus, it is lawful. However, the father has no say. If the father did something to cause the mother to lose the baby, he would be charged with murder. Common sense says if either does something to harm the unborn child, then whoever committed the act should be held accountable. And who is protecting the unborn child? Oh, I forgot, the child has no rights until it is born, unless the man does something. Then all of a sudden the unborn child has a right to life and the man is a murderer. Jesus Christ, are we all freaking nuts?

However, feminists, with their liberal posse, have been on the warpath for 40 years. It is time to stop the attack on men. Most of us care deeply about women and we are not the enemy. Some feminists, liberals, and government bureaucrats have labeled men as the oppressors to gain an advantage in our corrupt political system. Truthfully feminists are just another group with their own selfish agenda. Trying to castrate men, by twisting every law, is not going to make feminists happy. Accepting that you are a woman is not a tragedy. It is the hand that God has dealt you. Surely he has a purpose for each one of us or do you not believe?

And the fact still remains that the Supreme Court had no authority to legalize abortion. Congress shall make laws, not the Supreme Court. There is nothing in the Constitution that grants any court the authority to legislate social discourse based on personal agendas. And the "***eternally damned***" nine Supreme Court Justices that legalized abortion through a falsified case (Roe vs. Wade) are going to be held accountable in the "*Highest Court*".

I believe in equal pay for equal work based on merit. If two people are equally qualified, but one has more experience, the person with the most experience should make more money unless that person's job performance is not up to par. However, men of the same age, on average, will always be physically superior to their counterparts (there are a few exceptions). Therefore, men will always outperform women on jobs that demand physicality as a prerequisite (again there are a few exceptions). And lowering standards in the military branches, law enforcement, or any other physically challenging careers, to be more inclusive, is not going to change the facts that men are genetically stronger, faster, have quicker reflexes, more endurance, more tolerant to pain (having a baby maybe painful, but it does not compare to being tortured by an enemy), more durable (women are fragile), and handle pressure better because women are often too emotional. That is why four people are dead in Atlanta when a male inmate overpowered a female guard and went on a killing spree in March of 2005. Having a female FBI agent as one of the arresting officers of Brian Nichols was a photo opportunity to appease the public's questions of how such an incident could occur. Is does not change the fact that four people are dead because of Affirmative Action for women. And his defense attorneys first tried to plead insanity and now are using the new mentally retarded defense to avoid the death penalty. In the end (over three years later) a Black Jury refused to give Mr. Nichols the death penalty, thus justice was not served (exception to the rule). Most American victims seem to have no rights unless they are liberals.

Why don't we let blind people fly our commercial planes? Would you be comfortable with me flying your nonstop flight to Washington? Next, we could start letting our children drive their own school buses. Hell, let's allow the inmates to sentences themselves for their violent crimes. Our pro athletes are already performing this task. And maybe we could let foreigners acquire their own businesses in America with a one hundred and fifty percent (150%) government low interests loan, using no collateral, and not having to pay any taxes. Whoops, sorry this unconstitutional bullshit is happening throughout America. Every gas station, every hotel, and half the fast food chains are being acquired by foreigners that are gaining unfair business advantages with the aid of our federal government which American business owners can not compete with. There is no gray area, these unrighteous bureaucrats, with their liberal agendas, are just damn crazy.

Women are entitled to equal access and equal pay based on their qualifications. And Billie Jean King beating a blind, fat, out-of-shaped man twice her age, who hadn't played competitively in over a quarter of a century, doesn't mean *Jack*. Because Arthur Ashe or Jimmy Connors would have skunked Miss King 6-0 (love) on their worst day. And Venus nor Serena Williams, or any other top female tennis player, can beat a single male pro on tour today. These female players would be embarrassed by their ass whipping. Hell, next women will think they can compete with male boxers. But the truth is a heavyweight male contender could kill a woman with one punch. And I personally do not want to see a woman get seriously injured.

Equality in the workplace is a given. If a woman is qualified and is capable of doing the job (fulfilling the requirements), she deserves a fair shake. But trying to impose quotas and lowering physical standards is unconstitutional. There is a whole lot more to War than firing a gun. And there is no female soldier in our military that can beat a trained male soldier in a hand-to-hand combat situation. But the only reason our military includes women now is because they are being forced to do so by politicians. Congress and our Bureaucratic Government withhold resources (financial and operational equipment) if our military leaders don't comply with Affirmative Action for women.

Just because Hollywood portrays women as bad asses in movies doesn't make it so. It is a fictional depiction of women. And it is a miracle that hundreds of female police officers aren't killed by criminals every day. In less than a second, a male thug can overpower a female law enforcement officer and do whatever he wants. For a punch to the jaw or kick to the stomach will incapacitate most women. And maybe I am wrong, but I just am not comfortable with putting women in "*Harm's Way*". If women use steroids for the next fifty years, men would still be physically stronger because that is the way we are genetically designed. We need to be realistic and feminists need to let go of their jealousy.

Intellectually, we are equal. There are plenty of women smarter than me and that's ok. All I have is the tools that God has given me and ain't nothing going to change that. Some might say I got a raw deal, I say there is reason for my uniqueness. Any man that doesn't believe in equal access for women based on their skills and abilities should be ashamed of himself. But no man should be ashamed of wanting to protect women from the horrors of war or the violence of today's streets. It is a natural reaction of our biological makeup. But, why do feminists always take offense to everything? There are biological difference between men and women and that will never change no matter how many new laws are created to castrate the male population. If we put more time into recognizing our differences and working together for a more harmonious society; equality could be achieved.

Resolutions

Simple, stop hating and let's find some common ground. There are so many important issues that we could be working together on. If you want to know who is responsible for the oppression of women, it is a very small percentage of the wealthiest male assholes in the world. And I didn't do it-for I love women. Believe it or not, I even love feminists, but I don't agree with some of your liberal bullshit. For I support equal access based on merit, but I do not support lowering standards as a means of inclusion and I will never agree that affirmative action can fix injustice.

And I will not apologize for my beliefs on abortion. So I guess it best to say we agree to disagree and move forward. Most feminists need to understand that not everything is going to go your way that is the way of the world. Hell, if I had my way there would be no war, no poverty, no drugs, and everyone would own their own home. But unfortunately, most people struggle through life and few achieve financial independence or peace of mind. Maybe it is God's way of testing our faith.

And even though women will never be (on average) genetically as strong as men, doesn't mean we are on different teams. We should be on the same team and that is "*Humanity.*" If we are going to clean up the corruption in our government and develop a new political system, we need to pool our resources. Again, each group has to put aside personal agendas for the good of the whole. And I do not buy into clichés like "Rome wasn't built in a day." Rome fell because of its social and political corruption. And this is the current path of America and most Western Cultures.

If feminists can't join the rest of us in *Common Senseville*, then they must be left behind with the others who are lost in *Crazyville* or Vermont, Massachusetts, and California. No one person or group is more important than society. Hell, I could bitch and complain all day about the unfairness that most of us in the *Blind Community* have dealt with throughout history. But to build a better future, it is more important to remember the past, than to live in it. Changing society for the improvement and inclusion of everyone is not a game, so feminist need to quit acting like spoiled brats that didn't get their daily dosage of anti-male depressants. And men are not the enemy for the enemy is the feminist's jealousy of men.

It is time for feminists to let go of some of their liberal doctrine and join the *Community of Hope.* For no one forced some ambitious feminist to blow her way to the top. Now they seem to hate every man, especially moderates and conservatives because of their own bad choices. Becoming rich and famous isn't enough because sometimes the sin of getting there are unforgivable. And destroying every man except maybe a few pussified liberals that lack the *cohunes* to stand up to them will not cleanse their souls. Barbara Walters, Barbara Streisand, Barbara Boxer, and the other man hating feminists need to repent.

The 2008 Presidential election should be an eye-opening experience for all women. For what the Media and the Democratic Party have done to Hillary Rodham Clinton may have a negative affect on women in politics for many years. Barack said Hillary's referrals to her husband's experience would be like his wife trying to take credit for his Senate experience. But his supporters like Ted Kennedy and John Kerry know Barack hasn't actually done anything of any real significance since he has been in the US Senate, so they are trying to give him credit for what others have done. While at the same time, they have ridiculed Hillary who has achieved much more in her legislative efforts. In the Democratic Party it appears to be legal to belittle women, but to criticize African American candidates is illegal even when the facts support the criticism.

I have illustrated this same *double standard bias* throughout my book. Trying to create experience for Barack Obama where there is none is fictional propaganda used to deceive voters who don't follow politics closely. As I have indicated many times, I am not a supporter of Hillary, but the hypocrisy of the old Democrats supporting Obama is mystifying. Ask Barack where he stands on an issue and it usually depends where he is because he is very adept at standing on both sides of the fence. An allusive lawyer skilled in spinning his answers of controversial questions sounds like the same old Washington political insider too me. Shame on the Democratic Party for it has betrayed many women who have supported Democrats for the last forty years.

Women's sports are wonderful activities for young girls. These sports provide extracurricular opportunities for young women to set and achieve goals that will empower them to reach new heights. But, Title IX is unfairly balanced. Men's college football and basketball programs bring in the largest majority of funds for most university's athletic departments. Some women's basketball teams are now bringing in funds, but football is the lifeline of most institutions. The cost of football should be deducted before the funds are split, with a limit of no more than twenty percent (20%). After the cost of football there would be a forty percent (40%) to forty percent (40%) split for the rest of the men's and women's sports programs. Men's wrestling and gymnastics programs are usually the first cuts thanks to Title IX. Now, there is a push for women to get sixty percent (60%), because women make up close too fifty-nine percent (59%) of most college enrollments, of the funds in the athletic department. Are feminists servants of the devil? Of course, doing away with scholarships and making a college education as universal as a high school education would help, but there would still be fighting over the financial resources of the athletic department. And the majority of the female coaches make more than their male counterparts except for the men's football and basketball head coaches. Maybe the rest of the underpaid male coaches should start suing universities for discrimination in salaries. And why aren't these universities hiring gay coaches? If you think gay people are not playing football, basketball, and baseball, you probably are out of touch-at least in the real world. Oh that's right most universities preach diversity and practice liberal exclusion.

Early August of 2005 on a Friday afternoon my phone rings. I had just recently finished my last semester in college. A familiar voice speaks "Hello Jimmy I heard you just finished your degree." We began a cordial conservation for a few minutes. During the conservation she asked "Jimmy I need you. Would you like to come back to the Academy and teach?" I had worked there as a paraprofessional until DRS stepped in and assisted financially with the costs of my last two semesters. And I responded "I think we need to set down and discuss some concerns I have before I give you my answer." So we set up an appointment for the following Monday.

That Monday she told me she needed a mentor for a new P.E. teacher just out of college with no work experience especially with blind children. First, I ask for more pay and second I said I would stay for one year if things went smoothly while that little voice we all hear kept saying "Say no and walk away." And I should have quit the first day when I realized the new graduate with no work experience (her first job) thought she knew everything and was unreceptive to any advice. Several incidents occurred because she was unwilling to listen, but like a spoiled child it was always someone else's fault. But bureaucrats doing what bureaucrats do let her slide because they had a difficult time replacing the last P.E. instructor because of his conduct.

About two months into the school year, I get called in to the office. And the same person who begged me to help was now shouting at me. As I have on many occasions in meetings with unprofessional bureaucrats I listened to her tirades. Many of the teachers had complained about her antics, but now I was witnessing it first hand. That night at my apartment I thought to myself "You know I went back to school to become a writer and I don't have to put up with this type of nonsense." But I had promised a friend I would help chaperone a trip so I waited until after we returned before I resigned.

An American Institution

Personally I believe in a strong military because we live in a crazy chaotic world. If the world changed for the betterment of all, my point of view would probably shift. I wanted to serve in the military, but could not because of my vision. I could have used a 3 year commitment in the military because when I graduated from high school, I was clueless about where I was headed in life. And I would have loved to become a Ranger in the Army, but it would have had to been a communications officer, because I struggle with the idea of taking another human life.

Truly the US Military is another bureaucratic agency. However, I believe there are more good people in the Armed Forces than in all the other federal bureaucracies combined. One must remember there has always been a code of honor in the United States Military except during the Civil War and for about thirty years afterwards. That does not mean that every soldier follows the code of conduct and there was racial discrimination that can't be overlooked. But honor, duty, freedom, and a belief in God are the values on which the US Armed Forces were established. General Grant and Sherman were a disgrace to the uniform, but their atrocities were buried in the corruption of Washington. Unfortunately politicians and government bureaucrats dictate the US military's agenda. And military personal are trained to take orders, not question the rationality behind the decisions.

Streamlining the military is the right thing to do. We can't have purchases of nine hundred dollars ($900.00) for a hammer, six hundred dollars ($600.00) for a screwdriver, or fifteen hundred dollars ($1,500.00) for a toilet seat. Anytime a company, foreign or domestic, excessively over bills our military or any other governmental agency, the executives of these thieving companies should go to a state penitentiary for at least twenty (20) years. And those in charge of the accounting in the military or government agencies should be prosecuted when these types of fraudulent activities are not reported. For we need a stronger more efficient American Military until the world is more stable.

Four of my mother's brothers served in the military. One served in World War II and one served in the Korean War. And one of my good friends served in Vietnam so I have nothing but respect and admiration for those who have served or continue to serve. But I personally would like to see the military allow people with disabilities to serve. Though we can't serve in combat, we could serve in administrative roles because most of us are just as patriotic as anyone else. Just because I clamor on about social issues does not mean I don't love my country, but any successful relationship has to have mutual affection.

Whether we agree with a military engagement or not, those who die so we can enjoy a cup of coffee at the local diner, read a book, take a walk in the park, or sit and play a game of chess are heroes. And we must never forgot "those who gave all" for they sacrificed their lives for you and me and that is the true meaning of love. For serving others is the enlighten path to redemption.

21

The Entertainment Industry

"What is written is not always true and what is true is seldom written"

What happened? Where did we go wrong? Common Sense has left our society. For we have become commodified products of capitalism. And we no longer think for ourselves, we are being programmed by the wealthy controllers who influence our opinions and dictate our existences. We are like puppets being dangled on strings while the puppet master has us dancing and singing like the careless fools we have become. And we can no longer rationalize and reason because we have put our faith in empty rooms of illusionary dreams with no exits. Our blind faith in belief systems of control has left us powerless and wondering in the valley of darkness where there is no light.

Modern television in Western Cultures exemplifies how low our society will go. What happened to the quality of the programs? There are too many young dumbass executives that don't know anything about life. These inexperienced cocksuckers have not lived long enough to understand pop culture or genre. Even on shows like *CSI, Bones,* and *Law & Order,* there is a liberally biased agenda often surfacing in the scripts. And there were a few good comedies in the recent past such as *Seinfeld* and *Everybody Loves Raymond.* But in the distant past (60's) some of the greatest comedy shows ever written were *The Beverly Hillbillies, Green Acres, The Andy Griffith Show* (the first five years), *Bob Newhart, The Flintstones* (best cartoon in history), and *The Adams Family.* And who could forget the awesome police shows in the 60's and 70's such as *Hawaii Five-O, Ironside, Mod Squad, Starsky and Hutch,* and *Police Story.* But *Scifi* also made an impact with *The Twilight Zone,* and *Star Trek* which took our imagination to new places. Moreover, the western genre was very successful with *Gunsmoke, Bonanza, Daniel Boone, Maverick,* and *The Big Valley.* And the comic book heroes like *Superman* and *Batman* are still very popular. In the 70's *Barney Miller, Sanford and Son, MASH, Taxi, The Jeffersons,* and the original *Saturday Night Live* tickled audience's funny bone. While the detective genre was popularized in the 1930's with characters like *Dick Tracy, Sherlock Holmes,* and *The Shadow*, they still remain a huge favorite of modern audiences. For the list of the quality programs of the past is a huge library of different genres and the writers and producers were actually talented.

Today the quality of writing for television is so poor that I sometimes think they are all smoking crack. It seems like Hollywood is full of people with their G.E.D. that can't even spell the word English. All that cocaine in the 1980's fried the television executive's brains and now anybody that writes an idea on a napkin is "*magically gifted*". There is a reason why your gardener is a gardener and your maid is a maid, or the local waitress is a waitress; it is because of bad choices or it may be the best they can do-for there are no Mark Twains' or Charles Dickens without at least some knowledge of the *English Language.* The cook at the local *Denny's* is not an undiscovered actor, writer, or producer. And the garbage man on your route is not the next great comedian. Sometime ordinary people are just that, ordinary people who in times of crisis rise to meet extraordinary challenges.

And why do these stupid executive pricks cancel good shows like *Murder She Wrote* when its ratings are still respectable? Corporate sponsors have far too much influence in television programming. And these same corporate sponsors try and reach our children through mindless entertainment. The dumbass executives that work at the Networks of CBS, NBC, FOX, and ABC have forgotten that people of all ages watch television, not just teenagers. And I am sick of corporate sponsor's names on College Bowl Games. It should be the Rose Bowl sponsored by the following. But it will take an act of Congress to remove the corporations from their thrones of dictatorships. Their way of trying to reach teenagers is just as dishonest with the same intent as the tobacco companies trying to create a lifelong dependency of their products.

But the current reality shows are so trite that our dogs are beginning to question who the master really is in the relationship. The popularity of the reality fad can be attributed to people's desire to see that others lives are more messed up than their own. And talk shows that resemble something out of "Deliverance" are bombarding our homes. Dr. "*Dumbass*" Phil (if you are listening to Dr. Phil you probably are beyond help), Jerry "*Trailer Park Trash*" Springer (the worst show of all time), Montel "*Smokem Peacepipe*" Williams (Montel is too busy getting high to know what's up; oh I forgot it is for medical purposes even though the FDA says that is bull....), Maury "*whose your daddy*" Povich (the new pimp of the ghetto), Oprah "*QueenBee*" Wimphrey (Oprah changed her show into a feminist buffet line, it use to resemble Springer), and Tyra "*the brainless*" Banks (even a blonde bimbo on crack is more coherent). For some reason these trivial talk shows seem to be in vogue. Did we wake up one morning and lose our freaking minds or did the networks mindrape us during intermission?

There are a few witty and insightful talk shows like Comedy Central's *Daily Show* with Jon Stewart. And Stephen Colbert is also quite humorous. For I think both of these guys are comedic geniuses. But I didn't understand why David Letterman (who is one of the best talk show hosts in network television) invited Bill O'Reilly on his show and then proceeded to verbally assault him. For it is unprofessional for any talk show host in the entertainment industry to argue over differences in political ideology. That is why NBC hired Jay Leno because he rarely takes a position. It is ok to disagree with someone else's point of view, but no one has the right to get hostile over that person's beliefs and if you don't care for the person then don't book them on your show. Since this incident, Mr. O'Reilly has appeared on *The Late Show* with David Letterman several times, but any objective observer can tell Dave dislikes Bill. But that is the way most liberals are; if someone disagrees with them, they tend to exhibit extreme hostility or disdain toward that individual.

During the Presidential Election of 2008, if a conservative, moderate, or even liberal pointed out a negative fact regarding Barack Obama, media pundits and political surrogates of Obama would begin to rant and rave "That's a lie (even though the statement was actually true), Your a racist (anyone white who didn't support Barack Obama was labeled a racist or bigot), or It's not fair to criticize Barack (so Barack's inexperience, troubling associations, and lack of legislative achievement were dismissed)." And *Hollywood* joined in with its television and internet adds proclaiming that Barack Obama was the "chosen one". How could we not elect "*The Great Orator*" shouted his faithful followers. Jeremiah Wright was "right" when he said Obama had to tell the people what they wanted to hear to get elected. Suppose the American people knew Barack Obama was really an atheist like his mother, what if they knew his wife joined a racist Church because of her animosity toward whites, imagine if the public knew Organize Crime purchased Barack Obama's soul in 1996, and how would the public react if they knew the mainstream media deliberately withheld damaging information about Obama-for if the truth had been told Barack Obama would have never become President. This same con (fictional fabrication of the media) was run by the wealthy elite and their media surrogates on the *American People* for FDR in 1932. And today there are still loyal followers of FDR drinking the "*poisoned Kool-aid of hypocrisy*"

Though my time with the "*Idiot box*" has diminished and our quality time is getting shorter. Sometimes I watch a good movie, a college game once and a while (although some of the commentators are as insightful as the village idiot), and a few pro games. But today's network programming lacks creativity and there are too many commercials during a game. Every viewer should start suing the networks (another rule exception) for home invasion and the theft of our sanity. What good does it do to surf with our "clicker" when the same mindless dribble is on every channel?

The officiating, especially in the pro games, has gotten so bad that it is starting to resemble boxing, and I use to watch boxing before the fights were predetermined like pro wrestling. Any close game's outcome can be determined by one bad call late in a contest. It is no secret that the pro leagues front offices would prefer the large market teams to meet in the championship game every season. I use to watch some portions of the WWE programs and that is because I was an amateur and a pro wrestler even though I didn't get to realize my dream on the big stage. And Vince McMahon loves to push the envelope. But after the deaths of Eddie Guerrero and Chris Benoit, some of my enthusiasm was lost. And if I want to watch some women in panties or sexually provocative outfits,

I will order the adult channel or head to the nearest beach. For the female wrestlers matches even look faker than fake and they can go back to dancing on the pole as far as I am concerned. But some of the WWE's shows are mimicking Jerry Springer which reflects our culture's decline. Still, if an incompetent jury had not been swayed by a high priced defense with no integrity, maybe a hundred professional wrestlers might still be alive today. For if Hulk Hogan had testified against Vince McMahon it would have damaged his reputation and ended both of their careers, so what do you think he was going to say? And if Vince McMahon had gone to prison based on the evidence the steroid scandals in professional sports might have been addressed before the usage got out of hand. Another prime example of how double jeopardy benefits the rich and famous.

When the WWE had competition from WCW, the programming was much more entertaining. But WCW was run into bankruptcy by morons like Ric Flair, Dusty Rhodes, and Eric Bischoff. Ric Flair was one of the greatest professional wrestlers of all time, but when did acting become a prerequisite for management. Now he looks more like Methuselah, trying to hang on too past glory or maybe he is broke. And if he hadn't retired, I was thinking about a comeback. But Bischoff was a brown nosing asshole that didn't get his job on merit and Dusty Rhodes is a self-serving clown that is as bright as an Alabama graduate. "*The American Dream*" that's crap-more like the lard ass poster boy for *Krispy Kreme.* And his stick was lame and his wick blew out twenty years ago. Who was minding the store (WCW) with four-hundred million dollars of debt? I guess the inmates were definitely running the asylum with the head quack Ted Turner and they ran it out of business. But do not worry, for Vince McMahon is one of the biggest egotistical assholes in the northeast. Maybe the steroids have eroded his brain cells for he has become a senile old coot. One minute he wants to run the program and the next minute he wants to star in the program. Set your old ass down because you look like a fool.

For many years, Vince McMahon has used pro wrestlers to make his fortune. After he is done exploiting them, he discards them as though they were empty steroid needles. Many wrestlers have died on his watch and he feels no responsibility or remorse. When a journalist (HBO REAL SPORTS) questioned Vince about this, he responded by slapping the journalist's note pad and physically threatened him. Try that on me Vincent Kennedy McMahon and you will get a free ride in an ambulance to the nearest local hospital (exception to the rule).

Most of the ex-pro wrestlers that have bled for this tyrant (Vince McMahon) are left broke and penniless (Tony Atlas, Jake Roberts, etc.). Very few leave the game financial secure like Hulk Hogan or Bret Hart. McMahon seems to be resentful because these two didn't allow him to screw them, at least not financially. But Vince McMahon is the Don King of professional wrestling. Still, I was shocked NBC partnered with this jackass again after the two billion dollar bust of the XFL. And Jay Leno is right "Nobody is watching NBC" maybe that is why they purchased the USA Network.

If it were not for Randy Orton, Chris Jericho, and Edge the WWE would have no show. These three along with Kurt Angle are the best in the business. But Triple H married the boss's daughter to further his career which should be near an end. And John Cena never paid his dues and his in-ring performances are still unpolished. However, Cryme-Tyme is an embarrassment to the professional wrestling industry and the only crime is these two are getting paid. Moreover, the only thing more humiliating than being forced to lose to Rey Mysterio (a 4'11" 135lb midget/acrobatic circus clown) is a wrestler being told they have to lose to Shane or Vince McMahon.

Who will Vince leave his Wrestling Empire to a moronic son (Shane), a psychotic bitch (his daughter Stephanie), or a gold-digging son-in-law (Triple H)? As a man draws closer to meeting his maker, he should try and make amends for his misdeeds. For what many in every corporate industry not just the WWE characterize as business decisions (claiming nothing personal) fail to recognize is their decision affect "real people". We are all connected and we will all be held accountable in the end.

Most of the big budget films made today are repeats from the past. Hollywood, at times, believes its own hype. Keep on paying crazy salaries for "Big Stars" and you will keep getting humped in the booty, but maybe that is the way you like it. My favorite film stars are Bruce Willis, Johnny Depp, and Julia Roberts, but I would not pay twenty five ($25) million dollars to Jesus Christ to star in my film and he is the son of God. Western culture seems to always make things more difficult than they actually are. If there are no dark clouds, no thunder, and no lightening on the horizon, then the storm is just a moorage.

My strategy would be to produce a quality film that makes a profit. Simple and easy to follow even for the Californian heathens. I prefer the James Bond films where sex was presumed. And I don't care to see a sex scene in an action film. If I want to view sex in a film, I can order a porn pay per view. But I do love great fight scenes in action film like "*The Matrix*". As a kid, I use to love too watch the gangster films. It didn't make me want to become a criminal and I don't approve of organized crime's violent ways. But I view action films as entertainment for the male audiences. Most men, which I feel is a part of our genetic code, are violent and aggressive creatures of nature. Our self control and moral consciousness stops us from acting out, but we can enjoy our fantasies through films.

And comedy films are also a favorite of mine. But I am not big on the tear jerking (chick flicks) films that gay critics love.

However, I do enjoy romantic comedies, mysteries, westerns, science fictions, horrors, animated, mythical, adventures, suspense, and almost every genre except for love stories. But instead of looking for new stories, the film industry keeps recycling the same old stories. With all the new advances in technology and special effects, films should reflect new ideas. It takes foresight to change the way an industry operates and those who have the vision usually enjoy the rewards.

Resolutions

For starters Bill Cosby would be a smart hire to help NBC in developing new (more inclusive) comedy shows. Friends should have been called *Crackers* (I never could watch the garbage). And paying any actor or actress one million dollars an episode is insane. But most of the cable networks have better programs than NBC. If NBC is going to continue its association with the WWE, then require the board of directors to replace Vince McMahon. For professional wrestling can work on network television with oversight and the right people producing the shows. And Steven Spielberg would be a great choice to oversee all movie projects of NBC, the USA network, and Paramount or any other *Film Industry Giant.* All dramas need to reflect the quality of former shows like *Hawaii-Five-O* and *Gunsmoke.* And they also need to be cutting edge dramas, similar to the past, such as the *X-Files* and *The Pretender.* But experienced executives and writers with moral fiber are the essentials needed for success.

The *Flintstones* was the greatest cartoon series ever made along with the *Jetsons* and *Scooby Doo.* FOX and Comedy Central have proven cartoons can be successful in today's television industry. *Star Trek* was thirty years ahead of its time. *Diagnosis Murder, Murder She Wrote, Columbo*, and *Matlock* were well written shows with an older audience. The target demographics should include a wide range of people. That is why most of Spike Lee's films fail and suck because his films are not inclusive. For the fact is that the majority of white people are fed up with the race card playing nonsense of the media and some blacks using it as an excuse for poor social behavior or trying to lay a guilt trip on decent folk. All filmmakers have to broaden their genre to draw more diverse audiences. If a film doesn't appeal to a large spectrum (populous), the chances of financial success are lessened. And common sense is lacking in both the network and film industries. If we can put a man on the moon then why can't Network and Hollywood executives develop more intuitive programs?

Many of the problems in the film industry could be attributed to foreign buyouts. Japanese and Koreans do not have a firm grasp on American culture. The Japanese cartoons lack the artistic details of the American cartoons. *Scooby Doo, Masters of the Universe*, and *Spiderman's* graphics are much more realistically defined. Hanna-Barbera and Walt Disney's cartoons were more life like, while foreign cartoons resemble newspaper comedy stripes. If foreigners are going to continue to buyout American corporations, they need to leave veteran American executives in charge of the day-to-day business operations. Hell, I would not be able to run a Japanese or Korean company in Japan or Korea because I don't have a full grasp of their culture, so I don't expect them to fully understand ours.

CBS's coverage of pro football and basketball use to be the best. And NBC did a great job with pro baseball and ABC's coverage of college football was fantastic. What happened? First, the cameras use to follow the ball and the player in position of the ball; stay on the player with the ball. Now, they are too busy trying to show everything. Quit splitting my screen and take the highlighter away from the children. As I said earlier, there are too many commercials. And please stop breaking into the action with an interview in the stands by some pretty face, posing as a sports journalist, asking irrelevant questions. Jim Gray is one of the few that has the balls to ask the tough questions that are relevant. And Jim Lampley is another, but there are few Howard Cossells left in the sports industry of today.

It seems like most of the current commentators are pussified liberals that either fear reprisal (getting fired) or lack the courage to call it like it is. If a player's conduct is socially unacceptable the broadcaster should be on his ass like a roommate in prison. Keith Jackson was one of my favorite, but he has semi-retired. Most of the up and coming broadcasters are afraid of their own shadows. Joe Buck (FOX) is one of the best just like his dad and he does point out bad calls and unprofessional behaviors, but he also acknowledges the great plays and good calls as well. Jim Nance of CBS is another that captures the essence of the moment and he should be in charge of the studio Pregame. That is the way a great announcer should approach his job; "call it like you see it". Skip Carey also called the game with integrity and he will be missed. Though, most broadcasters appear to be the dogs on a short lease of their masters (Network and Corporate executives) that bark when they are told.

And I have always thought the best announcers are the ones that describe the game as though I were there. When I can picture the game with my eyes closed, it is as though I were reading a wonderfully written descriptive novel by a great author like Louis L'Amour. Sports broadcasters currently are constantly pushing liberal agendas rather than calling the game. I agree there should be more black head coaches in college football, but ESPN and these shallow commentators think that every head coaching or manager vacancy in all sports should be given to blacks whether they are qualified or not. What about Latino head coaches, or gays, and who says people with disabilities can't coach? Why can't women be head coaches of men's sports? Shoot, there are sure a lot of males coaching female sports. Just call the damn game and leave your political ideology and personal tirades at the *Super 8*.

Personally I feel head coaching and managerial opportunities should be more inclusive for all people. First, there has to be training opportunities in place for all minorities to gain the needed experience to become head coaches, managers, or sports executives. Equal access, not affirmative action is the key. Then decisions should be made on merit based on job performance and an individual's qualifications. And we should not forget owners and colleges have the right to choose the candidate they feel is the most qualified.

However, networks should never push political ideology. Discussing issues is one thing, but trying to force your opinion down America's windpipe is unacceptable. It is almost impossible for a sports journalist to stay unbiased, but don't just blab out your opinion, be ready to intelligently defend it. For I am capable of defending everything I have said in *The Invisible Man*. And I believe right and wrong are clear no matter what side of the fence one is standing on. There is no such thing as a gray area, but there are exceptions to almost every rule. And no, professional soccer will not ever catch on in America because it is too slow and boring. Watching a 1-0 (nil) game is absolute torture for even the worse sports fan. And I would rather watch hockey or golf (both of which I dislike) before watching five (5) minutes of a soccer game. For watching soccer is the only time suicide is forgivable.

Responsibility for the current runaway train we identify as television falls upon those in charge of the programming. American television use to have standards, but today we have unregulated garbage. And fining CBS a half-a-million for Janet's vanity is not effective oversight. I love Eddie Murphy and Richard Pryor was one of my favorite, however, they weren't undressing on stage. And I also use bad language, although I am trying to cut back because it is not good for youths to identify with adults using profanity.

Why spend 300 million dollars on a film when the studios could spend one-hundredth or less on a quality film with talented unknowns. The risks are smaller and the profit margins are much higher. It simply defies logic or common sense. And it is not as hard as the industry would have us believe. First, a producer finds a good story. If it is a novel, it has to be developed into a screen play and he or she has to acquire the rights and sells the idea to potential investors. Next, the producer goes out and hires the most talented and least expensive director, writers, actors, actresses, and crew. Then he or she chooses a location for the shooting and away everybody goes. I believe films can be shot, edited, and ready for markets a lot quicker if directors aren't having to baby sit spoiled rotten big name stars.

It is time for change in Hollywood. Anyone under 40 has not experienced enough in life to decide what should be broadcasted on network television. And the networks should drug test all their executive employees because if they are not on drugs, then what in God's name is wrong with these pretentious pricks. Hire some intelligent executives not still in dippers and talented writers not sucking on a crackpipe before you make managerial decisions on programming. Entertainment is supposed to be entertaining not painstaking.

Finding Redemption

Once upon a child was born who God endowed with many talents. But to test his faith, God took away his vision. As the child grew into a man, God closed all the doors of opportunity for even a man with a dream and the talent to achieve can't succeed without opportunity. For many years the man blundered through life and cursed God for his suffering. "Why would a loving God do this to anyone" he cried? Even though every dream encountered disappointment the man never relinquished his hope. Something inside would not let him quit for he knew deep down there had to be a purpose for his existence.

Constant battles with depression made the journey more difficult because each failure nips at a person's soul. Satan called "Give up you stupid fool for nobody cares. Submit and accept your place." But the man replied "Although I have succumbed too many of your temptations, my fate is not in your hands." So the man continued to look forward for tomorrow always brings forth the promise of new possibilities. One day the man was sitting in his recliner drinking his coffee as he often did before beginning his writing. This ritual was used to focus on the work at hand, but this day was different. As he pondered many of the mistakes he had made during his life, he asked himself "Could I have grown as a human being without the rocky roads I have traveled and the many poor decisions it seems I have made?" Pausing for a moment, as though a light switch had been turned on, a thought emerged "If a person doesn't feel suffering how will he recognize its pain? If a person doesn't experience disappointments how will he understand its failures? And if a person doesn't face challenges how will he solve its difficulties?" For every problem there is a solution and for every question there is an answer. Whether we like it or not doesn't matter for the truth is impartial.

Enlightened by his revelation the man hurried to his computer. Tap-tap goes the keystrokes as he puts his thoughts onto the page. For ten years earlier he had realized that life is a continual learning process that never ends for those who seek knowledge until we cross over. And he now understands that God's plans do not correlate with an individual's time tables for his wisdom is beyond man's understanding.

To redeem itself the Catholic Church must give away all of its wealth to the impoverished and it must stop taking confessions (for this task can only be administered by Jesus). But the Vatican must also confess and denounce its lust for wealth and power and it must hand over all child molesters to the proper authorities (law enforcement) for prosecution. Moreover the Catholic Church must clean up all the corruption (academic fraud and payoffs) in its high schools and college's athletic departments. However, this includes all Christian Universities. And the Roman Catholic Church must abandon its association with organized crime and it cannot accept any of the Mafia's blood money for those who choose a path of crime and violence have purchased their one way ticket to Hell. Finally, the Catholic Church must continue to stand up against and lead on conservative principles such as abortion, marriage, genocide, poverty, and oppression throughout the world for the goodwill in the Church must replace the political corruption of the Church.

Now if the Mormon Church wants to gain its redemption, it must reject Joseph Smith's *Fable of the Golden Plates.* And just like the Catholic Church, the Mormon Church must give away all of its wealth to the impoverished. But the Church must also discard the *Book of Mormon* and replace it with the *Holy Bible* for the Bible is the blueprint for all Christian denominations.

Furthermore, any Jew who denies Jesus Christ as the son of God will be denied by God. And it is imperative in these troubled times that the Jewish Community stand up against those in their community who have chosen to profit from immorality. Jews who seek wealth at the expense of others such as laundering blood money from unlawful and immoral acts, predator lending, or corporate greed will answer to God and the leaders in the community who neglect to challenge these few unrighteous men and women will by Judged accordingly because of their silence.

But the Muslin Community must also accept Jesus Christ as the Son of Allah or they will not enter the Kingdom of Heaven. And all Muslins who believe in the All Knowing and All Wise must solemnly commit to prevent and actively condemned all acts of violence for to take a life without just cause is to condemn one's soul to the Chastisements of Hell. For all believers of every religious order are commanded to serve our brothers and sisters humbly and quietly, but we must also stand together against oppression, immorality, greed, and corruption.

President Barack Hussein Obama has two paths to choose from just like James Leonard Nobles or anyone else. One leads to *Salvation* and the other leads to *Eternal Damnation.* For President Obama will be *Judged* by *God* and not by a *Godless Media.* If President Obama honestly wants to build a great legacy, he must first cleanup his corrupt partisan administration filled with political appointees. Truthfully the most vile cabinet since President Grant and FDR's administrations overflowing with incompetent selfish crooks.

Vice-President Joe Biden in the pocket of Labor still controlled by the Mafia, lies every day and a disingenuous media says "That just Joe". But this same supposedly unbiased media pounces on every word Sarah Palin utters. President Barack Obama must publicly criticize the mainstream media for its unfair treatment of Sarah Palin and Hillary Clinton. And President Obama must publicly acknowledge his poor choices for cabinet positions and replace these partisan surrogates with competent independent personnel.

Moreover, President Obama must also relinquish his foolish pride and intolerable arrogance before he can find redemption. For every decent man and woman dreams of "*World Peace*", but "naïve inexperience" cannot replace "rational logic". And President Obama's success depends on him becoming a moderate pragmatic leader that puts "the will of the majority" before partisan ideology. Eventually the truth will unfold and the dishonest will meet the "Reaper" for in the end we all answer to a higher authority.

22

Revelations

"With every ending there is a new beginning"

Anyone who reads Revelations with objectivity would probably admit that much of what is written is far fetched. For I would equate its imagery and descriptive folklore to that of *Greek Mythology*, but I do believe Jesus will return. Many stories in the *Bible* seemed to be over-exaggerated. Still, I believe in the message for the truth is there. However, our receding values and distortion of what is "right" assures me *Armageddon* is approaching.

And the end may be near. It could happen in the next ten years or in the next hundred years. But I still believe we can change our ending of *Manifest Destiny.* Though I believe Religion has to become one nondenominational entity; One Religion. Here the members believe in one God. No one is perfect, but believers must try and obey God's laws. The Christian and Jewish Churches in Western Culture have become socially tolerant of almost every sin against God's commandments. What is next? Is our society going to accept murder, rape, and molestation like the NFL and Catholic Church? And I also believe the *Koran* of Islam may be the closest religious text to the truth in our current world. Jihad that represents a man's commitment to become a better human being every day of his life should be recognized as "truth." But a Jihad call for violence is wrong and must be condemned, though I understand the frustration. Moreover, murdering powerless men, women, and children, who are themselves oppressed, gives the capitalist pagans more power and control. There will be a time when we all rise up as One Religion, One Nation, and slay the *Dragons of Lucifer.*

> Revelations 1:8; I am the Alpha and the Omega, the beginning and the ending.

Only God and his son Jesus know what day the wickedness shall end. But when the *Four Horsemen of the Apocalypse* ride and the *Angels of the Seven Churches* come forth it will be too late for the deceivers of men.

> Revelations 22:14; Blessed are they that do his commandments, that they may have right to the tree of life, and may enter in through the gates into the city.

These two passages are the truth of God and he will deliver us from the evildoers. But few will enter Heaven unless God's grace delivers us from our evil ways. For most of us (that includes me) have fallen prey to the wolf. And the dawn of darkness is waiting to extinguish the light-for without it how will we find our way.

But the *New World Order* is upon us. And the end of days is near. Globalization by the wealthy elite has been masked through corporate domination of all the world's markets. The wealthy elite figured out the way to control the masses can be achieved by controlling all the mediums. But we meaning ninety-nine point nine-nine percent (99.99 %) of the population are being manipulated every day by what is presented as news or sometimes referred to as "the truth". Eventually a leader will emerge from these unholy giants and he or she may be the *Antichrist.* And I know some religious sects believe the United States is the son of Satan, but they are wrong. Though I would agree that many of his followers are here disguised as C.E.O.'s, politicians, lawyers including prosecutors and judges, high level government officials, some religious leaders, psychologists and psychiatrists, and many wealthy families from new and old money. And the Antichrist will probably descend from either Europe or the United States and he or she will use the media to fool the people.

What Satan has underestimated is the control of the militaries by his followers. Our Militaries have killed for these jackals for thousands of years, but that will eventually backfire. For honorable military leaders of the free world have always known there is a higher power and when the time is right, they will choose God and his oppressed people. Another predictable event is that people will unite against the Antichrist. It is true the mediums of the world have us divided today, however that will change and we will all rise up and strike Satan and the Antichrist down.

But I believe we can change our current path today because we have the power of unity. And we don't have to play out the final act of Revelations. Satan must be a magician because the leader of the Fallen Angels has convinced many in the postmodern world that he or she doesn't exist. If the majority of us rebel against the disintegration of morality we could avoid the dark days of Revelations. Through a unified social and moral awakening, we could change our destiny.

Resolutions

There is a holy place of serenity connected by three bridges where Muslins, Judeans, and Christians will gather as ONE. And we will praise Allah together for it is his will. There will be no war, no hungry, and no suffering. Each man and woman and every child will join hands as a community of faithful servants. And the name of this holy oasis is *Paradise*; the gateway to the *Promised Land*.

For I am not a Prophet nor am I a Saint, I am not a Messenger-I am a flawed sinner that possesses nothing but my honesty and integrity. And I am not always right but I will always say what I believe. Do not be offended by what I have said because I speak the words in my heart and mind that have come to me over a lifetime of trials and tribulations. And a life can not be fulfilled unless one seeks the truth amidst the "sea of deception".

Those in control are in the process of programming (influencing) our way of thinking through relentless imagery and distortions of the truth. If one is constantly bombarded with information that the world is flat, eventually he or she will begin to believe it. An a prime illustration is the 2008 Presidential Election. The Western Capitalists are the New World Order. And their Globalization is a hostile takeover of our world. And WE hath to rise up as a ONE to stop the onslaught. For the Antichrist will come from one of these Capitalist Pagans which will use the Media to persuade the people that he or she is an honorable person. And China and Russia may become powerful allies of the "*Beast*" if World War III befalls us. The end of the Cold War is a media created myth. Our awakening is the *SHIELD* against indoctrination, our courage is the *ARMOR* of the believers, and our unity is the *SWORD* of the reckoning.

Revelation speaks of the mark of the beast and the wrath of GOD that will come down on those who worship Satan. And those who follow Satan will suffer the agony of the fire for eternity. Now I know, for many the *BIBLE* seems like a book filled with fairy tales, but God's words were written by prophets, not storytellers. Even I think some of the stories are exaggerated. But our current Western Civilization has become so tolerant of everything; it no longer stands for anything. Do you want to face the Apocalypse unprepared? And we are all imperfect mortals that have the free will of choice. Personally I believe we can change the ending with a new beginning. And together we can change the fate of the world, but divided we will endure the end of the humanity.

No one should cast stones, but we all do. This seems to be our nature. Revelations may be headed our way, yet as I said before we can change its course, if we change our direction. If we are able to find agreement, at least within principle, then there is still hope for humanity. Gene Roddenberry's *Star Trek* was hundreds of years ahead of it's time. A united *EARTH* where the mission was peaceful, the outreach was a unified space initiative, diversity was the norm, and cultural differences were de-emphasized.

And I do not believe that God kills people with natural disasters. Most of these disasters occur because of our abuses of the earth's resources. *Mother Nature's* wrath can be devastating and these major disasters will continue to occur around the world until balance is restored. Al Gore is doing a great service by trying to educate the public about the dangers presently happening throughout the world. Simply put, there are consequences for our destruction of nature and killing off of species. We are disrupting the harmony and balance of nature and the outcomes are going to continue to be catastrophic. The key to understanding and overcoming is that we (society) have to recognize that there is no weakness in admitting we are wrong. Actually, being able to admit being wrong and working to correct these misguided delusions is a quality of strength. It is time for us to suppress our agendas and come together as *ONE NATION* of *ONE WORLD* under *ONE RELIGION* with *ONE GOD*. Thus, there can be only *ONE RACE* and that is the *HUMAN RACE*.

If I Thought

If I thought about the American service men and
women dying in Iraq and Afghanistan,
If I thought about all the children starving in Africa,
If I thought about the genocides of Rwanda, Bosnia,
and Darfur,
If I thought about the children being sold into
prostitution and slavery throughout Asia,
If I thought about the drug and alcohol addictions that
are fracturing families throughout the United States,
If I thought about my Irish kinsman who used violence
as a voice against Imperialism,
If I thought about my Native American brothers who
have been deceived by the allure of profits from
gambling casinos on their lands,
If I thought about young Muslims willing to kill
themselves and others for their beliefs,
If I thought about the Royal Families in the Middle
East enjoying hundreds of billions of dollars from oil
profits while most of the people live in poverty,
If I thought about the poverty and lack of a better
quality of life for many people in South America,
If I thought about young people joining gangs as a
substitute for family,
If I thought about the obesity epidemic spawn by fast
food and junk food corporations in the United States,
If I thought about people with cancer linked to tobacco
and other unhealthy addictive products,
If I thought about the rising number of children with
learning disabilities because their mothers indulged in
drugs and alcohol during their pregnancies,

If I thought about how the Russian and Chinese Governments maintain control over their people with the use of force,
If I thought about the Ozone being destroyed by irresponsible corporations and governments as a byproduct of greed,
If I thought about the pollution of our water resources by toxic chemicals, nuclear waste, and garbage,
If I thought about the political corruption in the United States and throughout the Western World,
If I thought about how the majority of religions have become a part of the secular world,
If I thought about the epidemic of violence throughout Western and Eastern Cultures,
If I thought about the cowardly countries that lack the courage to stand up to oppressive nations during international diplomacy,
If I thought about nations hunting endangered species to the brink of extinction,
If I thought about a nuclear holocaust and the end of civilization,
If I thought about all these senseless acts, I would find myself weeping every awakened moment.
Because these inhumane tragedies touch my heart and speak to my soul, I deem this as proof there is a God. Otherwise, I might become one of the eternally damned that has traded their souls for a few ounces of fool's gold.

Conclusion

I chose the title "*The Invisible Man*" because I have often felt unnoticed or acknowledged as an equal. But now I have added a subtitle "*Awakening the Human Consciousness*" to distinguish my book from similar titles. The intent of my book is to invoke thought, thereby creating an opportunity for effective communication. It has noting to do with if one agrees or disagrees. The important question is why one agrees or disagrees? The language in my book is a reflection of my frustration with a corrupt system out of touch with the people it is supposed to represent.

We have been betrayed by our leaders and deceived by the powerbrokers. Our village has been damned because we turned away from God. Humanity serves God, it doesn't replace God. Rick Warren's *The Purpose Driven Life* is a must read. At times it felt like a sermon. Moreover it seeks to indoctrinate. Often it requires patience and thought. Personally I found identity in chapters eleven and twelve. Sometimes I found myself in disagreement. But just meeting the challenge of the forty day commitment took a concerted effort. Still I believe it has something to offer anyone who is searching for reasonable answers to faith based questions. If we don't start somewhere then we will never get anywhere. But we must also be honest with ourselves. If most of us had the opportunity, we would whore ourselves out for a chance at the illusive "*American Dream*".

And it is true I was very critical of the Catholic Church. Even though the Catholic Church does good work, do the good deeds outweigh the evil deeds? In *God's Eyes*, I would say no-for a church that serves its own self-interests does not serve the Father. Moreover, priests and nuns should be allowed to marry because married people can serve God too-for all men and women have sexual desires and suppressing their nature heightens their inner inhibitions. But the cheating of Christian Universities in college athletics is indefensible no matter "What cuckoo flew over the ESPN nest of excuses" says. At the same time, the Mormons do good work as well, but their founders thought they were the second coming of Jesus which is as loony as it is blasphemous. So the Mormon Faith was founded by false prophets and that's just the cold hard facts. But that doesn't mean Mormons aren't good people-it means their religion is a *Cult.*

And anyone objectively observing the fact that a large portion of top journalists, television executives, entertainment executives, corporate executives, professional sports executives, television and radio personalities, broadcasters, financial executives in banking, fund management, lending institutions, and Wall Street, government bureaucrats, Washington lobbyists and corporate lawyers, and members of Congress are either Catholic or Jewish might question the injustice of equal access and lack of diversity. For the Catholic and Jewish disproportionate representation along with the corruption of many of these institutions is very disconcerting. Therefore I believe the people have a right to challenge these powerbrokers of which many have betrayed the public's trust.

But in moving forward we have to recognize there has to be a partnership between the organization, those who work for the organization, stakeholders in the organization, and the clients of the organization (Government Agency, government employees, taxpayers, and recipients of benefits). And this approach applies to all Businesses (Corporation, corporate employees, investors, and consumers), Government agencies, and Religion institutions (God, employees, communities, and members) for we all share responsibility in the success or failure of an organization. Thus, the outcome of any organization depends largely on the cooperation or lack of cooperation between their partners.

Throughout my book, I was very critical of certain individuals and some groups. But I believe we are all brothers and sisters and I refuse to hate someone because I disagree with a belief or disprove of an act. And there are plenty who disagree with me and that is ok for I never claimed I am right; I just expressed my beliefs. At times I used satire or sarcastic remarks to illustrate a point or poke fun of a silly notion.

Often, Bill O'Reilly observes injustices that a bias media on many occasions buries because it doesn't fit into their agenda, but even Bill takes a left at Jupiter sometimes. Nonetheless, many of the examples in this book I used are to point out the failures of our social, educational, economical, political, and judicial systems that continually ignore the voices of the majority. *We* are here, *We* are not Queer, and *We* are fed up with the Bullshit.

Truthfully, it didn't matter who the *Democratic Nominee* is, for if any reasonable voter objectivity compared Barack Obama or Hillary Clinton to John McCain on questions of integrity, character, leadership, bipartisanship, experience, honor, fiscal conservatism, commitment, national security, sacrifice, earmarks, legislative achievements, service, conservative record, selflessness, and courage; the voter would have realize Senator McCain was the most qualified Presidential candidate. And John McCain is the only candidate who could have actually delivered on a promise of change because America is facing serious foreign and domestic challenges that require strong leadership. Thus, John McCain was the best choice for *Commander and Chief* in 2008 and no amount of deceptive hype by a democratically biased media (much of which is owned by the wealthiest liberals in America) can change that fact.

Personally, I could easily imagine myself being close friends with both Ann Coulter and Bill Maher. Just because we disagree doesn't mean we can't love one another. And I am also a fan of Michael Moore-*Roger and Me* is one of my favorite documentaries. So our political disagreements should never dictate our friendships for each one of us is unique. Though I must admit I am attracted to intelligent creative people-maybe that is why I hope President Obama is successful, but I will not be blinded by a propaganda machine that has decided to rewrite history by not reporting or distorting the facts. The American people desire the truth for a strong nation is built on mutual trust. And a community should always be inclusive if we are to have balance in our lives. For there is no rule that says we have to dislike someone because we disagree with his or her point of view. Heck, if we are what we eat then I would be a fried chocolate donut-for I love fried foods, fresh baked bread, and chocolate, but I also love people who are true to themselves for that is what makes life delicious.

It still comes down to choice. Will we continue to fight amongst ourselves or will we work together to improve the quality of life for everyone? For the power of unity is the most logical solution for a new political and social revolution. Jesus, Gandhi, and Dr. King were right-peaceful resolutions are the essential components needed to end "the reign of our oppressors". But it requires facing our fears and relinquishing our ignorance. Right now we stand at the fork of fate. One path is the end and the other path is a new beginning. Thus, we must choose wisely because there is no going back.

Humanity's greatest danger is ignorance.
Humanity's most difficult dilemma is suffering.
Humanity's hardest obstacle to overcome is fear.
Humanity's largest challenge is hopelessness.

Humanity's grandest chance for success is understanding.
Humanity's best hope is compassion.
Humanity's strongest ally is courage.
Humanity's perfect solution is a moral constitution.

"I stood on the tower of ignorance
and I wasn't impressed by its illusion of grandeur"

Thanks and have a great day

The End

Acknowledgements

Everyone's life is influenced or impacted by others. There are both positive and negative experiences that shape who each one of us become. My mother instilled the idea that honesty and integrity cannot be purchased for any price. And my stepfather showed me that common sense is just as important as education on our lifelong journey of learning. For each choice there is a consequence and all will be held accountable that day when we stand before the Lord Almighty.

So, I give thanks for my mother. Through my mother's eyes, I have witnessed the strength, humility, and love of a woman. I am also grateful for the sacrifices my stepfather and my mother made for my brothers, sister, and me. But I cannot leave out my wife, my two brothers, my sister, and my uncle because they have had to endure my "soapbox" over the last two and a half years as I constantly revised my work-for without family and friends life has no meaning. And every honest man's path is often forged with immeasurable hardships during his life-but he must stand like an oak for his roots will sustain him.

However, it would be impossible to thank everyone who has touch my life for I am blessed with many friends, but my high school wrestling coach was more than just a teacher, coach, and friend. He was a role model, a mentor, and a father for me and hundreds of other young boys far away from our homes. And even though he had a family, we were also a part of his family. For he and my grandfather are the only two righteous men I can personally vouch for in heaven.

And to those I didn't mention who have positively impacted my life, I thank you. For every journey in life has a beginning, a middle, and an end. While it is true I have reached the middle, I still have a lot to learn and a long way to go. And even though I am dissatisfied with the hypocrisy of many churches, I know without God's grace and Jesus's sacrifice my path toward enlightenment would be incomplete.

Bibliography

Ankerberg, John, and John Weldon. The Facts on The Mormon Church. Eugene: Harvest House Publishers, 1991.

Arberry, A.J. The Koran: Interpreted: A Translation. New York: Touchstone, (1955) 1996.

Barnes and Noble Books. The Constitution of the United States of America. New York: 2005.

Bradley, Bill. The New American Story. New York: Random House Inc., 2007.

Coulter, Ann. Godless: The Church of Liberalism. New York: Crown Publishing Group, 2006.

Darwin, Charles. The Origin of Species. New York: Random House Inc., (1859) 1993.

Gore, Al. An Inconvenient Truth. New York: Rodale, 2006.

Gray, John. Men are from Mars Women are from Venus. New York: HarperCollins Publisher Inc., 1992.

Hayek, Friedrich A. The Road to Serfdom. *The Definitive Edition* Chicago: University of Chicago Press, 2007.

Kagan, Neil, and Stephen G. Hyslop. Eyewitness to the Civil War. Washington: National Geographic, 2006.

Jewish Publication Society. The Torah: The Five Books of Moses. 3rd ed. Philadelphia: 1992.

Marx, Karl., and Friedrich Engels. The Communist Manifesto. New York: New American Library, (1848) 1998.

Morris, Dick., and Eileen McGann. Because He Could. New York: HarperCollins Publishers Inc., 2004.

Obama, Barack. The Audacity of Hope. New York: Crown Publishing Group, 2006.

Orwell, George. 1984. New York: Penguin Group, (1949) 1983.

Pederson, William D. Presidential Profiles The FDR Years. New York: Infobase Publishing, 2006.

Sagan, Carl. The Demon-Haunted World. New York: Ballantine Books Random House Inc., 1996.

Schreck, Alan. The Compact History of the Catholic Church. Cincinnati: St. Anthony Messenger Press, 1995.

Signerolli, Anthony. Call to Liberty: Bridging the Divide Between Liberals and Conservatives. Minneapolis: Scarletta Press, 2006.

Steele, Shelby. The Content of Our Character. New York: HarperCollins Publishing Inc., 1990.

Talbot, David. Brothers (The Hidden History of the Kennedy Years). New York: Free Press, 2007.

Tzu, Sun. Cliff Road Books. The Art of War. China: Sweetwater Press, 2006.

Warren, Rick. The Purpose Driven Life. Grand Rapids: Zondervan, 2002.

Woodward, Bob and Scott Armstrong. The Brethren (Inside the Supreme Court. New York: Simon & Schuster, (1979) 2005.

Zondervan Publishing House. Holy Bible. Grand Rapids: 1994.

Bibliographical Page References

www.ingramcontent.com/pod-product-compliance
Lightning Source LLC
Chambersburg PA
CBHW022351280326
41935CB00007B/156
9781926585383